Celeste's Best

Gluten-Free, Allergen-Free Recipes

Over 250 Recipes Free of Gluten, Wheat,
Dairy, Casein, Soy, Corn, Nuts and Yeast

Celeste's Best

Gluten-Free, Allergen-Free Recipes

Over 250 Recipes Free of Gluten, Wheat, Dairy, Casein, Soy, Corn, Nuts and Yeast

LUMINARY
PUBLICATIONS

SUMMARY
1. Gluten-Free, Allergen-Free, Wheat-Free, Dairy-Free, Casein-Free, Soy-Free, Corn-Free, Nut-Free, Yeast-Free, Potato-Free, Cookbook, Special Diet
2. Gluten Intolerance, Celiac Disease, Food Allergies, Food Sensitivities

This book is dedicated to all those
who must avoid gluten and other allergens
and thought they'd have to eat a restricted diet
without all the foods they once loved.

This book is especially dedicated to
my daughter and my nephews
and all the children,
who avoid gluten and other allergens in their diet
so that life can be full of more possibilities and smiles,
and less about things in life you can't have.

<u>*Acknowledgements*</u>

To my sister Elizabeth, for truly inspiring me to write this cookbook, never knowing that one day it would help her own children who were later diagnosed with celiac disease.

To my husband Eddie, my incredible partner in this endeavor, for his unending show of complete support! You've been nothing short of amazing!!!

To my daughter Kelly, the true reason behind writing this book. Thank you for being the book's first editor and finding all the little errors I had overlooked. Thank you for all you did to help bring this book to publication. And thank you for your willingness to test all the recipes over and over and over again.

To Mom and Dad, for continually supporting me, especially through months and months of creating the gluten-free, yeast-free bread recipes. (And I'm so happy I will never have to hear the infamous question I've been asked at least three times a week since I started the cookbook, "Is it done yet?" followed by, "Well, when do you think it will be done?")

A very special thank you to my sister-in-law Susan, for all her help and encouragement and for the days she called to tell me how much she loved my cakes, pies and bread recipes! And most especially for the day she ate my gluten-free, yeast-free multi-grain bread for the first time and excitedly phoned to tell me, "Everyone should be eating this bread. No, I mean everyone in the world!"

To my editor Beth Balmanno, whose belief in this cookbook empowered me. My profound thanks for your patience, advice, guidance and extreme attention to detail. I truly appreciated all your editorial comments and suggestions which helped me create the book I had envisioned.

To all my wonderful friends who cheered me on and helped keep me focused and energized: Christine Faverio, Tammy and Sherman Glavan, Jose and Maria Gomez, Mark Solazzo, Phil and Jackie Van Campen, and the countless others.

And a huge note of gratitude to all my cookbook testers: Melanie Thompson Cindric, Jennifer Ellis, Katherine Emmons, Susan Garramone, Andria Love, Mary McCarthy, Elizabeth O'Flaherty, Donna Warren, Dorothy Warren, Shirley Warren and Patti Zimmerman. Your feedback helped the cookbook be the best it could be!

To my nephews: Anthony, Matthew, Joseph, John and Christopher so that you all will always be able to eat the foods you love!

CONTENTS

INTRODUCTION

If someone had asked me ten years ago what gluten was, I'm not sure I would have known other than the fact that I thought you needed it to make bread. But then my nephew Anthony became ill. He was five years old, weighed a mere 28 pounds and had been diagnosed with "failure to thrive." It was a long road that led to discovering the cause of his illness and his delay in growth. Fortunately, my brother Tony and my sister-in-law Susan were finally able to find a doctor who recognized that all my nephew's symptoms could be attributed to celiac disease.

Celiac disease (also known as celiac sprue or gluten-sensitive enteropathy) is an autoimmune disease which affects the digestive system. It's estimated that 1 in every 133 people have celiac disease. When people with celiac disease eat foods or use products containing gluten, their immune system responds by developing antibodies. These antibodies often damage or destroy the villi – the tiny, finger-like protrusions lining the small intestine. Villi normally allow basic nutrients such as proteins, fats, vitamins, and minerals from food to be absorbed through the walls of the small intestine into the bloodstream. When the villi are damaged, a person becomes malnourished, no matter how much food he or she may eat. And understanding this, clearly explained why my nephew had failure to thrive. He was eating what would be considered by most to be a healthy diet, but his body was unable to break down the gluten protein and he couldn't gain the proper nourishment from any of the food he ate.

At the same time my nephew was diagnosed with celiac disease, my daughter Kelly was diagnosed with Candida, yeast overgrowth in her body. The best treatment for this was a change in diet. That meant removing wheat, milk and sugar from our diet. We maintained this way of eating for almost a year, then when she was well, we slowly resumed our normal diet again.

But when we began adding wheat, milk and sugar back into our diet, for the first time in my daughter's life I think, she told us she was not hungry for dinner. She would skip dinner, then later in the night she'd become very hungry and would try to eat a little something, only to feel sick to her stomach again. This lasted for almost two weeks. After the second week of this, we decided to have her tested for celiac disease. I knew the genetics of the celiac condition and that there was a strong possibility Kelly might also have the disease since her cousin had already been diagnosed with it. The prevalence of developing celiac disease if you have a second-degree relative (aunt, uncle, and cousins) diagnosed with celiac disease increases to 1 in 39.

We had her tested through Dr. Fine at Entero Lab because this was the most sensitive and least invasive testing we could find. The results - Kelly tested positive for sensitivity to gluten, milk, egg yolk and yeast. We also discovered that she had two genes for celiac disease, one she'd received from me and the other from her father. Later we came to find out that Candida may be a catalyst that triggers the onset of celiac disease.

From that point on, we, as a family, all began following a gluten-free, milk-free, yeast-free and egg yolk free diet. And once these foods were removed from our diets, my husband and I quickly realized once we ate the offending foods again that we could not tolerate some of these foods either and so we began strictly following the diet as well.

Having been on a wheat-free diet for almost a year, you would have thought making the transition to a gluten-free diet would have been easy.

Nope. Not even close.

Instead, I was completely overwhelmed and the rest of my life was put on hold as I tried to figure this all out. Being wheat-free and gluten-free are very different. To our surprise, we found that gluten was hidden in so many processed foods.

I remember being especially thankful for my sister-in-law Susan, my nephew Anthony's mother, and all the insightful advice she lent my way to help get me started. I was also thankful for the Internet which allowed me to find ideas and information from other people who had been diagnosed with the disease or had children who had celiac.

And I realize now probably what caused me the most difficulty in those early days was the pressure I put on myself to make my house completely gluten-free and allergen-free very quickly. I tried, believe me I tried. But it really took months for me to figure this all out and to truly say my house was gluten and allergen-free.

When I first began gluten-free cooking, I used a very basic gluten-free flour mix as a substitute for wheat flour. A combination of brown rice flour, tapioca starch and potato starch. This basic mix allowed me to bake again. We were still learning so much about gluten-free living and back then, nearly ten years ago, almost all of the gluten-free flours we used could only be obtained online (thankfully things have changed so much now!).

Although I was baking again, the gluten-free food didn't really taste or have the same texture as the foods we used to enjoy. And we had a long running joke in our family that whenever I baked something the best comment we could muster was, "Not bad." Never a "Wow!" or even a "Mmmm…," just the lackluster, "Not bad."

Trying to overcome this stigma regarding my gluten-free baking, I ordered a special gluten-free flour mix I found online from a company in California. This not only cost an incredible $10 for a three-pound bag, but it also had the added expense of shipping costs. Not very economical or practical I'd have to say, but something good came from that experience. For the first time we had a taste of a flour mix that produced soft, appetizing baked cakes and cookies.

I realized then that I had let myself believe the myth that gluten-free foods would always taste inferior to gluten filled foods. But now that I had seen a glimpse of what was possible I decided that I wasn't going to settle for foods that tasted any different than those we ate before my daughter was diagnosed with celiac disease and the other food intolerances. So for the next few years, I worked on developing my own flour mix.

Testing and retesting. Mixing and remixing.

Then something crazy happened.

I made a loaf of Irish soda cake to take to a function and a few people asked me for the recipe. I gave it to them and substituted "flour" for my mix. Oddly, they asked for the recipe for my flour mix. At the time, I have to admit, I brushed it off and attributed it to them just being kind.

A while after this, my daughter had a holiday party at our house and I baked up some cakes and cookies for the event. The moms who came loved my sugar cookies. They told me my cookies tasted better than those made with wheat flour and again I was asked for the recipe for my mix.

A short time later to help introduce a few of my daughter's friends to eating gluten-free, I invited some of them over and we made pizzas using my flour mix. I sent home recipes with everyone, again simply substituting the word "flour" for my mix. One mom emailed me a couple days later and wanted the recipe for my gf flour mix, because her son told her the pizzas he'd had at my house just tasted better. At the time, I couldn't believe that anyone who could use wheat flour would ever want to substitute it for my gluten-free mix.

But even though I had received some positive comments regarding my flour mix, we had begun to develop food sensitivities to corn and nuts. So I went back to the kitchen again and remixed and remixed and set out to develop a mix free of most common allergens. I began adding sweet rice flour to my mix. This was a great find that helped add moisture. And then I discovered white bean flour. White bean flour is an extremely mild bean flour. I had tried the garbanzo and garfava bean flour in my earlier days of gf baking and had been totally turned off by the strong bean taste. (In my mix you may notice a slight bean taste in uncooked foods, but once cooked it is almost completely undetectable. And if you ever do bake something with my mix and notice a bean taste, it usually means the food is undercooked.)

Through all my testing, I found the true test of a gluten-free flour mix is to bake a perfect yellow cake. I've never been much of a yellow cake eater myself, more of a chocoholic, truth be told, so yellow cakes had never been our usual family dessert. And at first, my husband who had always preferred and pretty much begged me to bake yellow cake, was pleased with all the golden cakes he was asked to sample. But somewhere around the fortieth night of yellow cake for dessert, though, we began to refer to it in our house as "The Yellow Cake Reign of Terror."

Finally, I think after some sort of divine intervention – or maybe the forces of the Universe just knew my family could not possibly endure one more night of yellow cake for dessert – there it was. The sweet taste of success. A moist, delicious yellow cake.

I haven't kept count as to exactly how many versions of my flour mix I've created and tested, but I'd guess that this is somewhere around version #157. (Which is nothing compared to how many versions I went through to create a gluten-free, yeast-free loaf of

A Few Things to Note

Recipes, like fine wine, get better with age. Each time I make a recipe I might make subtle changes or revisions which often improve it and make it even better. So to me, in actuality, a cookbook is never really finished once published, but will continue to be an ongoing testing and improving of all recipes.

For instance, I originally made the mayonnaise recipe with one egg but later found that it produced a much better tasting spread using two eggs. Then I discovered that I could replace the eggs with flaxeggs and create an eggless spread that still tasted great. And I'm currently developing an eggless mayonnaise recipe that doesn't use any egg or egg substitute at all and still maintains the consistency, texture and taste of mayonnaise.

The bread recipes also were continually tested, reworked, tested again, revised, tested again, rewritten, etc. That's how a recipe becomes a great recipe. Slight modifications here, a change or two there and voilà, next thing you know, you have an amazing recipe!

Please check www.celestesbest.com, www.CBglutenfree.com or my facebook page Celeste's Best Gluten-Free, Allergen-Free Recipes at www.facebook.com/CBglutenfree for updates and improvements to recipes in the book.

I hope many of you will share your suggestions and modifications for any of the recipes you try through the forum on our website. Your comments and ideas may also help others who read the book.

Bread Recipe Notes and Revisions

Gluten-Free, Yeast-Free Bread

How to Measure Ingredients

The single most important thing you need to know when baking and cooking is how to measure ingredients correctly. A recipe is like a mathematical equation:

$$3 + 2 + 1 + 2 = 8$$

3 **bananas** + 2 **eggs** or equivalent substitute + 1 cup **sugar** + 2 cups *Celeste's Best Baking Mix* = **Banana Bread**

Measuring any ingredient incorrectly in a recipe throws these numbers off and can seriously affect the finished result. I think this is especially true in gluten-free baking and cooking.

Each cookbook may use a different method to measure ingredients so it's important to know which method the author used to obtain the best results.

There are two basic methods used to measure dry ingredients:

Spoon and Sweep: Lightly spoon powdery, dry ingredients into your measuring cup, overfilling it until it creates a small dome over the top. Then using a knife or spatula sweep off the excess at the top so the surface is level. Do not tap the measuring cup down or shake it during this process as this will add more flour to the recipe than needed.

All the recipes calling for flour are measured using the Spoon and Sweep method of measuring dry ingredients.

Scoop and Sweep: Scoop measuring cup or spoon into the ingredient, then sweep off the excess with a knife or spatula so that surface is level.

This method is used for sugar, sea salt, baking powder, cream of tartar and spices.

INGREDIENTS AND SUBSTITUTIONS

Measuring Gluten-Free Flour

Flours

One question I'm often asked is, "Why can't I just replace my regular wheat flour with one cup of a gluten-free flour?" The answer is simple. There isn't one gluten-free flour that will single handedly replicate all the characteristics of wheat flour. In order to replicate the effects of gluten in wheat flour, you need to use a blend of different flours when cooking and baking gluten-free foods.

Celeste's Best Gluten-Free Flour Mix is comprised of three flours: white rice flour, sweet rice flour and white bean flour. This flour blend is the basic flour mix used for the majority of the recipes in this book.

To bake the yeast-free breads arrowroot starch/flour, sweet potato flour and tapioca flour are also used to create light, airy breads. To bake the Multi-Grain loaf of bread amaranth flour, ivory teff flour and quinoa flour are added.

The flours listed below are the gluten-free flours used throughout the cookbook.

White Rice Flour:

White rice flour is produced from rice that has had the bran and germ removed. Then the rice is ground into a fine powder.

White rice flour is one of the least allergenic flours to use for baking for anyone following a gluten-free diet. White rice is also easier to digest and assimilate than other grains.

White rice flour is the backbone of my gluten-free flour mix. It has a neutral, mild taste which does not alter the taste of your baked goods.

> - Some white flours may be milled more finely than others. It is important to use only those that are finely milled to obtain the best taste and texture in your cooking.

Sweet Rice Flour:

Sweet rice flour is a gluten-free flour milled from white glutinous short grain rice. Don't be alarmed – it is only called glutinous because of its sticky nature. Sweet rice flour does not contain any gluten. It does, however, contain more starch than regular rice flours.

It is also an excellent thickener for puddings, gravies and sauces. And one of my favorite properties of sweet rice flour is that it retains moisture which helps keep baked goods soft, light and airy.

White Bean Flour:

White bean flour is ground from white beans or great northern beans. The addition of this mild flavored flour adds extra fiber and protein to the flour mix without imparting the usual aftertaste or bitterness normally associated with some bean flours such as garbanzo or fava bean. (If you ever find your baked goods have any bean taste after cooking them, it usually means the foods were undercooked.)

Konjac Powder:

In order to bind and hold gluten-free baked goods together, you will occasionally need either konjac powder or xanthan gum. Konjac powder is used as a thickener, stabilizer, and emulsifier in gluten-free cooking. It is a bit expensive, but you only use a very small amount in most recipes.

Xanthan Gum:

Xanthan gum is a polysaccharide used as a binder in many gluten-free products. In the production of xanthan gum, sucrose or glucose is fermented by a bacterium, Xanthomonas campestris. Xanthan gum can be derived from corn, soy, or wheat.

The three additional flours used to create the gluten-free, yeast-free breads are:

Arrowroot Starch/Flour

Arrowroot flour is a starch that is a tasteless fine powder derived from dehydrated arrowroots. Arrowroot flour is easy to digest and is often used as a thickening agent.

Sweet Potato Flour:

Sweet Potato Flour is an incredible addition to gluten-free baking. I find this flour vital to making the gluten-free, yeast-free breads in this cookbook. The sweet potato flour is a starchy flour derived from white sweet potatoes. As an added benefit, the flour is high in fiber.

Tapioca Flour:

Tapioca flour is a starchy flour ground from the root of the Cassava plant. Tapioca flour is another important ingredient in making the gluten-free breads in this cookbook.

There are also three additional flours in the Multi-Grain loaf of bread:

Amaranth Flour:

Amaranth flour is ground from the cream colored seed of the amaranth plant. Amaranth is an herb that originates in South America where it has been grown for over 5000 years. Amaranth is an easy to digest complete protein containing all of the essential amino acids needed by the body. It is also a good source of calcium, fiber, magnesium, phosphorus, manganese and iron.

Ivory Teff Flour:

Ivory teff flour is an ancient grain flour from Ethiopia. Teff is a nutritional powerhouse. The ivory teff is slightly milder than the traditional brown teff, but just as nutritious. Teff is high in calcium and iron. It also is low in fat, high in fiber and a good source of protein.

Quinoa Flour:

Quinoa flour is ground from the quinoa plant. Like teff, the quinoa seed is also a powerhouse of nutrition. It's high in vitamins, minerals and fiber. It has all the essential eight amino acids, making it a complete protein. It also contains zinc, iron, calcium, vitamin B, phosphorus, potassium, magnesium and manganese. This nutritious seed has been cultivated in South America for over 3000 years. Quinoa was a staple food, revered by the Incas for the strength and endurance it gave people who consumed it. It has a slightly nutty taste.

How Do I Get Started?

Once people find out about my recipes, their first question is usually, what do I need to do to get started?

The list to the right is the one I usually give them which details the basic ingredients used throughout the cookbook.

You don't have to get everything right away. Start with the three flours in the main mix and the ingredients needed for the baked goods. Then after that, you can slowly begin adding in the remaining ingredients.

You can find up-to-date lists of the best places to purchase gluten and allergen-free ingredients at the most affordable prices by visiting www.celestesbest.com or www.CBglutenfree.com. You can also visit my facebook page at www.facebook.com/CBglutenfree. My website has additional resources and links to sites with shopping guides for the grocery store to help you make safe gluten and allergen-free food buying choices.

Always confirm that all ingredients you use to prepare the recipes are free from those foods you and your family may need to avoid. This is especially true in regards to corn. Corn is in almost every processed food imaginable and many fruits and vegetables are coated with a corn based wax or oil. This coating may also contain gluten.

Getting Started Shopping List:

To make the basic flour recipe:

> white rice flour
>
> sweet rice flour
>
> white bean flour

For many of the baked goods, you will need:

> cream of tartar (found in spice aisle)
>
> baking soda
>
> konjac powder or xanthan gum
>
> (most brands of xanthan gum contain corn)
>
> lemon juice
>
> extra light olive oil
>
> golden flaxseed meal
>
> eggs or egg substitutes
>
> milk or non-dairy milk substitute
>
> pure cane sugar or palm sugar (if you have sensitivity or intolerance to corn)
>
> vanilla extract (see website for listing of corn-free extracts)

Flours in the bread mixes:

> amaranth flour
>
> arrowroot starch/flour
>
> ivory teff flour
>
> sweet potato flour
>
> tapioca flour
>
> quinoa flour

Celeste's Best
Gluten-Free Flour Mix

This is my basic flour mix. In most recipes, it will replace wheat flour cup for cup. Occasionally you may find that some recipes will require an extra ¼ cup of additional liquid be added. Since the flours comprising this mix do not contain any gluten, a very small amount of konjac powder (glucomannan) or xanthan gum is used in most recipes as a binding agent to help hold things together.

To measure the flours, gently pour them straight from the bag or box into the measuring cup. Then use the flat edge of a knife or spatula to level them off. Place measured flours in mixing bowl and beat on medium speed for 1 – 2 minutes using whisk attachment until well blended.

I usually make two batches of this recipe quadrupled (11 cups) and store them in resealable gallon-sized plastic bags in the refrigerator.

Use the following recipes based on your need.

2 cups **white rice flour**
½ cup **sweet rice flour**
¼ cup **white bean** or **great northern bean flour**

Yield: 2¾ cups

Be sure all the flours are well mixed.

To double the recipe:

4 cups **white rice flour**
1 cup **sweet rice flour**
½ cup **white bean** or **great northern bean flour**

Yield: 5½ cups

To triple:

6 cups **white rice flour**
1½ cups **sweet rice flour**
¾ cup **white bean** or **great northern bean flour**

Yield: 8¼ cups

To quadruple:

8 cups **white rice flour**
2 cups **sweet rice flour**
1 cup **white bean** or **great northern bean flour**

Yield: 11 cups

This recipe will just about fill a gallon-sized plastic food bag.

Use this chart as a handy reference:

	2¾ cups	**5½ cups**	**8¼ cups**	**11 cups**
White Rice Flour	2 cups	4 cups	6 cups	8 cups
Sweet Rice Flour	½ cup	1 cup	1½ cups	2 cups
White Bean Flour	¼ cup	½ cup	¾ cup	1 cup

Yield:

- To help preserve the freshness of gluten-free flours, store in a cool place such as the refrigerator or freezer.

- You can make your own bean flour by grinding beans in a high-powered blender or grain mill until they become a fine powder. They can also be milled using a coffee grinder. When using a coffee grinder, I prefer to grind the beans then sift them through a fine mesh strainer and then process them a second time to produce an even finer flour.

- Because of the integral part each flour plays in this recipe, it is important to use only the flour listed and not to substitute with any other flour to create this mix.

- Many ethnic markets sell gluten-free sweet rice flour locally as do many online stores which makes the flour as affordable as any of the other flours in the mix.

Binders in Gluten-Free Cooking

The gluten in wheat is elastic and expands when baked, allowing cakes, cookies and dough to maintain their shape without falling or crumbling. However, since the flours used in gluten-free baking do not contain gluten, something must be added as a binder to create these same elastic qualities and help goods hold their shape.

When I first began cooking gluten-free more than ten years ago, there were two main binders people generally used to replace wheat gluten in gluten-free goods. Xanthan gum and guar gum. In the beginning, I used only xanthan gum, then I switched to guar gum for a while and then back to xanthan. Xanthan gum is a polysaccharide used as a binder in many gluten-free products. In the production of xanthan gum, sucrose or glucose is fermented by a bacterium, Xanthomonas campestris. Xanthan gum can be derived from corn, soy, or wheat.

In the last year, I have stopped using any gums in my cooking. Our diet is a fairly natural one and I didn't feel these gums were something I wanted to be eating. I also felt my daughter was having a reaction to them. Some common reactions include migraines, skin itchiness, nose and throat irritation and gastrointestinal symptoms such as bloating, gas, and diarrhea. Searching on the web, I found many others were beginning to discover that these gums may be an issue for them, too. I began experimenting with different ingredients to replace these gums. I tried psyllium husk powder, which works quite well by the way. But for me personally, it caused a bit of stomach discomfort. I also tried fruit pectin. Did not have much luck with that or gelatin for that matter. They did not produce the results I was after. Nor did I have much luck with agar-agar, inulin or acacia root.

Then I tried konjac powder or glucomannan. This water soluble fiber is derived from the konjac gluco-mannan root plant. It's simply ground-up, dried konjac root. It is a dietary fiber that has been used in Asia for centuries. This fiber can be used as a gelling agent, thickener, emulsifier, stabilizer as well as a soluble fiber source.

Some of the believed benefits of konjac fiber include: regulation of lipid metabolism, reduced blood lipid and cholesterol; the reduction of blood glucose; reducing risk of constipation and cancer of lower digestive tract; and improvement of diet for diabetics. Adding konjac glucomannan fiber to one's diet slows the absorption of sugar and cholesterol from the digestive tract, helping to control sugar levels in diabetics and reducing cholesterol levels.

Konjac powder proved to be the most successful in gluten-free cooking and baking. In most of my recipes, I was able to substitute the same amount of konjac powder in place of the xanthan gum. A few recipes needed to be adjusted by adding slightly more konjac, usually an extra ¼ teaspoon per cup of flour.

Baking Powder

You may notice looking through the cookbook that none of the recipes contain baking powder as an ingredient. Not all baking powders are gluten-free and commercial baking powder often contains fillers such as cornstarch or potato starch. Some brands also contain aluminum.

An easier substitution is to replace baking powder with a combination of cream of tartar and baking soda. Mix 2 parts cream of tartar with 1 part baking soda. So if a recipe calls for 1 teaspoon baking powder, that can instead be replaced with ½ teaspoon cream of tartar plus ¼ teaspoon baking soda.

Use the chart below as a reference:

Substitute with:

Baking Powder Needed:	Cream of Tartar	Baking Soda
½ teaspoon	¼ teaspoon	⅛ teaspoon
1 teaspoon	½ teaspoon	¼ teaspoon
2 teaspoons	1 teaspoon	½ teaspoon
3 teaspoons (1 tablespoon)	1½ teaspoons	¾ teaspoon

If you prefer, you can make a baking powder substitute to use in your own recipes by combining the following ingredients:

1 tablespoon **baking soda**
2 tablespoons **cream of tartar**
1½ tablespoons **arrowroot starch/flour**

Keep stored in a tightly sealed container. One teaspoon of this homemade baking powder equals 1 teaspoon of commercial baking powder.

- To test the effectiveness of your baking powder as a leavening agent, dissolve a teaspoon or so in a couple tablespoons of water. It should bubble vigorously. If you are making your own baking powder, keep it in a sealed container to avoid exposure to moisture, which will lessen the powder's effectiveness.

- Using too much baking powder can have the same result as using too little – baked goods that won't rise. Also using too much can impart a bitter taste on the foods you're baking.

Butter Substitute - Extra Light Olive Oil

Extra light olive oil is the perfect substitute for butter or margarine. This is a terrific replacement for those who are avoiding dairy and it's a healthy one at that. Whenever a recipe calls for butter or margarine, substitute extra light olive oil. Recipes can be replaced with a reduced amount of oil using the recommended quantity shown in the chart below:

Butter or Margarine	Extra Light Olive Oil
1 teaspoon	¾ teaspoon
2 teaspoons	1½ teaspoons
3 teaspoons (1 tablespoon)	2¼ teaspoons
2 tablespoons	1½ tablespoons
¼ cup	3 tablespoons
⅓ cup	¼ cup
½ cup	¼ cup plus 2 tablespoons
⅔ cup	½ cup
¾ cup	½ cup plus 1 tablespoon
1 cup	¾ cup

Olive Oil Butter Recipe

Whisk together in a small bowl:

½ cup **extra light olive oil**
1 teaspoon **sea salt**

Pour mixture into a small container and freeze overnight, or until solid. Then place container in refrigerator and use just as you would use butter. (Unfortunately not a suitable substitute for butter in baking.) Olive Oil Butter melts extremely fast once removed from refrigerator and exposed to warmer temperatures.

- Be sure to use **"extra light olive oil"** and not just "light olive oil" as there is a difference in taste which could affect baked goods.

- Many wholesale clubs sell extra light olive oil at an affordable price.

Cake Release

Cake Release is a combination of flour, oil and shortening that I use to grease most of the pans I prepare for my baked goods. The wonderful part about using this mixture is that most baked goods can effortlessly be removed from the pan.

Makes 1½ cups

Place the following in mixing bowl and beat on high speed for 2 – 3 minutes or until smooth and free of any lumps:

1 cup *Celeste's Best Gluten-Free Flour Mix*
1 cup **extra light olive oil**
1 cup **shortening**

Store in an airtight container in refrigerator.

To use: Remove Cake Release from refrigerator and allow to warm slightly as you prepare your recipe. Using a folded paper towel, sweep across the top of the mixture and then place a thin coating where needed.

Egg Replacer

Eggs are sometimes difficult to substitute in recipes simply because they perform different functions in each recipe. Often they are needed for their moistening properties. In some recipes, they are necessary to help leaven. Other times, eggs are needed to help bind ingredients.

In some recipes, I've found this egg replacer recipe works best as an egg substitute and in others flaxeggs recipe (on the following page) seems to create the best results.

For recipes that call for more than two eggs, sometimes I use a combination of this recipe along with flaxeggs.

Please note: You will need an **immersion** or **stick blender** for this recipe.

To replace 1 egg:

In a two cup measuring cup place the following:

3 tablespoons **water**
1 tablespoon **sweet potato flour**
1 tablespoon **extra light olive oil**
¼ teaspoon **cream of tartar**
¼ teaspoon **konjac powder** or **xanthan gum**
⅛ teaspoon **baking soda**

Blend on high speed for 10 – 15 seconds or until mixture has thickened and is frothy like beaten egg whites.

To replace 2 eggs:

¼ cup plus 2 tablespoons **water**
2 tablespoons **sweet potato flour**
2 tablespoons **extra light olive oil**
½ teaspoon **cream of tartar**
¼ teaspoon **konjac powder** or **xanthan gum**
¼ teaspoon **baking soda**

Flaxeggs - Egg Substitute

This is an excellent substitute for eggs using ground flaxseeds. We actually find we prefer this substitute instead of eggs in many recipes. In the pizza crust recipe (see pages 194 – 195) I definitely prefer the crust prepared with flaxeggs over real eggs.

You'll find this flax substitute works well in a wide range of recipes such as muffins, breads, cakes, cookies and pancakes. Flaxeggs work best when the eggs called for in a recipe are needed to bind the ingredients together.

I originally prepared my flaxeggs using 1 tablespoon of flaxseed meal per 3 tablespoons of water. At that time, I only whisked the mixture together. When I began using the immersion blender to whip them up, I found using only 1 teaspoon of flaxseed meal produced the best consistency and much better results when baking. If I need the egg substitute for its binding abilities, then I do still use the 1 tablespoon flaxseed meal.

Place in a measuring cup or a small bowl:

1 teaspoon **golden flaxseed meal**

Add:

3 tablespoons **hot water** (heat to almost boiling)

Pour water over flaxseed meal. Blend with an **immersion** or **stick blender** on high speed for 10 seconds or until mixture becomes bubbly and frothy. Let rest for 1 – 2 minutes, then blend again for 10 seconds or until mixture gels and thickens.

Store prepared flaxeggs in covered containers in refrigerator until needed. Best when used in 3 – 5 days.

To replace eggs in a recipe, use the following ratios:

	Flaxseed Meal	**Water**
1 egg	1 teaspoon	3 tablespoons water
2 eggs	2 teaspoons	6 tablespoons water
3 eggs	1 tablespoon	9 tablespoons water
4 eggs	1 tablespoon + 1 teaspoon	12 tablespoons water

- Whole flaxseed does not need to be refrigerated but can simply be stored in a cool, dark place out of direct sunlight. Ground flaxseed should be stored in the refrigerator or freezer to maintain freshness.

- Golden flaxseed meal will produce a flaxegg that is lighter in color and less noticeable in baked goods.

- You can quickly and easily grind flaxseed in a coffee grinder.

- Sprinkle flaxseed meal on cereal or salads to add additional fiber to your diet.

- You can make a large quantity of this flaxseed egg substitute and refrigerate it up to 1 week and use as needed.

- ¼ cup of whole flaxseed = approximately ½ cup of ground flaxseed.

Flaxeggs can be used in many recipes but does not work in recipes that are dependent on eggs such as cream puffs, éclairs (still working on developing recipes for these) or egg-based custards.

Using flaxegg as your egg substitute will produce a speckled appearance in your lighter baked goods. The Yellow Cake recipe though (see page 312), contains no eggs to circumvent this problem.

Foods baked with flaxeggs will often not rise quite as high as those baked with eggs.

Although the cookbook is free of many allergens, it isn't labeled "egg-free" because I'm still in the process of testing all the recipes with the egg substitutes.

If I've tested a recipe with one of the egg substitutes, you'll find a comment in the note box letting you know which worked best.

Homemade Confectioners Powdered Sugar

Many frosting and dessert recipes often call for powdered sugar or confectioners sugar. Since powdered sugar normally contains cornstarch, many who must avoid corn in their diets may be happy to know that you can easily make your own powdered sugar at home.

Makes about ½ cup

Put the following in a coffee grinder and process at highest speed for 15 – 20 seconds or until desired consistency is reached:

½ cup **sugar**
½ tablespoon **sweet rice flour**

Let sugar settle before removing lid. Use in any recipe that calls for powdered sugar or store in an airtight container for use later.

- This recipe will also work in a high powered blender. (Never realized how high powered my first blender was until it broke. The newer model was unable to process the sugar.)

- Sugar crystals can sometimes etch into the sides of plastic blender pitchers.

- The sweet rice flour helps prevents clumping and also helps improve the thickening ability of the sugar, which is important when the sugar will be used to make frosting.

Quick and Easy Rice Milk

Many commercial non-dairy milk substitutes have a starchy, bitter aftertaste or are loaded with sugar. It wasn't long before I tired of paying for and lugging home cases of rice milk and set out on a quest to make my own.

This is the fastest, easiest way to prepare rice milk. One day I was in a rush and needed milk quickly. Normally I prepared the milk the way I describe in the Non-Dairy Rice Milk recipe which follows on pages 26 – 27, but then I thought why do I have to cook the rice for 20 minutes, then process it into milk?

Since rice flour is simply milled rice, why couldn't I cook that for only a few short minutes and blend it? Happy to say it led me to perfect rice milk with almost no waste!

My daughter is the true taste tester for milk substitutes. There are few she'll actually drink. This one though has a pleasant taste that even my daughter will drink and she prefers it unsweetened. And even though she can prepare the milk herself, she is always happy to see a full pitcher ready and waiting for her in the fridge when she's thirsty.

Makes approx. 8 cups (½ gallon)

On stovetop in a 5-quart pot on medium heat, add:

2 cups **water**
¼ cup **white rice flour**

Bring pot to a light boil stirring often until mixture thickens into a slurry, about 3 – 4 minutes.

Remove from heat and add to pot:

4 cups **water**
3 cups **chopped ice**
½ teaspoon **sea salt**
sweetener to taste (optional)
1 teaspoon **vanilla extract** (optional)

Process in pot on high speed with **immersion** or **stick blender** for 30 seconds or until well combined and milk is frothy.

Pour milk into a glass container and refrigerate. Shake well before serving. Best when used within 3 – 4 days of preparing.

- If you need to make 1 gallon of milk, it's best to make a half gallon at a time (in two separate pots) instead of doubling this recipe. Doubling it and using ½ cup of rice flour makes a very thick base for the milk.

- Different brands of rice may produce a starchier milk and you may have to add more water to achieve the proper consistency.

- Please note though, unlike commercial brands, this milk isn't fortified with added minerals and vitamins.

- I use this milk unsweetened in all my recipes. The vanilla version is best for drinking and not for cooking.

Non-Dairy Rice Milk

I debated whether or not I should even put this rice milk recipe in the book since the recipe on the previous page is so much easier to prepare, but decided some readers may still need to prepare milk from a grain.

Jasmine rice makes the best tasting rice milk. It's incredible to believe that it takes only ¼ cup of rice to make a half gallon of milk.

This recipe is more time consuming than the one on the previous page but it is still a simple process.   Cook rice. Process it. Add water. Strain it. Strain it again. Add sea salt and any optional flavoring. Done.

Makes approx. 8 cups (½ gallon)

On a stovetop in a 5-quart pot, add:

1½ cups **water**
¼ cup **white jasmine rice**

Bring pot to a boil. Cover and reduce heat to low. Continue cooking for 25 minutes.

Remove from heat and add:

2 cups **water**
2 cups **chopped ice**
½ teaspoon **sea salt**
sweetener to taste (optional)
1 teaspoon **vanilla extract** (optional)

Using an **immersion** or **stick blender**, process for 30 seconds on high or until you no longer see any individual grains of rice and milk is frothy. Add an additional:

3 cups **water**

Process again. Then strain rice through a very fine, double mesh strainer. Discard any rice in the strainer. Then strain one additional time to further remove any large pieces. Using the immersion blender again, mix until milk is smooth and free of lumps.

Pour milk into a glass container and refrigerate. Shake well before serving. Best when used within 3 – 4 days of preparing.

- Need to make milk in a hurry? Use 4 cups crushed ice and omit the 2 cups water.

- If you need to make 1 gallon of milk, it's best to make a half gallon at a time instead of doubling this recipe. Doubling it by using ½ cup of rice makes a very thick base for the milk and it's very difficult to strain.

- Different brands of rice may produce a starchier milk and you may have to add more water to achieve the proper consistency.

- Please note though, unlike commercial brands, this milk isn't fortified with added minerals and vitamins.

APPETIZERS AND DIPS

Baked Chicken Wings

Artichoke Bean Dip

This dip combines artichoke and great northern beans. An unusual combination that is surprisingly delicious.

Makes 3 cups

Rinse and drain in a strainer:

1 (15 ounce) can **great northern beans**

Place the following in food processor:

1 (14 ounce) can **whole artichoke hearts**, drained
2 **green onions**, chopped into ½-inch slices
¼ cup **olive oil**
2 tablespoons **lemon juice**
2 **cloves of garlic**, minced
1 teaspoon **sea salt**
½ teaspoon **dried oregano**
½ teaspoon **dried thyme**
¼ teaspoon **black pepper**

Add the drained **great northern beans** and process for 1 – 2 minutes or until smooth. Serve with vegetables (carrots, celery or broccoli) or flatbread (see pages 183 and 187). Also tastes very good with thin slices of Gluten-Free, Yeast-Free Multi-Grain Bread (see pages 175 – 176).

> ▪ Most processed artichokes contain citric acid which can be an issue for those who are sensitive to corn.

Artichoke Green Olive Dip

Another artichoke dip that is easy to make. The pairing of artichoke hearts and green olives produces a dip that's creamy, yet free of dairy products.

Makes 3 cups

Place in food processor and process until finely chopped:

1 cup pitted **green olives with pimentos**

Drain:

2 (14 ounce) cans **whole artichoke hearts**

Lightly pat hearts dry with paper towels and place in food processor along with:

½ cup **olive oil**
2 teaspoons **lemon juice**
1 **clove of garlic**, minced
¼ teaspoon **black pepper**
¼ cup finely chopped **fresh parsley**

Process for 2 – 3 minutes or until smooth. Serve with vegetables or flatbread (see pages 183 and 187). Also tastes very good with thin slices of Gluten-Free, Yeast-Free Multi-Grain Bread (see pages 175 – 176).

> ▪ Most processed artichokes contain citric acid which can be an issue for those who are sensitive to corn.

Baked Chicken Wings

An appetizer we often serve up as a dinner. Team up your wings with Ranch Dressing (see page 51).

Makes 15 – 20 wings

Preheat oven to 425 degrees. Spread or brush across the bottom of a large baking sheet:

2 tablespoons **extra light olive oil**

Place the following in a large zippered plastic bag:

¼ cup *Celeste's Best Gluten-Free Flour Mix*
1 tablespoon **paprika**
1½ teaspoons **garlic salt**
½ teaspoon **black pepper**
⅛ - ¼ teaspoon **cayenne pepper**
⅛ - ¼ teaspoon **chili powder**

Shake bag until all ingredients are thoroughly mixed. Then add:

2 pounds of fresh **chicken wings** and **drumettes**

Place one pound of wings in the bag at a time. Shake bag until all pieces of chicken have been well coated. Place floured chicken in single layer on baking sheet, rolling and coating chicken in oil in pan. Bake in preheated oven for 30 minutes then turn wings over and bake for an additional 15 – 20 minutes or until chicken is no longer pink inside.

- Frozen wings and drumettes (even when thawed) tend to release moisture when cooking and the wings will not be as crispy.

- For a spicier wing, add the full ¼ teaspoon cayenne pepper and ¼ teaspoon chili powder.

Black Bean Dip

Great with homemade tortilla chips.

Makes 2 cups

Place the following in a food processor:

2 **green onions**, chopped
2 (16 ounce) cans **black beans**, drained
¼ cup mild chopped **green chilies**
2 tablespoons **tomato paste**
¼ cup **water**
3 **cloves of garlic**, minced
1 tablespoon **lemon juice**
1 teaspoon **sea salt**
¾ teaspoon **cumin**
¼ teaspoon **cayenne pepper**

Process ingredients until smooth. Serve with chips or vegetables.

Herb Dip

A creamy mayonnaise based dip with parsley and tarragon.

Makes 1 cup

Mix together the following in a medium sized bowl:

1 cup **mayonnaise** (see page 362)
2 tablespoons chopped **fresh parsley**
1 **green onion**, finely chopped
1 small **clove of garlic**, minced
½ teaspoon **dried tarragon** or ½ tablespoon chopped **fresh tarragon**
¼ teaspoon freshly ground **black pepper**

Then sprinkle on top:

1 tablespoon chopped **fresh parsley**

Serve with cut up vegetables such as peppers, carrots, and celery.   Refrigerate any leftover dip for up to 3 – 5 days.

Marinated Mushrooms

Marinated mushrooms are great served as an appetizer or as a side dish to accompany a meal. This is one of our favorite recipes.

Serves 4

In a large bowl or serving dish, whisk together:

⅓ cup **olive oil**
¼ cup **lemon juice**
½ teaspoon **sea salt**
½ teaspoon **pepper**
1 tablespoon **dried basil** or **fresh basil**, finely chopped

Toss in:

1 (8 ounce) package **sliced fresh mushrooms**
12 ounces **cherry tomatoes**, halved
2 **green onions**, thinly sliced

Cover and chill in refrigerator for several hours before serving.

> - Freeze dried basil tastes like fresh basil and is often available in many grocery stores. If you are unable to find it, replace it with finely chopped fresh basil or dried basil.

Stuffed Mushrooms

There are many ways to stuff mushrooms. This recipe is the way my mother always prepared them.

Makes 20 mushrooms

Preheat oven to 350 degrees and grease a large cookie tray. Wipe clean with a mushroom brush or dampened paper towel:

20 large **mushrooms** or 9 medium sized **portabella caps**

Cut the very ends of the stems of the mushrooms and discard. Remove stems and finely chop in small food processor.

In a medium sized skillet on medium-low heat, add:

¼ cup **extra light olive oil**
2 **cloves of garlic**, minced
chopped **mushroom stems**

Sauté until lightly browned. Add:

2 tablespoons **fresh parsley**, finely chopped

Stir the parsley into the pan, then remove pan from heat and add:

½ cup **gluten-free bread crumbs** (see page 181)
½ teaspoon **sea salt**
¼ teaspoon freshly **ground black pepper**

Combine all ingredients until well mixed. Place mushroom caps on cookie tray. Spoon a small amount of filling into each cap, completely filling the cap without packing the filling too tightly. Drizzle a small amount of **extra light olive oil** on top of each cap and bake for 20 minutes.

Swedish Meatballs

My mom always made Swedish Meatballs as one of her appetizers when guests were coming to visit. Sometimes we prepare this recipe as an appetizer, but we also often serve it as the main dish with a few side dishes to accompany it.

Makes about 45 meatballs

In a large skillet over medium heat, add:

2 tablespoon **olive oil**

Then add:

¼ cup finely chopped **onion**

Sauté until soft, about 2 – 3 minutes, then remove from heat.

Meanwhile in a large bowl, combine the onions with the following:

1 pound **ground beef**
1 cup **gluten-free bread crumbs** (see page 181)
2 **eggs** or equivalent substitute
1 teaspoon **sea salt**
½ teaspoon **black pepper**
¼ teaspoon **nutmeg**
¼ teaspoon **allspice**

Add the sautéed onions to the mix and shape the meat into small 1-inch balls. (If mixture seems dry add up to ¼ cup **beef stock**.) And in the large skillet over medium heat add:

¼ cup **extra light olive oil**

Then add half the meatballs, turning each with a spoon, to cook until well browned on all sides. Remove meatballs and place on a plate lined with paper towel to trap excess grease. Keep cooked meatballs warm while preparing second bath.

Once all meatballs have been cooked and removed from skillet, reduce heat to low and add:

¼ cup *Celeste's Best Gluten-Free Flour Mix*

(continued)

Then slowly add:

4 cups **beef stock**

Cook for 5 – 7 minutes, stirring often, until the stock has thickened into a gravy. Return meatballs to pan and reduce heat to a simmer and cook an additional 2 – 3 minutes. Serve hot.

> - This appetizer becomes more of a meal when served over a bed of gluten-free fettuccini noodles.

SALADS AND SALAD DRESSINGS

Tomato Salad

Chicken Salad

This chicken salad tastes great served over a bed of lettuce or wrapped up in a tortilla (see recipe on pages 191 – 193).

Serves 4 – 6

Place in a large pot:

8 skinless, boneless chicken breast halves

Fill pot with water until chicken is covered. Bring water to a boil, cooking chicken until no longer pink inside and when cut with a knife juices run clear.

Drain pot and allow chicken to become cool enough to handle. Cut cooled chicken into bite-sized pieces and place in large bowl.

In another large serving bowl mix together until well blended:

1 cup **mayonnaise** (see page 362)
2 tablespoons **fresh parsley**
2 tablespoons **lemon juice**
1 teaspoon **dried dill**

Then add:

cut chicken cubes

Stir salad until well blended. Refrigerate and serve chilled.

- Sometimes I'll make chicken salad from cut-up chicken pieces instead of the breasts. It's a little more work but then I use the water I boiled the chicken in as my base for a pot of chicken stock (see page 60).

- Short on time? Replace chicken breasts with 3 (13 ounce) cans of gf chunk chicken breast in water.

Cold Pea Salad

A refreshing salad, perfect as a side dish on a hot summer day.

Serves 4 – 6

Place in a colander:

2 (1 pound) bags **frozen baby peas**

Thaw peas slightly by placing colander under water faucet with cold water, just until no longer frozen, but not all the way thawed.

Allow peas to drain. In a small bowl, combine:

½ cup **mayonnaise** (see page 362)
2 tablespoons **lemon juice**
1½ tablespoons **sugar**
½ teaspoon **sea salt**

Place drained peas in a large bowl. Add mayonnaise mixture and stir well, then add:

3 **scallions**, sliced
½ cup **grated carrots**

Combine all ingredients well, then refrigerate and chill for at least an hour before serving.

Macaroni Salad

It's wonderful to still be able to enjoy macaroni salad even while following a gluten-free diet. We just made this salad for our 4th of July celebration along with some hamburgers and hot dogs.

The addition of green olives in this recipe truly enhances the taste of this salad.

Serves 4 – 6

Bring a pot of water to boil in a stockpot. Add:

1 bag (16 ounces) **gluten-free elbow pasta**

While the macaroni is cooking, place the following salad ingredients into a large bowl:

3 **stalks celery,** each sliced lengthwise and then sliced thinly horizontally
1 **medium onion**, chopped
½ cup **green olives**, sliced in half
½ cup **mayonnaise** (see page 362)
2 tablespoons **milk** or **non-dairy milk substitute**
2 tablespoons **lemon juice**
1 tablespoon **sugar**

When elbows have finished cooking, place in a colander and rinse thoroughly under cold water. Mist with extra light olive oil to prevent sticking and let drain completely, then add to salad ingredients. Mix well and refrigerate for at least an hour or more. Serve cold.

Shrimp and Calamari Salad

One of my daughter's favorite salads to prepare.

Serves 2 – 4

Bring a medium pot of water to a boil on the stove.

Meanwhile thaw in a colander under cold running water:

2 cups **frozen calamari rings**

Once water is fully boiling, add rings and cook for only 1 minute or according to directions on bag. Overcooking calamari will cause it to become tough and chewy. Drain rings and then submerge them in ice water.

Then thaw in colander under cold running water:

2 cups **fully cooked frozen shrimp**

While the shrimp is thawing, in a medium sized bowl, combine:

1 stalk of **celery,** cut length wise and sliced
2 **cloves of garlic**, minced
¼ cup **olive oil**
2 tablespoons **lemon juice**
2 tablespoons **parsley**, chopped
½ teaspoon **sea salt**

Toss all ingredients together and chill for 30 minutes or longer.

▪   Add cooked scallops, octopus or even mussels to the salad.

Tomato Salad

My dad is famous for his tomato salad. I personally prefer to eat this with my steak dinners instead of the usual ketchup.

Serves 4 – 6

In a medium sized bowl, combine:

¼ cup **olive oil**
½ teaspoon **dried basil**
½ teaspoon **sea salt**
1 **clove of garlic**, minced

Stir dressing with a fork. Then add:

1½ pounds **juicy tomatoes**, cut into wedges

Mix all ingredients, tossing gently. Season with additional sea salt if desired. Best served at room temperature, but leftover salad may also be refrigerated and eaten the following day.

- It's important that your tomatoes are slightly soft, ripe and juicy for this recipe. I cut tomatoes on a plate and then transfer slices and the juice from the tomatoes to a bowl.

- The best part of the salad is the liquid that remains after the salad has been eaten. Be sure to enjoy it and not let a drop go to waste.

- Try dehydrated basil in place of dried basil for the best taste. It is now readily available at most grocery stores and is usually found in the produce section.

- Garlic lovers can add an extra clove of minced garlic.

Tuna Pasta Salad

This is one of those old "stand by" recipes we've been making for years. Great to pack up and take for lunch, too.

Serves 4 – 6

Bring a large pot of water to a boil, then cook according to package directions:

1 pound **gluten-free elbow macaroni** or **shell pasta**

Meanwhile, drain in a colander:

2 (7 ounce) cans **tuna in water**

In a large bowl, whisk together:

½ cup **mayonnaise** (see page 362)
2 tablespoons **ketchup** (see page 360)
½ teaspoon **sea salt**

Then add the drained tuna and also add:

3 **scallions**, finely chopped
3 **medium tomatoes**, peeled and coarsely chopped
1 **cucumber**, peeled and finely chopped

When pasta is cooked, pour into a colander and run cool water over it. Drain well and add to salad. Toss all ingredients until well combined. Refrigerate and chill for at least an hour before serving.

> ▪ Quicker method: Drain pasta, then while still in colander add one cup of ice cubes (crushed works best) and toss gently with your hands until all ice has melted and pasta has cooled.

Tuna Salad

This is a very tasty salad that's great over a bed of lettuce, stuffed in a tomato, stacked high on top of a gluten-free cracker or sandwiched between two slices of any of Celeste's Best gluten-free breads.

Serves 4 – 6

In a large bowl, combine and mix well:

1 cup **chopped celery**
1 cup **mayonnaise** (see page 362)
1 cup **chopped onion**
¼ cup **fresh parsley**
2 teaspoons **lemon juice**
1 teaspoon **garlic powder**
½ teaspoon **sea salt**
½ teaspoon **pepper**

Then add:

4 (6 ounce) cans of **tuna**, drained

Mix in tuna, breaking up any large chunks. Refrigerate until chilled and serve.

> - This is usually a lunch we'll take with us if we'll be away from home for the day. We make a loaf of bread and slice it and bring that along with the tuna salad. Then we prepare the sandwiches in the car.
>
> - If you're using tuna packed in oil, simply drain the oil. You do not need to rinse the tuna before adding it to the salad.

Citrus Herb Vinaigrette

This is a copycat recipe to one served in restaurants. My husband prepares a jerk seasoning (see page 372) grilled chicken salad with tomatoes, avocados and mangoes and then tops it with this wonderful citrus herb vinaigrette.

Serves 4 – 6

Whisk all the ingredients together in a medium sized saucepan:

1⅓ cups **olive oil**
¼ cup plus 2 tablespoons **water**
¼ cup **vinegar** (see note box below)

½ cup **sugar**
6 **cloves of garlic**, minced
2 tablespoons **Dijon mustard** (see note box below)
3 tablespoons **lemon juice**
1½ tablespoons **fresh parsley**, minced

1 teaspoon **dried basil**
½ teaspoon **dried oregano**
½ teaspoon **sea salt**
¼ teaspoon **black pepper**

Bring to a boil over medium heat. Then continue cooking for 1 more minute. Remove from heat. Let cool slightly, then chill for several hours before serving.

- The recipe for jerk seasoning can be found on page 372.

- Those with corn sensitivities would need to use corn-free vinegar (or try replacing the vinegar with lemon juice) and corn-free Dijon mustard, or you can even make your own Dijon mustard. We have also made this dressing by substituting the Dijon mustard with a teaspoon of mustard powder.

French Dressing

Commercial salad dressings can contain any number of allergens, preservatives and who knows what else these days. The good news, though, it's very easy to make your own. We make one dressing a week and switch each week so we don't get tired of them.

Makes about 2 cups

Place the following ingredients in a food processor with a feeding tube and process for 1 minute or until well mixed:

½ cup **ketchup** (see page 360)
½ cup **lemon juice**
½ cup **sugar**
2 tablespoons **minced onion**
1 teaspoon **sea salt**
⅛ teaspoon **garlic powder**

Once well blended, begin to slowly dribble in:

1 cup **olive oil**

Continue adding the oil, steadily until all has been added and dressing has incorporated.

Pour into a jar with a tight fitting lid and refrigerate. Best when used within 7 – 10 days.

> ▪ We save our old glass jars and reuse them for our salad dressings.

Honey Mustard Dressing

This dressing is an oil based dressing and is perfect for those who have eliminated vinegar from their diets.

Makes about 1 cup

Whisk together the following in a small bowl or 1 cup measuring cup:

⅓ cup **honey**
⅓ cup **lemon juice**
⅓ cup **olive oil**
1 teaspoon **dry mustard**
1 teaspoon **sea salt**

Mix together all ingredients until well blended. Pour into a jar with a tight fitting lid and refrigerate. Best when used within 7 – 10 days.

Italian Salad Dressing

A perfect blend of spices. As an added bonus – this dressing also helps make a quick dinner. Mix up the dressing and pour a few tablespoons over chicken breasts placed in a baking dish. Bake for 45 minutes at 350 degrees.

Makes approx. 1¾ cups dry mix

Whisk together your spice mix in a small bowl:

¼ cup **oregano**

2 tablespoons **onion powder**
2 tablespoons **parsley**
2 tablespoons **sugar**

1 tablespoon **garlic powder**
1 tablespoon **garlic salt**
1 tablespoon **sea salt**

2 teaspoons **basil**
2 teaspoons **pepper**

½ teaspoon **celery salt**
½ teaspoon **thyme**

Store mix in an airtight container.

To prepare the dressing in a 2 cup measuring cup, combine the following:

1⅓ cups **olive oil**
½ cup **vinegar** or **lemon juice**
¼ cup **water**
¼ cup **prepared spice mix**

Whisk all ingredients until well combined. Store in a 16 ounce jar with a lid. Shake well or whisk before serving.

- We also sometimes simply sprinkle some of this on our salads and then drizzle olive oil and vinegar or lemon juice to taste.

- Those with corn sensitivities would need to use corn-free vinegar.

Ranch Dressing

My husband and daughter love ranch dressing whether they're enjoying it on a salad or simply to dip some carrots in for a snack. My daughter, as a small child, referred to this dressing as "dippings." When the family went dairy-free as well as gluten-free, we thought we might have to give up one of our favorite dressings. That was until we came up with this recipe. To us it's as close as you can get to Ranch Dressing when you're making it gf and df.

Makes 3 cups

Pour into a 4 cup measuring cup and whisk together or process with an **immersion** or **stick blender** on medium high speed for 10 seconds:

2 cups **mayonnaise** (see page 362)
1 cup **milk** or **non-dairy milk substitute**
½ tablespoon **lemon juice**
½ tablespoon **lime juice**

Then stir or whisk in:

2 tablespoons **dried chives**
2 tablespoons **dried parsley**
1 teaspoon **garlic powder**
1 teaspoon **onion powder**
¾ teaspoon **seasoning salt** (see page 374)
¾ teaspoon **black pepper**
¼ - ½ teaspoon **konjac powder** or **xanthan gum**

Once all ingredients are combined and mixed well, pour into a jar or bottle and refrigerate. Serve chilled.

- Adjust the konjac or xanthan amount according to how creamy you'd prefer your dressing. To serve as a dip, add ½ teaspoon.

- The salad dressing or dip will thicken as it sits, so refrain from adding additional konjac or xanthan until the dip or dressing has sat for at least a half an hour.

- Lime juice is the key to the taste of the dressing most closely matching Ranch.

SOUPS

Creamy Tomato Soup

Artichoke Bean Soup

Artichoke hearts and cannelloni beans come together to create an incredibly simple soup that tastes like you spent hours preparing.

Serves 4 – 6

Heat on low in a medium sized saucepan:

1 teaspoon **olive oil**
1 **clove of garlic**, minced

Meanwhile, place the following in your food processor:

1 (14 ounce can) **artichoke hearts**, drained
1 (15 ounce can) **cannelloni beans**, drained

Process for 2 – 3 minutes or until completely pureed.

Add artichoke/bean mix to saucepan. Then add:

2 cups **chicken stock**
sea salt and **pepper** to taste

Reduce heat to simmer and cook for an additional 15 – 20 minutes or until soup is thick and creamy and well heated.

> - If you enjoy this soup, be sure to try the Artichoke Bean Dip (see page 30).
>
> - Those who are sensitive to corn should use fresh artichoke hearts instead of canned which usually contain citric acid.

Asparagus Soup

The perfect soup to serve in the springtime when asparagus is in season. Utterly delicious!

Serves 4 – 6

Rinse, then snap off and discard the bottom tough ends of:

1 pound (1 bundle) **fresh asparagus**, cut into 1½-inch size pieces

Meanwhile in medium sized stock pot, whisk together:

3 tablespoons **extra light olive oil**
3 tablespoons ***Celeste's Best Gluten-Free Flour Mix***

Heat on medium heat until hot, then add:

1 quart (4 cups) **chicken stock**
asparagus pieces

Bring to a boil, then continue cooking for 15 – 20 minutes until asparagus is soft.

Remove from heat. Carefully, as soup will be very hot, puree with an **immersion** or **stick blender** until smooth.

Then slowly whisk in:

1 cup **milk** or **non-dairy milk substitute**
1 teaspoon **lemon juice**

Return soup to stove and reduce heat to a simmer and cook for an additional 5 – 10 minutes. Ladle into serving bowls. Season with **sea salt** and **pepper** to taste.

> ▪ Add one small onion, chopped, and sauté it in the oil until soft before adding the flour, for a slightly different taste.

Black Bean Soup

Creamy black bean soup ready in 25 minutes!

Serves 4 – 6

Add to a large stock pot:

2 cups **chicken stock**
2 **celery stalks**, finely chopped
2 **cloves of garlic**, minced
1 **onion**, finely chopped
½ cup finely chopped **carrot**

Bring mixture to a boil, then reduce heat to low and cook for 10 minutes. Then add:

1½ (15 ounce) cans **black beans**, undrained
1 teaspoon **cumin**
½ teaspoon **sea salt**
¼ teaspoon **chili powder**
⅛ teaspoon **cayenne**

Cook for 5 more minutes on low then remove from heat. Puree with **immersion blender** or **stick blender** until smooth. (Be careful during this step, as soup is hot.) Soup may also be placed in blender and pureed.

Return pot to burner. Then in a small bowl or measuring cup briskly whisk together until there are no lumps:

¼ cup **water**
3 tablespoons **sweet rice flour**

Add to pot and stir well. Then add:

½ (15 ounce) can **black beans**, undrained
1 tablespoon **lemon juice**

Continue to simmer and allow soup to thicken for 5 more minutes. Ladle into serving bowls. Season with **sea salt** and **pepper** to taste.

Chicken Noodle Soup

I remember the first night we made this soup. I just about jumped for joy! This so reminded me of the red and white labeled soup of my youth!

Serves 4 – 6

Bring a pot of water to boil on stovetop. Add:

1¼ cups **gluten-free spaghetti**, broken into 2-inch pieces

While the pasta is cooking, in a large pot add:

6 cups **chicken stock**
2 **boneless, skinless chicken breast halves**, diced (approx. 1½ cups)
1 tablespoon **minced parsley**
sea salt and **pepper** to taste

Bring to a boil, uncovered, then reduce heat to medium and cook for 10 minutes or until chicken is cooked. Cook pasta until al dente – almost fully cooked.

Then strain, rinse with a full glass of water and add drained pasta to the soup. Simmer for 5 – 7 minutes. Ladle into bowls and serve.

- This recipe is a great way to use up leftover chicken, too.

- Different pasta brands will impart different tastes. For this soup, I prefer rice pasta or a blend of quinoa/rice pasta.

- Originally I cooked the noodles in the soup water, but sometimes the gluten-free pastas can be starchy and thicken the soup too much, so it's best to cook it separately then add it to the soup. This is especially true if you double the recipe.

Chicken Pot Pie Soup

We like to make this soup to accompany Chicken Pot Pie Empanadas (see page 129). If you like Chicken Pot Pie, you'll love this soup.

Serves 4 – 6

In a small pot, boil until fully cooked:

2 **skinless, boneless chicken breast halves**

Allow to cool slightly, then cut chicken into bite-sized cubes and keep warm.

Meanwhile in a large pot, heat over medium heat:

¼ cup **extra light olive oil**

Whisk in:

⅓ cup *Celeste's Best Gluten-Free Flour Mix*

Then add:

1 quart (4 cups) **chicken stock**
¼ teaspoon **garlic powder**
¼ teaspoon **pepper**

Then slowly whisk in:

1 cup **milk** or **non-dairy milk substitute**

Add and continue to cook for 5 – 7 minutes as soup thickens, stirring occasionally:

cubed chicken
1 (10 ounce bag) **frozen peas and carrots**

Ladle into bowls and serve.

Chicken Soup for the Soul

When anyone in our house is feeling a bit under the weather there is always a pot of this soup simmering on the stove.

Serves 4 – 6

In a large stockpot, combine:

1 quart (4 cups) **chicken stock**
3 cups **water**
1 (14.5 ounce) can **diced tomatoes**
1 (13 ounce) can **chunk chicken breast in water**, undrained
1 cup frozen **chopped spinach**
5 **cloves of garlic**, sliced
½ cup **white rice**
1 teaspoon **sea salt**

Loosely cover pot and bring to a boil. Reduce heat and simmer for 30 minutes or until rice is fully cooked.

- You can substitute spaghetti broken in 1-inch pieces instead of the rice.

- You can cut up romaine and use in place of the spinach.

- This is a soup that we often add whatever ingredients we have on hand. Frozen green beans broken into pieces, sliced or chopped carrots, sliced celery, cut onion. If I have time instead of using canned chicken, I dice up one chicken breast and boil that first in the water and stock for 15 minutes before adding the other ingredients.

Chicken Stock

I think most people would be surprised at how easy it is to make their own chicken stock. Whenever we have roasted chicken, I save the bones in a bag in the freezer. Then when I get some time I pull them out and make some stock. I find that stock made from cooked bones produces a heartier stock.

Makes 8 quarts

In a large stockpot (at least 12 quarts) or a multi-pot (a stock pot with a colander insert) add:

the **carcass of one roasted or baked chicken**
10 **whole peppercorns**
4 unpeeled **carrots**, ends removed, washed and roughly cut
2 **bay leaves**
2 **stalks of celery**, ends removed, washed and roughly chopped
2 **whole cloves**
2 **cloves of garlic**, unpeeled
1 unpeeled **onion**, quartered

Add:

8 quarts of **water** (32 cups) or enough water to cover over the top of all stock ingredients by at least an inch.

Over medium heat, bring soup to a slow boil and as soon as it begins boiling lower temperature to simmer. Simmer stock for 2 – 4 hours.

Drain all the solids from the stock. This is where the multi-pot comes in handy. Using a fine mesh strainer will also help remove any small pieces from the stock.

To enhance the speed of chilling the stock, return stock to pot and place pot in sink surrounded by ice. Then place an ice pack in a plastic bag and place in pot. When soup has cooled, place in refrigerator.

Best when used in 5 – 7 days or freeze in resealable plastic bags in freezer.

Cream of Chicken Soup

A very simple soup that can be used as a replacement for condensed canned soup when called for in recipes or with the addition of a few more cups of chicken stock as a creamy soup to accompany any meal. This soup is a big hit with our family.

Makes 1¾ cups

In a medium sized saucepan over medium heat, cook the following for 3 – 5 minutes:

2 tablespoons **extra light olive oil**
3 tablespoons **fresh minced onion**
1 **clove of garlic**, minced

In a small bowl or 2 cup measuring cup, whisk together well:

1 cup **chicken stock**
½ cup **milk** or **non-dairy milk substitute**
⅓ cup *Celeste's Best Gluten-Free Flour Mix*
¼ teaspoon **black pepper**
¼ teaspoon **sea salt**

Add liquid mixture to saucepan and stir until soup reaches desired thickness, about 3 – 5 minutes. Use soup in any recipe calling for a can of cream of chicken soup.

To make soup for a meal instead of the 1 cup of stock, add:

4 cups **chicken stock**

Follow recipe as directed but cook an additional 7 – 10 minutes after adding the liquid ingredients, stirring often as soup thickens.

- Substitute 2 tablespoons dried minced onions if you don't have fresh.

- This recipe makes a slight bit more soup (about ½ cup) than the canned commercial version.

Cream of Mushroom Soup

This can be made as a soup or as a substitute for any recipe calling for a can of Cream of Mushroom Soup.

Makes 10¾ ounces (approx. 1¼ cups)

Place a medium sized pan on medium heat and add:

3 tablespoons **extra light olive oil**

Add and sauté until soft:

½ cup **fresh mushrooms**, finely chopped

Stir in:

3 tablespoons *Celeste's Best Gluten-Free Flour Mix*

Continue stirring until smooth (other than the bits of mushroom) and bubbly.

Remove from heat and slowly add while continually stirring:

½ cup **beef stock**
½ cup **milk** or **non-dairy milk substitute**

Return to medium heat and bring to a boil, stirring often until soup thickens. Season with sea salt and pepper to taste.

To serve as soup: Add an additional 1¼ cups water or beef stock. For a richer soup, add 1¼ cups milk or a mixture of ¾ cup milk and ½ cup of water.

Creamy Broccoli Soup

This is a tasty soup that is thick and creamy. An immersion blender is a handy tool to have to puree soups. Works well for many of the creamy soups in the cookbook.

Serves 4 – 6

In a medium sized stockpot, combine:

3 cups **frozen chopped broccoli** or **broccoli florets**
2 cups **water**
2 cloves **garlic**, sliced
1 **onion**, diced
¼ teaspoon **sea salt**

Cover pot and bring to a boil. Reduce heat and simmer for 15 minutes. Take pot off burner and puree with **immersion** or **stick blender** until smooth. (Be careful during this step, as soup is hot.) Soup may also be placed in blender and pureed. Return soup to stove; bring temperature up to medium heat. Meanwhile in a small bowl or measuring cup mix together with fork or small whisk:

1 cup **milk** or **non-dairy milk substitute**
2 tablespoons *Celeste's Best Gluten-Free Flour Mix*

Pour milk mixture into soup, mixing well until incorporated. Then stir in:

½ teaspoon **dried basil**
½ teaspoon **dried parsley**
½ teaspoon **sea salt**
¼ teaspoon **black pepper**

Cook soup an additional 5 – 10 minutes or until soup has thickened sufficiently. Ladle into bowls and serve.

Creamy Tomato Soup

An easily prepared creamy tomato soup. From stove to table in ten minutes.

Serves 2 – 4

Place a medium sized pot on medium heat and add:

3 tablespoons **extra light olive oil**

Add and sauté until soft:

¼ cup **chopped onion**

Then whisk in:

2 tablespoons *Celeste's Best Gluten-Free Flour Mix*

Puree with **immersion** or **stick blender** in bowl:

3 (14.5 ounce) cans **diced tomatoes**

Pour tomatoes into pot along with:

1½ cups **water**
1 (6 ounce) can **tomato paste**
1½ tablespoons **sugar**
1½ teaspoons **sea salt**
1 teaspoon **dried basil**
½ teaspoon **dried oregano**
¼ teaspoon **pepper**

Continue to cook for 5 – 7 minutes. Ladle into bowls and serve.

Mushroom Soup

A thick dairy-free soup that tastes as rich as those made with heavy cream. Using portabella mushrooms gives the soup a flavor that just can't be beat.

Serves 4 – 6

In a large soup pot over medium heat, add:

3 tablespoons **extra light olive oil**

Then add:

1 large **onion**, chopped

Sauté until soft and translucent, about 3 – 4 minutes. Reduce heat to low and add:

3 – 4 large **portabella mushrooms** (dark gills scraped out and discarded), chopped

Cover pot and cook until mushrooms are tender, about 10 minutes. Bring heat back up to medium and stir in:

3 tablespoons *Celeste's Best Gluten-Free Flour Mix*

Cook for 2 – 3 minutes, then add:

6 cups **chicken stock**
1 **bay leaf**
1 teaspoon **dried thyme**
1 teaspoon **sea salt**
1 teaspoon **sugar**
½ teaspoon **pepper**

Simmer soup on low for 10 minutes, partially covered. Take pot off burner and remove bay leaf and discard. Carefully, as soup will be very hot, use **immersion** or **stick blender** to puree soup until creamy.

Then slowly whisk into pureed soup:

1 cup **milk** or **non-dairy milk substitute**

Return pot to stove and continue to simmer for 5 minutes or until soup is well heated. Spoon into serving bowl and garnish with chopped **fresh parsley.**

(continued)

- Bay leaves are used to season many foods while cooking, but are removed before serving because they can impart a bitter or sour taste otherwise.

- A blender may also be used to puree the soup. Allow soup to cool slightly, though, before placing it in blender.

Pasta Fagioli

Pasta Fagioli is a hearty, meatless Italian soup comprised mainly of pasta and beans. The gluten-free version of this tomato based soup is made with gluten-free pasta and white beans.

Serves 4 – 6

Bring a pot of water to boil on stovetop. Add:

1 cup uncooked **gluten-free shell pasta**

While the pasta is cooking, in a large pot over medium heat, add:

2 tablespoons **olive oil**

Then add and cook for 8 – 10 minutes until soft and golden brown:

1 cup **chopped onion**
3 **cloves of garlic**, minced
¼ cup finely chopped **fresh parsley**

Then add and bring to a boil:

2 (14.5 ounce) cans **petite-diced tomatoes**
2 quarts **chicken stock**
1 (15 ounce) can **cannellini beans** or **great northern beans**, undrained
1 teaspoon **dried basil**
¼ teaspoon **black pepper**

Reduce heat and simmer for 7 – 10 minutes. Drain and rinse the cooked pasta then add to pan and continue to simmer for an additional 5 minutes.

Season with sea salt, pepper and a small amount of crushed red pepper flakes if desired. Then drizzle some additional olive oil on top.

Swiss Chard and White Bean Soup

Swiss chard belongs to the same family of vegetables as beets and spinach. It is a highly nutritious leafy green that provides an excellent source of vitamins K, A, C and E, plus several B vitamins, magnesium, manganese, potassium, iron and dietary fiber. It is also a source of calcium.

Serves 4 – 6

In a stockpot, add:

8 cups **chicken** or **vegetable stock**
1½ pounds **Swiss chard**, ends cut, rinsed, torn into 2-inch pieces
3 **cloves of garlic**, sliced

Bring to a boil over medium heat, and cook for 5 – 7 minutes. Then reduce heat to a simmer and add:

1 (15 or 19 ounce) can **white beans** (cannellini or northern beans)
⅛ - ¼ teaspoon **crushed red pepper flakes**

Continue to simmer for 10 minutes. Ladle into bowls and serve. Add **sea salt** and **pepper** to taste.

> - Add an additional can of beans to make a meal out of the soup.
>
> - Instead of Swiss chard, you can substitute kale.

VEGETABLES

Artichokes

Vegetable Cooking Times

Eating vegetables provides more fiber, nutrients and antioxidants in your diet. We try to eat one or more vegetables with each meal. Most nights we steam our vegetables in a steamer pot. Steaming is an easy way to prepare vegetables. It also maximizes taste and color, while retaining most nutrients in vegetables.

Below is a chart of cooking times for steaming vegetables. Cooking times are based on one pound of vegetables, placed in a steamer basket over 2 inches of water.

A couple of tips for steaming vegetables:

1. Cut or slice vegetables into uniform slices to ensure even cooking.

2. Fill your steamer pot with at least 2 inches of water. The water should fill the bottom of the pot but not touch the food itself.

3. Once your pot is filled with water, place your vegetables in steamer insert. Cover pot and place over high heat and bring to a boil.

4. Reduce heat to medium.

5. For longer cooking times, such as with artichokes, check water levels and refill if needed. (Absolutely nothing worse than trying to clean a steamer pot that has gone dry.)

6. Steamed vegetables are best when cooked tender-crisp. Simply pierce them with a fork to test for doneness. Overcooking will produce mushy vegetables.

7. A few simple and easy toppings for steamed vegetables:

   * Our personal favorite: drizzle extra virgin olive oil and a sprinkle of garlic powder or fresh minced garlic and sea salt over vegetables.

   * Sprinkle fresh or dried chopped herbs such as parsley, thyme, or dill over steaming vegetables.

   * For vegetables like broccoli, green beans, and summer squash try adding a few slices of lemon or lemon zest to vegetables while they cook or you can also add lemon juice to the steaming water.

VEGETABLE	METHOD	COOK TIME (in minutes)
artichokes, baby	Pull off tough outer leaves; cut off top quarter and trim stem.	15 – 20
artichokes	Pull off tough outer leaves; cut off top quarter and trim stem. (Check water levels throughout cooking time.)	60 – 75
asparagus	Trim ends; stand upright in asparagus steamer.	4 – 6 depending on thickness, or until tender.
beets	Peel. Cut beets into quarters.	12 – 15
broccoli	Cut off florets; cut stalks in half lengthwise and then into 1-inch-thick pieces.	7 – 10
Brussels sprouts	Peel off outer leaves; trim stem.	6 – 8 or until tender
carrots	Cut ¼-inch thick.	6 – 8 or until tender
cauliflower	Cut into 1-inch-wide florets, discarding core and thick stems.	5 – 13, depending on the size of the pieces
green beans	Pinch off stem ends.	5 – 7
peas	Snap off the top and the bottom of the pod, then pull off the string along the seam. Open the pod and use your thumb to remove the peas.	4 – 7
spinach	Cut off the thick stems of the spinach and discard.	3 – 4
squash and zucchini	Slice into ½-inch-thick rings.	5 – 7
sweet potatoes	Peel. Chop ends. Cut into 1-inch pieces.	7 – 10 or until tender

Artichokes

Growing up we often ate artichokes. But I know many people might be intimidated when it comes to preparing this fiber-filled vegetable. And fiber is something often missing from a gluten-free diet.

And I can't tell you how many times the checkout clerk at the grocery store has asked me "What are these?" before she rung up these tight, compact green globes. But truthfully this recipe is very easy to prepare and one our family really looks forward to eating. You can steam artichokes, but we prefer them boiled and seasoned.

Buy one artichoke for each person you plan to serve. Choose artichokes that have compact leaves and are firm and heavy for their size.

Using a knife, cut one inch off the entire top of the artichoke. Then cut the stem off getting as close to the base as you can so that the artichoke will sit level in the pot.

Some people skip this next step, but I like the way it makes the artichokes look. With a scissor, trim the pointy leaves of the artichoke and discard.

Place your thumb in the center of the artichoke being watchful for any pointy leaves which may not have been trimmed and loosen the leaves.

Rinse artichokes and leave upside down to drain. Then thinly slice:

1 **clove of garlic**

Stuff slices between the leaves of the artichoke. Place in cooking pan with enough water to cover the bottom quarter of the artichoke.

Sprinkle on top of each artichoke:

1 teaspoon **fresh parsley**

Then drizzle over each artichoke:

1 teaspoon **lemon juice**
1 tablespoon **olive oil**

Place pan on stove over high heat and bring water to a slow boil. Cover pan and reduce heat to a light boil and continue cooking for 60 – 75 minutes or for very large artichokes, an hour and a half. Check periodically throughout cooking to make sure there is still sufficient water in pot.

To eat, pull off outer leaves one at a time. Dip base of leaf into mayonnaise, then pull through teeth to remove soft, pulpy portion. Continue until all leaves have been removed. Use the side of your fork to scrape away fuzzy, inedible center at base and discard. The bottom of the artichoke – the heart – is completely edible. Slice into small pieces and dip into mayonnaise and enjoy.

- Chop fresh parsley and store in freezer so it will be handy for recipes like this one.

Escarole and Beans

Over the years, every time I've made this side dish, I've called my mother to ask, "How do you make escarole and beans again?" until luckily one day I decided to write a cookbook and finally wrote down this simple recipe.

Escarole is part of the chicory family. The minced garlic and cannelloni beans in this recipe are perfect compliments to this leafy green. You'll usually find heads of escarole in the produce section near the romaine and lettuce.

Serves 4 – 6

Wash and let drain in a colander:

2 heads **escarole**

In a large skillet heat on medium heat and add:

2 tablespoons **olive oil**
2 **cloves of garlic**, minced

Heat garlic until lightly browned, then add:

Slightly damp **escarole**
¼ teaspoon **crushed red pepper flakes**

Cook, stirring often, until escarole wilts and softens, about 7 – 10 minutes. Add:

2 (15 or 19 ounce) cans **cannellini beans**

Turn heat down to low and cook for an additional 5 minutes.

Fried Onion Strings

You may notice there are not many fried foods in this cookbook. We try to keep on the healthier side of things when we cook.

But there are a few items I can't help but indulge in occasionally – fried oysters (my personal weakness and our traditional Christmas morning breakfast), doughnuts and I'd absolutely have to add to the list - fried onion strings.

These onion strings would make the perfect topping to a green bean casserole.

Serves 4 – 6

Slice very thinly (so that you can see through each slice):

2 large **onions**, peeled

In a large measuring cup, whisk together:

3 cups **milk** or **non-dairy milk substitute**
3 tablespoons **lemon juice**

Place sliced onions in a large bowl and cover with milk and let sit for one hour. Meanwhile in another large bowl, whisk together:

2½ cups *Celeste's Best Gluten-Free Flour Mix*
1½ teaspoons **sea salt**
½ teaspoon **cayenne pepper**
¼ teaspoon **black pepper**

When onions have finished soaking, heat a frying pan on medium heat with a sufficient amount of **vegetable oil**. (We prefer to have about ½-inch of oil in the pan.)

Place a good sized handful of onions into the flour mix, separating rings and coating well, then shaking off any excess. To check if oil is well heated (approximately 375 degrees) take a flour coated onion ring and place in pan. If oil is ready, it should bubble slightly and sizzle. (Note: If oil smokes it is too hot.) When ready, add remaining floured rings to pan.

Cook each batch for 3 – 5 minutes or until golden brown. Remove with a slotted spoon or tongs and place on a plate covered with paper towel to drain. Continue with remaining onion rings until all have been floured and fried.

Lemony Green Beans

This is an extremely easy recipe, and it is also one of our family's favorites. I sometimes prepare this for company or as a take along side dish for a buffet get together.

Serves 4 – 6

Place into a large serving bowl:

1 (6 pound, 5 ounce) or 2 (50 ounce) **cans of green beans**, drained

In a small bowl, combine:

¼ cup **olive oil**
1 teaspoon **sea salt**
1 tablespoon **lemon zest**
2 tablespoons **lemon juice**

Pour olive oil mixture over green beans and toss all ingredients together until well mixed. Serve.

- You can also serve this dish with fresh or frozen green beans you steam, then immerse in ice cold water to cool off. Drain, then toss with remaining ingredients.

- Some brands of canned green beans taste better than others.

Marinated Artichoke Hearts

Our family loves artichokes. Making your own marinated artichoke hearts is simple and takes only a few minutes.

This recipe is for using a large jar of hearts that you might get at a warehouse shopping club. To scale the recipe down to use for canned or even a 9-ounce box of frozen artichoke hearts, simply cut the recipe in half.

Makes one 2 pound, 1.4 ounce jar of artichoke hearts

In a small bowl, whisk together:

1 cup **olive oil**
¼ cup **lemon juice**
1 teaspoon **sea salt**
1 teaspoon **dried thyme**
1 teaspoon **dried oregano**
¼ - ½ teaspoon **crushed red pepper** (based on taste)

Drain:

1 (2 pound, 1.4 ounce jar) of **artichoke hearts**

Return artichokes to jar and add oil marinade until artichokes are fully covered. Shake well. Allow flavors to marinade overnight.

Serve or refrigerate for 7 – 10 days to use in recipes or on salads.

- Most processed artichokes contain citric acid which can be an issue for those who are sensitive to corn.

Onion Rings

My husband called on his way home from work one night and asked if I could make onion rings. I had tried twice before to make them and even though they required a lot of effort to prepare, we were less than satisfied with the end result.

But you know what they say about that magical "third time" – definitely true in this case. Onion rings! Actual onion rings!

Nevertheless, this recipe comes with a warning – making onion rings is time consuming. Still, that hasn't stopped us yet from making a batch.

Makes 20 – 25 rings

Preheat oven to 350 degrees. Line two large baking sheets with parchment paper.

Cut:

1 large **onion** sliced ½-inch thick, separated into rings

Meanwhile in a quart-sized zippered plastic bag, mix together:

¾ cup *Celeste's Best Gluten-Free Flour Mix*
½ teaspoon **sea salt**
½ teaspoon **Italian seasoning**
½ teaspoon **Cajun seasoning**
½ teaspoon **black pepper**

And in another quart-sized zippered plastic bag, place**:**

1 cup **gluten-free bread crumbs** (see page 181)

Prepare each of the following in their own shallow bowl or container:

½ cup **milk** or **non-dairy milk substitute**
2 **eggs** or equivalent substitute

Place 2 – 3 onion rings at a time into the milk, letting the excess milk drip off. Then dip rings into bag of seasoned flour mix, shaking the bag well to coat the rings. Then into egg, again letting excess drip off. Lastly, dip rings into the bag of bread crumbs.

So you are dipping in this order: **milk, flour, egg** then **bread crumbs**.

Place rings in single layer on baking sheet. Mist over tops well with **extra light olive oil**. Bake in oven for 25 – 30 minutes.

- Line up your ingredients for the batter in order ending with your baking sheet to save time.

- If your bread crumbs are frozen, take them out several hours before using in this recipe so they have sufficient time to thaw, otherwise they'll likely be too damp and have a tendency to clump up. If your crumbs are still slightly wet, spread the thawed crumbs on a baking tray and toast them in the oven for a few minutes.

- Be sure the bread crumbs are finely processed. I often run them through the food processor once again before making this recipe. Finer crumbs adhere better to the rings.

Roasted Italian Vegetables

My husband came up with this recipe and we so enjoy it each time he makes it. It's very simple, just slicing up a few ingredients and drizzling with some olive oil and - Voila! An incredibly delicious side dish!

Serves 4 – 6

Preheat oven to 375 degrees. Line two baking sheets with parchment paper.

Peel and slice into ½-inch size pieces:

10 **carrots**

Cut into bite-size cubes:

2 medium sized **eggplants**, peeled, sliced ½-inch thick
2 **yellow squash,** sliced ½-inch thick
2 **zucchini,** sliced ½-inch thick
2 **onions,** peeled, sliced ½-inch thick

Evenly divide the vegetables and spread across the parchment paper on the two trays. Place in oven and bake for 30 – 40 minutes or until tender.

> ▪ We prefer to make this side dish when we have eggplant, carrots and onions on hand. But you can use whatever happens to be in season. Sometimes we also cut tomatoes into ½-thick slices and then into bite size pieces and add that, too. Red onions are also a nice variation as well.

Sweet Potatoes Cubes

Sweet potatoes consistently show up on top ten lists of healthy foods. They're a nutritional powerhouse. They're full of carotenoids, vitamin C, potassium, and fiber.

This is one of our favorite ways to eat sweet potatoes. Slightly spicy and quickly bakes up in half an hour.

Serves 4 – 6

Preheat oven to 400 degrees. Grease 2 large cookie trays. Peel and cut into 1-inch cubes:

4 – 6 medium sized **sweet potatoes** (about 10 – 12 cups)

Place sweet potato cubes in a gallon sized resealable plastic bag along with:

3 tablespoons **extra light olive oil**

Shake bag well so that each cube is coated with oil. Meanwhile in a small bowl, mix together:

⅓ cup **sweet potato flour**
¼ cup **brown sugar**
2 teaspoons **seasoning salt** (see page 374)
½ teaspoon **chili powder**
½ teaspoon **black pepper**
⅛ teaspoon **cayenne pepper**

Sprinkle half the seasoning into the bag. Shake well. Add the remaining seasoning and shake well to evenly distribute seasoning on all the sweet potatoes. Spread half the sweet potatoes on each tray, one layer deep.

Place trays in oven and bake for 30 – 35 minutes.

- For spicier sweet potatoes, add ¼ teaspoon more chili powder and ⅛ teaspoon more cayenne pepper.

- Cooking the potatoes too long can cause them to become soft and mushy.

Sweet Potato Fries

Sweet potato fries are a terrific and healthy alternative to regular potato fries.

Serves 4 – 6

Preheat oven to 425 degrees. Grease two large cookie trays. Wash and peel:

4 medium sized **sweet potatoes**

Cut each sweet potato in half lengthwise. Then slice each half into ¼-inch thick slices. Cut each slice into ¼-inch fries. Place fries in a large bowl of water and soak for at least 1 hour.

Remove fries from water and towel dry.

In a large bowl, whisk together the following:

¼ cup **sweet potato flour**

and your choice of the following:

2 teaspoons **Cajun seasoning**

or

2 teaspoons **chili powder**
¼ teaspoon **garlic powder**
¼ teaspoon **onion powder**
¼ teaspoon **sea salt**

or

2 teaspoons **ground cumin**
1 teaspoon **chili powder**
½ teaspoon **sea salt**
1 teaspoon **onion powder**

Sprinkle flour and seasonings on fries. Continually toss the fries until all of the white from the flour disappears. Place fries on baking trays and cook in preheated oven for 15 minutes. Turn over fries with a spatula, then cook for an additional 15 minutes.

- Sweet potato flour produces the driest fries, but if not available other gf flours will help to prevent the fries from becoming overly mushy when baking, too. White rice flour works well, too.

- Variation: Replace spices above with just 1 tablespoon brown sugar and a teaspoon of both sea salt and pepper.

- Variation: Replace spices above with 1 tablespoon brown sugar and ½ teaspoon of both cinnamon and cayenne pepper.

Zucchini Boats

Zucchini boats (or sometimes called stuffed zucchini) have always been one of my favorite side dishes. I love the way the tomato, zucchini and bread crumbs complement one another.

Serves 4 – 6

Preheat oven to 350 degrees. Grease a 13 x 9 x 2-inch baking dish.

Wash and cut the stem end off of:

6 **medium sized zucchini** (smart tip: choose zucchini that will fit in your stock pot)

Fill a large stockpot with water. Place on high heat and bring water to a boil. Place zucchini in boiling water and parboil for 4 – 6 minutes. Then test to see if they are ready by inserting a fork into the flesh. Fork should go in easily and zucchini should still be slightly firm.

Remove zucchini from water and drain. When cool enough to touch, slice down horizontally and carefully cut each zucchini in half. With a sharp knife etch out a rectangle in the surface of each zucchini boat, being sure to leave at least ¼-inch thickness on all sides.

Using a spoon, scoop or scrape out the inside. Place zucchini boats in single layer in baking dish. Then coarsely chop scooped out portion of the zucchini and place in a medium sized bowl to be added later to the stuffing.

Heat a skillet over medium heat and add:

3 tablespoons **olive oil**

Add:

3 **cloves of garlic**, minced
½ cup **chopped onion**

Sauté for 2 – 3 minutes then add **chopped zucchini** and:

3 **large tomatoes**, peeled and chopped (or 1 (14.5 ounce) can **diced tomatoes**)
2 tablespoons **dried basil** (yes, 2 tablespoons!)
¼ cup **fresh parsley**

Cook for 5 more minutes. Remove from heat and place in medium sized bowl and add:

1½ cups **gluten-free bread crumbs** (see page 181)
½ cup **chicken stock**
3 tablespoons **olive oil**
½ teaspoon **sea salt**
¼ teaspoon **pepper**

Mix all ingredients together. Stuff shells with bread crumb mixture and place in prepared baking dish. Drizzle additional olive oil over each zucchini boat and place in preheated oven and bake for 30 – 35 minutes or until the shells are tender and topping is golden brown.

Zucchini Fritters

My mother used to make zucchini fritters when we were kids. Zucchinis always seem to be in such abundance during the summer. Thankfully there are an equally abundant number of ways to prepare them. My husband loves to fix these up and we always look forward to dinner when zucchini fritters are one of the side dishes.

Makes 12, four inch fritters

Grate over several sheets of paper towel or a clean kitchen towel:

2 medium **zucchini,** washed, ends removed, coarsely grated (3 cups)

Wrap up grated zucchini in paper or kitchen towel and squeeze out as much remaining liquid as you can. Preheat griddle or large non-stick fry pan to medium. Heat on medium low and add:

¼ cup **olive oil**

Meanwhile as oil is heating up, in a large bowl combine with a fork:

3 **eggs** or equivalent substitute
¼ cup **milk** or **non-dairy milk substitute**
½ cup *Celeste's Best Gluten-Free Flour Mix*
2 tablespoons **dried parsley**
1 teaspoon **sea salt**
½ teaspoon **black pepper**
¼ teaspoon **cream of tartar**
⅛ teaspoon **baking soda**

And then add:

drained zucchini

Continue to mix with a fork until well blended. Batter should have the consistency of a thin pancake batter. If your batter is too thin, the fritters will spread excessively when they are placed in the pan. If it is too thick, the fritters will not spread out enough to cook well. Add more flour or more milk as needed to create the right consistency.

When oil is hot and bubbles, drop 2 tablespoons of batter for each fritter into pan. Brown until golden on each side, turning once and cooking for roughly 4 – 6 minutes total cook time for each fritter. Place cooked fritters on plate lined with paper-towels. Best when served hot, but also taste good cooled.

BEANS, GRAINS AND PASTA

Baked Beans

Baked Beans

My husband and I both had cravings for baked beans – you know, the kind with the secret family recipe. But most brands have some allergen we're sensitive to. My husband was determined and he developed this recipe. I think you'll agree this comes incredibly close to the famous, secret recipe that only Duke, the dog, knows about.

Serves 6 – 8

Preheat oven to 350 degrees. Grease a 13 x 9 x 2-inch baking dish.

Cut into bite-sized pieces and place in large bowl:

1 (8 ounce) package uncooked **turkey bacon**

Then add the following and stir until well combined:

3 (15½ ounce) cans **great northern beans**, undrained
1 **small** onion, diced
1½ cups **ketchup** (see page 360)
1 cup **brown sugar**
½ cup **molasses**
2 teaspoons **dry mustard**

Pour all ingredients into prepared baking dish. Bake for 2 hours.

> ▪ For hot dogs and beans, add: 10 **hot dogs**, cut into 1-inch slices, during the last 40 minutes of cooking time.

Black Beans and Rice

We've been making this dish for years. A healthy, meat free meal.

Serves 4 – 6

In a stockpot over medium heat, add:

2 tablespoons **olive oil**

Add and sauté for 3 – 5 minutes or until soft:

1 **red pepper**, chopped
1 large **onion**, chopped
3 **cloves of garlic**, minced

Add:

¾ cup **white rice**

Cook for only a few minutes and then add:

2 cups **chicken stock**
1 (14.5 ounce) can **diced tomatoes** (drain juice slightly)

Bring mixture to a boil, then lower heat to a simmer and cook for 25 – 30 minutes (cook according to instructions for specific type of rice you choose to use.)

Then stir in:

2 (15 ounce) cans **black beans**, drained
¼ - ½ teaspoon **cayenne pepper** (depending on how spicy you like it!)
1 teaspoon **cumin powder**
1 teaspoon **curry powder**
2 tablespoons **fresh chopped cilantro**

Cook for 5 additional minutes or until beans are well heated. Spoon into bowls and serve.

Quinoa and Black Beans

A refreshing protein rich salad. Wonderful as a main dish served alongside a bowl of black bean soup (see page 56) or as a side dish with any meal. Tastes excellent hot or cold!

Serves 4 – 6

Cook one cup of quinoa according to directions. (Quinoa grains have a coating of saponin that creates a bitter-tasting cooked grain if it isn't removed first. Many brands of gluten-free quinoa are pre-rinsed. When using a brand that hasn't been pre-rinsed, before cooking simply rinse the quinoa with water in a fine mesh strainer until the water runs clear.)

Meanwhile in a medium sized bowl, mix together:

1 (15 ounce) can **black beans**, rinsed and drained
4 **scallions,** chopped
2 **tomatoes**, diced
¼ cup chopped fresh **cilantro**
zest of one lime
2 tablespoons **lime juice**
3 tablespoons **olive oil**
1 teaspoon **sugar**

Add the cooked quinoa to the other ingredients and lightly toss with a large spoon until well blended. Serve hot or cold.

Basil Chicken with Tomatoes over Penne

Chicken with a hearty helping of basil simmered in a fresh tomato sauce. This meal is great for company, too, because you can have all the ingredients ready and quickly throw them together in a few minutes.

Serves 4 – 6

Boil a large stockpot of water, then add:

1 (16 ounce) bag **gluten-free penne pasta**

Cook the pasta according to package instructions.   Meanwhile place in a medium sized stockpot:

2 pounds **skinless, boneless chicken breast halves**, (or 3 **chicken breast halves**) cut into ¼-inch cubes

Add enough water to cover chicken in pot. Bring to a boil and cook for 10 minutes. Then remove from heat, drain water, and keep chicken warm.

In a large skillet, add:

1 tablespoon **olive oil**
1 medium **onion**, chopped (½ cup)
3 **cloves of garlic**, minced

Cook onion on medium heat, until soft and translucent. Then reduce heat to low and stir in:

3 cups **chopped fresh tomatoes** (preferably grape tomatoes)
¼ cup **chopped fresh** or **dehydrated basil leaves**
¼ teaspoon **red pepper flakes**
½ teaspoon **sea salt**
⅛ teaspoon **black pepper**

Simmer for 5 minutes or until tomatoes have softened. Drain and rinse pasta, then add to pan along with the chicken. Cook for an additional 3 – 4 minutes and serve.

> ▪   Add ½ cup chicken stock if you prefer more sauce over your pasta.
>
> ▪   If you don't have fresh tomatoes use 2 (14.5 ounce) cans of diced tomatoes.

Dairy-Free Lasagna

A delicious, dairy-free alternative for those who love lasagna. This recipe is a bit labor intensive, but the result is amazing. And believe me, the Italian and Sicilian in me doesn't even miss the cheese one tiny bit.

Serves 6 – 8

Boil a large stockpot of water, then add:

1 (16 ounce) box **gluten-free lasagna noodles**

Cook the noodles for 12 – 14 minutes, or until just tender. (Lasagna noodles are easier to handle al dente and also noodles will continue cooking slightly while baking in the oven.)

Preheat oven to 350 degrees. Grease a 13x9x2-inch glass casserole dish. In a large skillet on medium heat, add:

2 tablespoons **olive oil**

Then:

1 **medium onion**, diced
2 **cloves of garlic**, minced

Cook until the onions become soft and translucent. Then add:

2 pounds of **ground beef**

Cook for 7 – 10 minutes or until the beef is cooked through.   Meanwhile in another pan set on medium heat, add:

2 tablespoons **olive oil**

Add and sauté until soft:

2 cups **diced eggplant**, diced (see note box on following page)
2 cups **yellow squash**, diced
2 cups **zucchini**, diced
2 cups frozen **chopped spinach**

Then stir in:

2 (15 ounce) cans **diced tomatoes**
1 (6 ounce) can **tomato paste**

Cook for 5 more minutes then add to meat sauce. Reduce heat to simmer as you prepare the white sauce.

In a medium sized saucepan, add:

¼ cup 2 tablespoons **olive oil**

Whisk in:

½ cup *Celeste's Best Gluten-Free Flour Mix*
1 **clove of garlic**, minced

Then slowly whisk in, creating a roux:

1½ – 2 cups **milk** or **non-dairy milk substitute**

Allow the white sauce to come to a gentle boil, whisking constantly, as sauce thickens. Add milk to reach desired consistency. Then remove from heat and also remove the meat sauce from heat.

Drain lasagna noodles and rinse well with water. Then spoon a thin layer of the meat/vegetable sauce on the bottom of the baking dish. Place a single layer of the lasagna noodles, topped with more meat/vegetable sauce, then the white sauce, and lasagna noodles again. Repeat for one more layer and finish with a light layer of the meat sauce.

Place in oven and bake for 30 – 35 minutes.

Add to the remaining meat/vegetable sauce and heat on simmer while lasagna cooks:

2 (15 ounce) cans **tomato sauce**

Remove lasagna from oven and spoon sauce over top and serve. Wonderful served with a loaf of Gluten-Free, Yeast-Free French Bread (see pages 173 - 174).

- Often eggplant can be bitter so it's best to slice it, and sprinkle some sea salt over it and cover it with a clean kitchen towel and let it rest for 30 minutes before dicing. The sea salt with draw out water and along with it the bitter alkaloid compounds.

- Rice lasagna noodles often break apart during cooking. Simply put all the pieces together to form long strips.

Kevin's Dinner

Growing up on Long Island in New York, we had terrific neighbors, Ed and Dede Vogl. This dish is named after their oldest son, Kevin, and is a combination of elbow macaroni and ground beef mixed with tomato sauce.

This recipe has been a staple on the dinner menu at our house for as long as I can remember. In fact, I don't think a month goes by without us enjoying this old family favorite.

Serves 4 – 6

Boil a large stockpot of water, then add:

1 (16 ounce) bag **gluten-free elbow pasta**

Cook the pasta according to package directions. (Pasta will continue cooking slightly when added to meat mixture in pan.)   Meanwhile in a large skillet, add:

1 tablespoon **olive oil**
1 medium **onion**, chopped (½ cup)

Cook onion on medium heat, until soft and translucent. Then add:

3 pounds **ground beef** (80% lean or better)

Cook the meat for 15 – 20 minutes or until it is well browned and fully cooked. Then drain meat of any grease if necessary and return meat to pan.

Add:

4 (15 ounce) cans **tomato sauce**
1 (6 ounce) can **tomato paste**

Stir well. When pasta has finished cooking, drain pasta in a colander and rinse well. Add to meat and sauce, again stirring well to combine. Continue to cook on low for 5 minutes, then serve.

> - Growing up we made this dish with more pasta than meat. As an adult, I prefer it with more meat than pasta. Adjust the dish to your own taste.

Pasta with Clam Sauce

I love this dish! Not only does it have an incredible taste, it's so easy to put together that you won't mind making it time and time again.

Serves 4 – 6

Boil a large stockpot of water, then add:

1 (16 ounce) bag **gluten-free fettuccini**

Cook the pasta for the recommended time or until desired tenderness is reached. Meanwhile heat in large skillet over medium heat:

¼ cup **olive oil**

Add and sauté for 5 – 7 minutes:

1 small **onion**, chopped (½ cup)
6 **cloves of garlic**, minced (yes 6!)

Then add:

1 (14.5 ounce) can **diced tomatoes**
1 (15 ounce) can **crushed tomatoes**
3 tablespoons **fresh chopped parsley**
1 teaspoon **sea salt**
¼ teaspoon **oregano**
¼ teaspoon **pepper**

Simmer for 10 minutes. Meanwhile open:

1 large (51 ounce) can or 7 small (6½ ounce) cans **chopped clams**

Drain the clams in a strainer reserving **2 cups** of the juice. When pasta is done, drain and rinse well and place in serving dish and set aside. Meanwhile stir into sauce:

reserved clam juice (for thicker sauce omit)
chopped clams

Cook for only 1 – 2 minutes to reheat the clams. Overcooking the clams will cause them to become tough and chewy. Remove pan from heat and pour sauce over fettuccini and serve.

Pasta with Sausage and Squash

Sausage and summer squash served over a bed of pasta.

Serves 4 – 6

Boil a large stockpot of water, then add:

1 (16 ounce) bag **gluten-free spaghetti pasta**

Cook the pasta for the recommended time or until desired tenderness is reached. Meanwhile, in a large non-stick skillet, add:

3 packages (4 links) **fully cooked sweet gf Italian chicken sausages**, cut into ¼-inch slices

Cook for 5 – 7 minutes or until sausage is fully reheated. Remove sausage from pan and keep warm. Reduce heat to medium low and add:

¼ cup **olive oil**

Once oil has heated add:

2 medium **yellow squash**, sliced thin
2 medium **zucchini**, sliced thin
1 tablespoon **minced onion**

Cook for 5 – 7 minutes or until vegetables are tender. Then add:

2 tablespoons **sliced green olives**
1½ teaspoons **Italian seasoning**
1 teaspoon **garlic powder**
½ teaspoon **crushed red pepper**

When pasta has finished cooking, drain pasta in a colander and rinse well. Add pasta to pan along with sausage and continue cooking on low for 5 minutes, then serve.

Spaghetti Sauce

This couldn't be any easier to prepare and yet the flavor reminds me of the sauce my mother used to make when I was growing up. Originally, I followed a long recipe and one night my husband whipped this up. I loved the simplicity and the taste and I've been cooking his version ever since.

Serves 4 – 6

In a large stockpot on medium heat, add:

2 tablespoons **olive oil**
2 **cloves garlic**, minced

Sauté garlic until lightly browned.

Meanwhile cut into 2-inch square pieces:

2 – 3 pound **pot roast** or **chuck roast**

Add meat to the pot, turning to brown on all sides.

Then add:

6 (15 ounce cans) **tomato sauce**
2 (6 ounce cans) **tomato paste**

Stir well to incorporate the paste into the sauce. Continue cooking on low heat as sauce that cooks on too high a temperature will burn the bottom of the pot and impart an unpleasant burnt taste to the sauce. Cook for 2 hours, stirring occasionally.

Meanwhile follow the recipe for meatballs (see page 108) and then add the cooked meatballs to the sauce. Cook an additional 2 hours until meat is tender.

The meat will become more tender the longer the sauce cooks. You can tell your sauce is ready when you no longer need a knife to cut the meat and it simply breaks apart with only a fork.

Add **sea salt** to taste. Serve over gluten-free pasta.

*Please see following page for cooking notes and suggestions.

- For the best tasting sauce, use a meat with a higher fat content. Leaner cuts aren't as tasty as a chuck roast.

- Many canned tomato products contain citric acid which may affect those who are sensitive to corn. Fortunately, there are many brands that are both gluten-free and corn-free.

- You may also add cooked pork or chicken sausage to the sauce if desired. Cook the sausage in oven or panfry until completely done, then add to sauce.

- This sauce can be made with just meatballs or meatballs and gf sausage and that would considerably cut down on cooking time. Then you will only need three (15 ounce) cans of sauce and one can of tomato paste.

- Another variation would be to cut up one medium sized onion and sauté that along with the garlic before adding the meat. Push the onions over to the side, and then begin browning the meat, before adding the sauce.

- My husband prefers a sweeter sauce and always adds a little sugar to his serving. My daughter and I like the taste just as it is and never add any sugar or salt to it.

Spaghetti with Vegetables

We used to be regulars at an Italian restaurant before going gluten-free and the owner made the most amazing spaghetti with vegetables dish. We were happily surprised how close this came to the dish we had loved and remembered so well.

Serves 6 – 8

Combine the following in a large bowl and puree with an **immersion** or **stick blender** until smooth:

1 (15 ounce) can **tomato sauce**
2 (14.5 ounce) cans **diced tomatoes**
2 (6 ounce) cans **tomato paste**

Pour pureed sauce into a large stockpot over medium low heat and add:

1 tablespoon **sugar** (optional)
1 teaspoon **dried basil**
1 teaspoon **dried oregano**
1 teaspoon **sea salt**
½ teaspoon **black pepper**

Meanwhile in a 6 quart saucepan over medium heat add 2 tablespoons **olive oil** and then add:

1 **onion**, finely chopped (1½ cups)
4 **cloves of garlic**, minced

Sauté onion and garlic for 3 – 5 minutes until soft and translucent.   Then add to skillet:

2 (10 ounce bags) **frozen chopped spinach**, thawed and drained
2 (8 ounce) packages of **sliced baby bella mushrooms**
4 cups **broccoli florets**

Sauté vegetables for 7 – 10 minutes over medium heat. Add ⅓ cup of water as needed, should the vegetables need additional liquid. Cook only until vegetables are "al dente" – warmed through but still slightly crisp. When sauce is well heated add the sautéed vegetables and:

1 cup sliced **green olives**

Reduce to simmer and cook for 3 – 5 minutes. Serve over gluten-free pasta.

BEEF

Beef Shish Kabobs

Beef and Bean Burritos

We usually make burritos with refried black beans and then top them with Burrito Sauce (see page 357).

Serves 4 – 6

Prepare a double batch (6 tortillas) of the tortilla recipe (see pages 191 – 193) and keep warm.

In a large skillet on medium heat, brown until well cooked:

1 pound **ground beef**

Drain excess grease if necessary. Then add:

¼ cup **tomato sauce**
1 (16 ounce) can **refried black beans**
½ cup **chopped onion**

And the following seasonings:

1 teaspoon **cumin**
1 teaspoon **sea salt**
½ teaspoon **chili powder**
½ teaspoon **coriander**
½ teaspoon **garlic powder**
¼ teaspoon **cayenne pepper**
¼ teaspoon **black pepper**

Reduce heat to low and continue cooking for 7 – 10 minutes. Spoon filling into prepared tortillas, wrap tightly and position on plates with seam side down. Top with Burrito Sauce (see page 357) if desired.

Beef (Carne Asada) Fajitas

This carne asada recipe is made with grilled flank steak. The meat is seasoned with a spicy rub.

Serves 4 – 6

Prepare a triple batch of **gluten-free tortillas** (see pages 191 – 193) and keep warm.

Whisk the following spices together in a small bowl to create a rub:

1 tablespoon **paprika**
1½ teaspoons **brown sugar**
1½ teaspoons **chili powder**
1½ teaspoons **sea salt**
¾ teaspoon **black pepper**
¾ teaspoon **cumin**

Place the following in a large baking dish:

1 **flank steak** (1 pound, ¾-inch thick)

Pour a small amount of **olive oil** across the steak. Season both sides of meat with the spice rub. Allow meat to come to room temperature, about 20 – 30 minutes. Preheat grill to medium high. Grill meat for 4 – 5 minutes per side. Meat should still be red inside, medium rare (125 – 130 degrees when tested with a meat thermometer) when removing from grill.

Place meat in a baking dish, pour 2 – 3 tablespoons lemon juice over it and cover with a cookie tray, allowing it to rest and steam for 10 minutes. This will promote juiciness and create a very tender meat. Slice thinly with a sharp knife at a 45-degree angle, against the grain of the meat.

While beef is steaming prepare the onions. Place in large sauté pan:

2 tablespoons **olive oil**
2 **onions**, cut in half and sliced

Cook for 5 – 7 minutes or until soft and tender. Spoon mixture into warm tortillas and top with sliced meat and serve.

- We like to spread mayonnaise on the tortillas before adding the onions and meat.

- The fajitas are also delicious filled with guacamole along with the meat and onions.

Beef Empanadas

One of my favorite recipes in the book is the empanada recipe. They are a bit more time consuming than many of the other recipes in the book but in my opinion so worth the extra effort.

Makes 22 – 24 empanadas

Prepare the **empanada dough** according to recipe instructions (see pages 327 – 328).

Preheat oven to 400 degrees. Line two large cookie sheets with parchment paper.

In a large skillet on medium heat, add:

2 tablespoons **olive oil**
1 cup finely diced **onion**
1 **jalapeno pepper**, minced (see note box on following page)

Cook for 5 minutes or until soft. Then add:

1 pound **ground beef**

Cook for 7 – 10 minutes or until meat is well browned and no longer pink. Then add:

¼ teaspoon **chili powder**
1 can (14.5 ounce) **diced tomatoes**

Lower heat to medium low and continue to cook for 12 – 15 minutes or until mixture has thickened. Season with:

½ teaspoon **sea salt**
¼ teaspoon **black pepper**

Then stir in:

½ cup **fresh cilantro**, finely chopped

Fill a very small bowl with water. Dip finger into water and moisten edges of dough. Place a teaspoon of meat mixture inside each empanada. Seal edges with fingers or by pressing with tongs of fork. Place on baking sheet. Mist tops with spray oil. Bake for 30 – 40 minutes or until crust has turned golden brown. Remove from oven and cover with a lightweight kitchen towel for several minutes to steam and soften the empanadas before serving.

- Jalapenos too spicy? Remove all the white ribs and seeds from inside the jalapeno to cut down on the heat.

- To freeze empanadas for later use: Place filled, uncooked empanadas on a baking sheet, place in freezer until firm, 3 hours, then remove from tray and freeze in plastic bags. To use: Remove from freezer and bake 45 – 50 minutes.

- Double the recipe and you'll have plenty of the beef mixture to eat along with the empanadas.

- If you have any leftover empanada filling, you can prepare some gluten-free pasta and top it with the filling for a tasty side dish.

Beef Shish Kabobs

This is a dish we usually make on special occasions. It's a simple marinade that perfectly complements the beef. Since this is a dish you can prepare ahead of time it is a perfect dinner to prepare for guests.

Best served with rice and Pineapple Salsa (see page 365).

Serves 4 – 6

Cut into 1-inch pieces and place into a large bowl or gallon-sized zippered bag:

1½ pounds **beef sirloin steak**, cut 1-inch thick

In a small bowl, whisk together marinade:

2 tablespoons **lime juice**
2 tablespoons **olive oil**
2 **cloves of garlic**, minced
1 **jalapeno pepper**, seeds removed, minced
½ teaspoon **ground cumin**

Pour marinade over beef and toss well to coat all pieces. Refrigerate for at least 30 minutes. Meanwhile on a large dish prepare the vegetables for the kabobs. You may use any vegetables of your choosing. The following are those we typically use:

mushrooms
cherry tomatoes
yellow squash
onions
zucchini
green, yellow and red peppers

Wash all vegetables and cut into pieces large enough to fit onto skewers. If mushrooms are small enough they may remain whole. Cherry tomatoes may also remain whole. Turn grill on to medium. Place meat and vegetables on skewers and cook on grill until done.

> ▪ Kabobs can also be baked in the oven at 350 degrees for 15 – 20 minutes.

Beef Stew

There is nothing quite as comforting as a bowl of hot beef stew on a cold winter day.

Serves 4 – 6

Place in a shallow dish:

½ cup *Celeste's Best Gluten-Free Flour Mix*
½ teaspoon **garlic salt**
½ teaspoon **black pepper**

Dredge in flour until well coated:

2 pounds cubed **beef stew meat**

Place in large skillet on medium heat:

3 tablespoons **olive oil**

Then add coated squares of beef and cook until evenly browned, about 7 – 10 minutes.
Transfer beef to a large stockpot and add:

1 quart **beef stock**
1 (1 pound) bag frozen **white pearl onions**
1 (16 ounce bag) frozen **diced peas and carrots**
3 **stalks of celery**, sliced
2 **bay leaves**
1 **clove of garlic**, minced
1 teaspoon **sea salt**
1 teaspoon **sugar**
½ teaspoon **black pepper**
½ teaspoon **paprika**
1 teaspoon **lemon juice**

Bring pot to a boil for 5 minutes, then simmer on low heat for 3½ hours or longer.
Remove bay leaves and spoon stew into bowls and serve.

- Substitute half a bag of frozen sliced carrots and half a bag of frozen peas for the peas and carrot mix. Use what you have on hand and it will still make a great stew.

- The last time we made this we didn't have any pearl onions and substituted 2 onions cut into chunk sized pieces.

Meatballs

I grew up in an Italian family and I don't think there was ever a week that went by that we didn't have Spaghetti and Meatballs. Does going gluten-free mean you have to give up an old favorite? Not at all!

Makes 20 – 25 meatballs

Preheat oven to 400 degrees. Grease a 13 x 9 x 2-inch glass baking dish.

In a large mixing bowl, combine the following:

1 **onion,** chopped and lightly sautéed
2 cloves of **garlic**, minced
1 **egg** or equivalent substitute
¾ cup of **gluten-free bread crumbs** (see page 181)
⅓ cup **fresh parsley**, chopped
½ teaspoon **Italian seasoning**
¼ teaspoon **red pepper flakes**
¼ teaspoon **sea salt**
¼ cup **spaghetti sauce** or **tomato sauce**

Mix well with a fork, then add:

2 – 2½ pounds of **ground beef**

Combine above ingredients with your hands until well blended. Form into 1½-inch balls and place on greased cooking dish. Cook for 20 – 25 minutes or until meatballs are browned, but still slightly pink on the inside. (You want them to have cooked long enough that they will not break apart when you try to pick them up with a set of tongs.)

Pick meatball up with slotted spoon or tongs to drain fat, then set meatballs gently into a pot of hot Spaghetti Sauce (see pages 96 – 97) and continue cooking for an additional hour or longer.

> - Flaxeggs work best as an egg substitute in this recipe because they will help to bind the ingredients.
>
> - Use ground beef with at least 80% fat. Most of the fat is cooked off the meatballs in the oven and then drained. Meat with little or no fat tends to produce a hard meatball.

Meatloaf

I like this recipe because it's very versatile. You can vary it to suit your tastes and ingredients you have on hand.

Makes one loaf or 12 mini meatloaves

Preheat oven to 375 degrees. Grease one loaf pan or one muffin tray. In a large bowl, mix together:

2 pounds of **ground beef**
2 cups chopped **baby bella mushrooms** or 1 cup **gluten-free bread crumbs** or 1 cup cooked **quinoa**
2 **eggs** or equivalent substitute
½ chopped **onion**
½ cup chopped **orange bell pepper**
1½ teaspoons **sea salt**
½ teaspoon **pepper**

Place meat mixture in pan and form loaf with hands. Or for muffins, form mixture into round shapes the size of a baseball and drop into muffin tray.

Prepare topping by briskly whisking together or processing for a few seconds with an **immersion** or **stick blender**:

⅔ cup **ketchup** (see page 360)
3 tablespoons **brown sugar**
1 teaspoon **ground mustard**

Spread ketchup mixture over loaf or muffins. Place in oven and cook 50 – 60 minutes for a loaf and 30 – 35 minutes for the muffins.

> - Be sure to place a drip tray underneath your pan in the oven to catch any grease that may spill over during cooking.

Pepper Steak

I always loved pepper steak but thought I might have to give up one of my favorites when we stopped eating soy as most recipes I had for this dish contained soy sauce. This recipe is soy-free and it's so tasty, you won't miss it one bit.

Serves 4 – 6

Prepare seasoning mix by whisking together in small bowl:

2½ teaspoons **paprika**
2 teaspoons **salt**
1 teaspoon **black pepper**
1 teaspoon **onion powder**
1 teaspoon **oregano**
1 teaspoon **thyme**
¾ teaspoon **cayenne powder**

Reserve 2 teaspoons of seasoning mix in small bowl. Sprinkle and rub remainder of mix over both sides of:

2 pounds of **flank steak**

Allow meat to come to room temperature, about 20 – 30 minutes. Preheat grill to medium high. Grill meat for 4 – 5 minutes per side. Meat should still be red inside, medium rare (125 – 130 degrees when tested with a meat thermometer) when removing from grill. Place meat in a baking dish, pour 2 – 3 tablespoons lemon juice over it and cover with a cookie tray, allowing it to rest and steam for 10 minutes. This will promote juiciness and create a very tender meat. Slice thinly with a sharp knife at a 45-degree angle, against the grain of the meat.

Meanwhile in a large skillet on medium heat, add:

2 tablespoons **olive oil**
¼ cup **water** or **beef stock**

Then add:

6 **bell peppers** in assorted colors, cored, halved, and thickly sliced
4 large **onions**, halved and thickly sliced
reserved **2 teaspoons of seasoning mix**

Cook onions and peppers for 8 – 10 minutes or until slightly softened, tender crisp and serve with meat. May be served over a bed of rice or lettuce leaves.

Pigs in a Blanket

Until I figured out how to make a great biscuit, Pigs in a Blanket were a less than stellar dinner in our house. Most of the time the hot dogs were eaten and the wraps were pulled off, untouched. Once we got the recipe down pat, we were ready to wrap them up once again.

Makes 63 pigs in a blanket

Preheat oven to 450 degrees. Grease two large cookie sheets or line with parchment paper.

You'll need:

3 **packs of gluten-free hot dogs** containing 7 hot dogs each

Dry off the hot dogs with a paper towel or kitchen towel, then cut each one into thirds.

Prepare **one recipe of biscuits** (see page 213 or 235). Follow the recipe almost to the end but do not pat the dough down. Once you have prepared the dough, leave it in a ball.

Gently tear off small amounts of dough, slightly bigger than marble size. Pat this down with care until you're left with a strip approx. ½-inch by 2-inches and wrap this around the hot dog. Roll back and forth gently in your hands and place wrapped hot dog on baking tray, seam side down.

Continue until all the hot dogs have been wrapped. Place in oven and cook until wraps have browned lightly on top, about 12 – 14 minutes.

> - Divide the dough in half before you start to help you better judge how much dough you will need to complete wrapping all the hot dogs.

Salisbury Steak with Mushroom Gravy

The first time I made this, I knew I was going to make a dinner made with ground beef, I just didn't know what it was going to be. I think most people are often faced with that challenge at dinnertime.

I have to say in regards to taste, the hamburger-like steaks surprised both me and our family. They were so good, everyone had more than one.

Makes 10 patties

In a large skillet over medium heat add and cook until onions and mushrooms are soft:

2 tablespoons **olive oil**
½ cup **diced onion**
2 **cloves of garlic**, minced
12 ounces **baby bella mushrooms**, sliced and diced

Allow to cool slightly as you prepare the rest of the ingredients. In a large bowl combine:

1 cup **gluten-free bread crumbs** (see page 181)
¼ cup **chopped fresh parsley**
2 **eggs** or equivalent substitute
½ teaspoon **sea salt**
¼ teaspoon **pepper**

Then add:

3 pounds **ground meat**

Work the meat into the mixture along with the cooled onions and mushrooms. Shape meat into oval patties, about ¾-inch thick.

Return the large skillet to medium heat and add:

2 tablespoon **olive oil**

Add patties, cooking 7 – 9 minutes on each side until browned and completely cooked. Remove patties and keep warm until ready to be served.

Meanwhile in a medium sized bowl, prepare the **Mushroom Gravy**. Briskly whisk together:

1 quart **beef stock**
¼ cup *Celeste's Best Gluten-Free Flour Mix*

Then stir in:

1 pound **baby bella mushrooms**, sliced

Pour gravy into the same skillet used to cook the patties if possible. Stir constantly while cooking over low heat for 5 – 7 minutes as gravy boils and thickens. Either return patties to skillet and simmer in gravy for 5 minutes or simply pour gravy on top of patties when serving.

Spinach Stuffed Meatloaf Roll

Not the usual boring meatloaf everyone fears. This meatloaf is stuffed with bread crumbs and spinach and will be a meal everyone will look forward to come dinnertime.

Makes one meatloaf

Preheat oven to 350 degrees. Generously grease a broiler pan.

In a medium sized sauté pan, heat:

1 tablespoon **olive oil**
1 **clove of garlic**, minced

Then add:

1 package (10 ounces) **frozen chopped spinach**
⅓ cup **water**

Continue to cook on medium heat, until spinach is cooked through, about 5 – 7 minutes. Allow spinach to completely drain in colander to remove any excess water.

Meanwhile in a large bowl, mix together:

2 **eggs** or equivalent substitute (see note box on following page)
¾ cup **gluten-free bread crumbs** (see page 181)
¼ cup **ketchup** (see page 360)
¼ cup **milk** or **non-dairy milk substitute**
½ teaspoon **sea salt**
¼ teaspoon **black pepper**
¼ teaspoon **dried oregano**

Add and mix until well combined:

2 pounds **ground beef** (80% lean or leaner)

Cut a sheet of aluminum foil 17 by 12-inches. (I cover foil with a sheet of parchment paper as I don't like my food to come in contact with aluminum.) Then spread meatloaf mix across paper making a rectangle 15 by 10-inches and 1-inch thick. Then layer cooked spinach evenly across the top of the meatloaf. Beginning on the longer side, carefully begin to roll up the meatloaf, using the foil to help lift it and maneuver it. Continue rolling and seal seam where ends meet by pressing along edge with fingers. Place on a broiler pan and cook for 40 – 45 minutes or until done.

- Flaxeggs work best as an egg substitute in this recipe because they will help to bind the ingredients.

- I sometimes use a 28 ounce bag of chopped spinach. It's a bit of a challenge to roll up the meatloaf, but very tasty.

- Instead of chopped spinach, try chopped broccoli.

Stuffed Peppers

For many years, I was unable to eat peppers. Their tough skins would often give me stomach discomfort. Then my husband began farming for a new farm that grew beautiful organic bell peppers. These peppers had a thinner, more digestible skin. I couldn't believe that I could once again eat peppers and began adding some of my favorite recipes to the cookbook including this one.

Serves 4 – 6

Preheat oven to 350 degrees. Fill a large stockpot with water and bring to a boil. Add and parboil, cooking for only 2 – 3 minutes (you may need to do this in two batches):

6 **green bell peppers**, tops cut away and seeds removed

Using tongs, remove peppers from water and set on a towel to drain any excess water. Empty water from pot and return to stove. Turn on medium heat and add:

2 tablespoons **olive oil**

Add and sauté until soft:

1 cup finely chopped **onions**
½ cup finely chopped **green bell pepper**
3 **cloves of garlic**, minced

Add:

1 pound **ground beef**
¼ cup chopped **fresh parsley**
1 teaspoon **sea salt**
½ teaspoon **black pepper**
⅛ teaspoon **cayenne pepper**
⅛ teaspoon **red pepper flakes**

Continue cooking for 7 – 10 minutes or until meat is browned and fully cooked. Add, stirring well:

2 cups cooked **white rice**
½ (15 ounce) can **tomato sauce**

Cook for an additional 2 minutes. In a 13 x 9-inch baking dish, pour in:

1 (15 ounce) can **tomato sauce** and remaining sauce left in can from previous step

Stuff the meat mixture into the peppers and place in baking dish.   Place in preheated oven and bake for 25 – 30 minutes.

- ■ You can make this with red or orange peppers, too, but I found I prefer the taste of the stuffed green peppers best. However, if you're preparing this dish for company, adding a red or orange pepper makes your serving tray more festive.

POULTRY

Chicken Scaloppini with Lemon Sauce

Baked Chicken

This is my husband Eddie's famous baked chicken. A very simple recipe, but oh, so good! Be sure to make some gravy to go along with it.

Serves 4 – 6

Preheat oven to 375 degrees. Grease a 13 x 9 x 2-inch baking dish. Combine the following in a plastic gallon-sized bag:

½ cup **Celeste's Best Gluten-Free Flour Mix**
1 teaspoon **fresh black pepper**
1 teaspoon **garlic salt**

Place 2 – 3 pieces at a time of a:

3 – 4 pound **chicken**, cut into 8 pieces (2 breasts, 2 thighs, 2 legs, 2 wings)

in plastic bag with flour and seasonings and shake until all pieces are well coated.

Continue until all pieces have been floured and seasoned. Place chicken in baking dish, skin side up. Drizzle **olive oil** over tops of chicken. Bake for 55 – 65 minutes or until cooked through and no longer pink inside.

To make gravy:

When chicken is done baking, remove chicken from baking dish to serving platter. Reserve 2 tablespoons of drippings from baking dish and place into a medium sized saucepan. Also scrape any brown bits stuck to the bottom of the baking dish. Heat on medium heat. Mix in with a spatula until well combined forming a paste or a roux:

¼ cup **Celeste's Best Gluten-Free Flour Mix**

Then whisk in:

2 cups **chicken stock**
⅛ teaspoon **sea salt**

Continually stir with whisk until gravy thickens, about 5 – 7 minutes. Pour into a gravy boat and serve over baked chicken.

Barbequed Chicken

This is an olive oil and lemon juice, herb based barbeque. Perfect for a summer barbeque.

Serves 4 – 6

Prepare the marinade by whisking the following in a medium sized bowl:

½ cup **olive oil**
¼ cup plus 2 tablespoons **lemon juice**
2 teaspoons **sea salt**
1 teaspoon **paprika**
1 teaspoon **onion powder**
1 teaspoon **dried basil**
1 teaspoon **dried thyme**
½ teaspoon **garlic powder**

Place the following in a shallow pan:

3 – 4 pound **chicken**, cut into 8 pieces (2 breasts, 2 thighs, 2 legs, 2 wings)

Pour marinade over chicken and refrigerate for several hours or overnight.

Preheat grill to medium. Remove chicken from marinade and place dark meat pieces on grill first as they take longer to grill. Add remaining pieces. Place smaller pieces of chicken around the outer edges of grilling surface, further away from the main heat source allowing them to cook more slowly.

Use tongs to turn chicken once during cooking time. Cook until done. Check for doneness by cutting into the middle of a piece of chicken. The juices should run clear when you cut into the thickest part of the piece.

> ▪ To save time, you can also partially cook the chicken in the oven for 40 minutes at 400 degrees and then continue cooking on the grill until done.

Chicken and Dumplings

This recipe is for the old fashioned, southern strip dumplings.

Serves 4 – 6

Preheat oven to 350 degrees. Grease a 13 x 9 x 2-inch baking dish.

Place in pan:

3 – 4 pound **chicken**, cut into 8 pieces (2 breasts, 2 thighs, 2 legs, 2 wings) or **8 skinless, boneless chicken breast halves**

Season with salt and pepper. Bake for one hour for the chicken pieces or 40 minutes for the breasts or until done and no longer pink inside. Allow to cool slightly.   When chicken is cool enough to handle shred chicken meat into bite size pieces.

Meanwhile, bring to boil in a large pot:

10 cups of **chicken stock**

Begin preparing dumplings by whisking together in mixing bowl:

2 cups *Celeste's Best Gluten-Free Flour Mix (CBGFFM)*
1 teaspoon **sea salt**
1 teaspoon **konjac powder** or **xanthan gum**
½ teaspoon **cream of tartar**
¼ teaspoon **baking soda**

Add and beat on medium speed for 30 seconds or until small crumbs form:

1½ tablespoons **extra light olive oil**

Then add and beat for 30 seconds on medium speed or until dough becomes a uniform mass:

1 cup **chicken stock**

Divide dough into two balls. Lay a large piece of parchment paper on your work surface. Sprinkle 2 tablespoons of *CBGFFM* evenly across paper. Place one ball dough on top and using a rolling pin roll dough to ⅛-inch thick. Sprinkle a few teaspoons of flour over surface as you roll if dough is sticky.   Then using a pizza cutter cut dough into 1-inch by 2-inch strips. Do the same with the other ball of dough.

Begin dropping the dumplings into the boiling stock one at a time as quickly as possible, stirring while you add them. Cook for 20 minutes, only occasionally stirring, very gently, so as not to break up the dumplings.

Then add the cooked chicken and serve.

- Make your own stock by following the recipe on page 60.

- Have leftover chicken you don't know what to do with? Instead of cooking the chicken use 3 cups leftover shredded chicken in this recipe.

- Variation: Add 1 (10 ounce) bag **frozen peas and carrots** to boiling chicken stock before adding the dumplings.

Chicken Cacciatore

Chicken in a tomato sauce with green olives. My mother used to allow us to choose whatever we wanted to eat for our birthday dinner – my choice was always Chicken Cacciatore.

Serves 4 – 6

In a large skillet on medium heat, add:

2 tablespoons **olive oil**

When oil is warm, add:

1 **onion**, chopped (½ cup)
3 **stalks celery**, diced

Cook onion and celery for 4 – 5 minutes or until soft and translucent. Push onions to the side and then add:

3 tablespoons **olive oil**
3 – 4 pound **chicken**, cut into 8 pieces (2 breasts, 2 thighs, 2 legs, 2 wings) or 8 **skinless, boneless chicken breast halves**

Cook chicken until fully done and no longer pink inside.

Add:

3 (15 ounce) cans **tomato sauce**

Bring to a boil, then reduce heat to low, cover pan and simmer for 15 minutes.

Add:

1 (10½ ounce) jar **green olives with pimento**, sliced

Cook an additional 5 minutes. Serve over rice or gluten-free pasta.

Chicken Crepes with Gravy

A bit time consuming because you'll need to prepare both the crepes and the filling so we usually simply make a garden salad to accompany the meal.

Serves 4 – 6

Prepare a batch of **10 crepes** (see pages 202 – 203). In a medium sized saucepan, combine:

3 **skinless, boneless chicken breast halves** cut in ¼-inch cubes
1 (10 ounce bag) **frozen peas and carrots** (1½ cups)

Add enough water to cover all ingredients in pot. Then bring to a boil and cook for 15 minutes.

Remove from heat, drain water. Preheat oven to 350 degrees. Grease a 13 x 9 x 2-inch baking dish.

Meanwhile, in a large skillet over medium heat, cook:

¼ cup **extra light olive oil**
⅓ cup **chopped onion**
½ cup **sliced celery**

While the onions are cooking whisk together in a small bowl:

⅔ cup *Celeste's Best Gluten-Free Flour Mix*
½ teaspoon **sea salt**
½ teaspoon **black pepper**

When onions are soft and transparent, reduce heat to medium-low and whisk in flour mixture. Then add:

4 cups **chicken stock**

Raise heat to medium. Bring to a boil for 1 minute while stirring often. Simmer on low for 3 – 5 minutes or until gravy has thickened.

Remove from stove. **Reserve 1½ cups gravy**.

Mix chicken and vegetables in skillet and coat with remaining gravy. Put ⅓ cup of mixture in center of each crepe and roll up. Place crepes seam side down in baking dish. Top with reserved gravy. Cook for 20 minutes.

Chicken Fajitas

A big favorite in our house. Grilled chicken and sautéed onions on a warm, soft, hot off the griddle gluten-free tortilla.

Serves 4 – 6

Prepare a triple batch of **tortillas** (see pages 191 – 193) and keep warm. Whisk the following spices together in a small bowl to create a rub:

1½ teaspoons **chili powder**
1½ teaspoons **garlic powder**
1½ teaspoons **paprika**
1½ teaspoons **sea salt**
¾ teaspoon **black pepper**
¾ teaspoon **coriander**
¾ teaspoon **cumin**

Place the following in a large baking dish:

6 skinless, boneless chicken breast halves

Drizzle a small amount of **olive oil** on each breast. Season both sides of each breast with the spice rub. Refrigerate for at least thirty minutes. Then grill chicken for 10 – 12 minutes over medium heat until done and the meat is firm and the juices run clear.

While chicken is cooking prepare the onions. Place in large sauté pan:

2 tablespoons **olive oil**
2 **onions**, cut in half and sliced

Cook for 5 – 7 minutes or until soft and tender. Slice grilled chicken into ½ -inch strips and place in pan with onions. Spoon mixture into warm tortillas and serve.

- The fajitas are also delicious filled with grilled eggplant, along with the chicken and onions.

Chicken Pot Pie

Although this meal is a bit time consuming, after the first bite you won't have any regrets!

Makes one pot pie

Preheat oven to 375 degrees. Grease a 9-inch pie pan. Prepare **two pie crusts** (see pages 318 – 319). Place one crust in the bottom of the pie pan. Then chill crusts in refrigerator until ready to fill.

In a medium sized stockpot, combine:

2 pounds, **skinless, boneless chicken breast halves**, (or 3 **chicken breast halves**) cut in ¼-inch cubes
1 (10 ounce bag) **frozen peas and carrots**
½ cup **sliced celery**

Add enough water to cover all ingredients in pot. Bring to a boil and cook for 15 minutes. Then remove from heat, drain water. Meanwhile in a saucepan over medium heat cook:

¼ cup **extra light olive oil**
⅓ cup **chopped onion**

Remove top crust from refrigerator and allow to come to room temperature to soften slightly to avoid cracking. While the onions are cooking, whisk together in a small bowl:

⅓ cup *Celeste's Best Gluten-Free Flour Mix*
½ teaspoon **garlic powder**
¼ teaspoon **black pepper**
¼ teaspoon **celery salt**
¼ teaspoon **sea salt**

When onions are soft and transparent, reduce heat to medium-low and whisk in flour mixture. Then add:

2 cups **chicken stock**
½ cup **milk** or **non-dairy milk substitute**

Simmer, stirring often, until sauce has thickened, about 5 – 7 minutes. Remove from heat. Add drained chicken and vegetables to the stock mixture and mix well to combine.

Pour the chicken and vegetable mixture into the prepared pie crust, spreading evenly across pan.   (continued)

Using the parchment paper for support, pick up top crust and quickly yet carefully lay over bottom crust. (Note to novices: it takes some practice to do this. In time you become more skilled at picking it up and placing it on the pie. If you need extra support use a thin, hard cutting board to help maneuver the top crust.) Tuck any excess pastry under the bottom crust and then crimp the edges using your fingers or a fork.

Using a sharp knife, cut 2-inch sized slits in top to vent crust, allowing steam to escape. For any cracks that may appear on the surface or edges, simply moisten your fingers with a small amount of water and smooth them out.

Bake in preheated oven for 40 – 45 minutes or until top pie crust is golden brown.

- I usually make two pot pies with this recipe, by adding an additional bag of peas and carrots and adjusting the amount of chicken stock to 3½ cups and the milk to 1 cup. I also use the recipe for 2 pie crusts and then roll them out very thin so that I can make four crusts from it.

- Use the remaining water from cooking the chicken and vegetables to make a quick soup by tossing in some chopped vegetables, garlic and ½ cup uncooked rice.

Chicken Pot Pie Empanadas

If you love chicken pot pie then you'll love this recipe. It's also a great way to use leftover chicken.

Makes 22 – 24 empanadas

Prepare the **empanada dough** according to recipe instructions (see pages 327 – 328).

Preheat oven to 400 degrees. Line two large cookie sheets with parchment paper. In a large skillet on medium heat, add:

2 tablespoons **olive oil**
½ **onion**, diced

Sauté onion for 3 – 5 minutes or until soft and translucent. Then stir in:

2 tablespoons *Celeste's Best Gluten-Free Flour Mix*

Stir constantly for 1 minute, then slowly add:

2 cups **chicken stock**

Cook for 3 – 5 minutes or until mixture has thickened. Then add:

2 cups **frozen diced peas and carrots**
2 **skinless, boneless chicken breast halves**, cooked and meat shredded
¼ teaspoon **sea salt**
¼ teaspoon **pepper**

Cook mixture for 2 – 3 minutes. Then remove from heat. Fill a very small bowl with water. Dip finger into water and moisten edges of dough. Place a teaspoon of meat mixture inside each empanada. Seal edges with fingers or by pressing with tongs of fork.

Place on baking sheet. Mist tops with oil spray. Bake for 25 – 30 minutes or until crust has turned golden brown. Remove from oven and cover with a lightweight kitchen towel for several minutes to steam and soften the empanadas before serving.

- To freeze for later use: Place filled, uncooked empanadas on a baking sheet, place in freezer until firm, 3 hours, then remove from tray and freeze in plastic bags. To use: Remove from freezer and bake 45 – 50 minutes.

Chicken Sausage and Rapini

This is an Italian dish that can be prepared in minutes. Rapini, a leafy mustard green, is also sometimes called Broccoli di Rape, Broccoli Raab, Broccoli Rabe or Broccoletti. One vegetable with so many names!

By whatever name you choose to call it, rapini is delicious and also a very healthy vegetable and a great source of vitamins K, A and C as well as calcium, folate and potassium.

Serves 4 – 6

Bring a large pot of water to a boil.

Wash:

1 bunch **rapini**

Remove the large tough leaves, leaving just tender leaves and flower buds. Trim ½-inch off bottom of each stem and discard. Cut remainder of each stalk into 2-inch pieces.

When water is in a full boil, add:

prepared **rapini**

Stir in greens and cook until wilted and tender, about 10 – 15 minutes.   (Rapini can also be steamed for 7 – 10 minutes or until wilted and tender.)   When rapini has finished cooking drain in a colander. In a large skillet over medium heat, add:

1 tablespoon **olive oil**
2 **cloves of garlic**, minced

When garlic is lightly browned, add:

1 package (4 links) **fully cooked gluten-free chicken sausages**, cut into ¼-inch slices
⅛ teaspoon **red pepper chili flakes**

Cook for 5 – 7 minutes or until sausage is fully reheated. Reduce heat to low, then add:

precooked **rapini**

Cover pan and cook for an additional 5 – 7 minutes. May be served over a plate of gluten-free pasta.

- This recipe can be made with any type of meat sausage. You can also use uncooked sausage, but fully cook it before adding the rapini.

- Rapini can also be cooked up as a side dish. Follow the recipe as instructed but omit the chicken sausage.

Chicken Scaloppini with Lemon Sauce

Chicken scaloppini is an easy dish using cutlets that have been pounded thin, coated with flour and sautéed. In this recipe the scaloppini is topped with a lemon sauce.

Serves 4 – 6

In a shallow dish, whisk together the seasoned flour:

½ cup **Celeste's Best Gluten-Free Flour Mix**
½ teaspoon **salt**
¼ teaspoon **black pepper**

Horizontally slice through:

6 skinless, boneless chicken breast halves

Then cut each piece in half. Place each section between two pieces of waxed paper and pound with flat side of a mallet to ¼-inch thick. (This step can also be skipped and the dish can be prepared with the chicken breast halves.) Dip chicken lightly into prepared flour mixture and coat both sides. (Save any leftover flour.) In a large skillet over medium heat add:

3 tablespoons **olive oil**

Once oil and pan have heated up, place chicken in skillet. Cook for 2 minutes on each side or until no longer pink inside. Place chicken on serving platter, cover and keep warm.

To prepare the lemon sauce combine the following in a medium sized bowl:

2 tablespoons **Celeste's Best Gluten-Free Flour Mix** or **leftover seasoned flour**
1 cup **chicken stock**
2 **cloves of garlic**, minced
grated rind of one lemon
⅔ cup chopped **fresh parsley**

Pour stock mixture into skillet and bring to a boil, stirring often until sauce thickens, about 2 – 3 minutes. Spoon sauce over chicken and serve.

> ▪ Instead of adding more oil when cooking the chicken I add small amounts of chicken stock as needed.

Chicken Souvlaki

The Latin word "souvla" means skewer. Souvlaki is a Greek dish consisting of small pieces of meat (and sometimes vegetables) skewered and grilled. This dish is so easy to prepare and because of the wonderful trinity of lemon, oregano and garlic it is fast becoming one of our favorite meals.

Serves 4 – 6

Cut into 1-inch strips (or 1-inch cubes):

6 skinless, boneless chicken breast halves

In a bowl large enough to hold chicken, whisk together:

¼ cup **lemon juice**
¼ cup **olive oil**
4 teaspoons **dried oregano**
2 teaspoons **garlic powder**
2 teaspoons **pepper**
2 teaspoons **seasoning salt** (see page 374)

Add chicken and toss until all pieces have been coated with marinade. Refrigerate for 30 minutes or longer.

(If you are using wooden skewers, you'll need to soak them for at least 30 minutes to prevent them from burning when grilled.)

Place the chicken on skewer. Grill over medium heat for 7 – 9 minutes on each side. This dish is wonderful served with rice couscous.

> ▪ Make a half batch of extra marinade to drizzle over chicken before serving.

Chicken Stir-Fry

We often used to have stir-fries, but all my old recipes included soy in the form of soy sauce. This recipe is terrific if you're eliminating soy from your diet, but still would like to enjoy eating a stir-fry.

Serves 4 – 6

Heat a large skillet on medium heat with 2 tablespoons **olive oil,** then add:

1 cup **chopped green onion**
3 **cloves of garlic**, minced
2 teaspoons **grated fresh ginger**

Also add to pan:

6 **skinless, boneless chicken breast halves**, cut into strips 2-inch by ¼-inch

Cook until chicken is cooked through, approximately 8 – 10 minutes. Remove the chicken from skillet and keep warm.

Add 2 more tablespoons of **olive oil** to the skillet and when oil is hot, add:

3 (16 ounce) bags of **fresh stir-fry vegetables** (broccoli, carrot, snow pea blend)
1 (8 ounce) package **sliced portabella mushrooms**

Cook on medium heat until softened, but still crisp. Meanwhile, whisk together in medium sized bowl:

¼ cup **sweet rice flour**
2½ cups **chicken stock**

Pour stock mixture into skillet along with vegetables and cook for 5 minutes until sauce thickens. Return chicken to skillet and cook an additional 5 minutes. Serve over rice or gluten-free thin spaghetti.

- Replace fresh vegetables with a blend of frozen vegetables.

- 2 teaspoons of grated ginger gives this dish a mild ginger taste. Add additional teaspoons to suit your own taste.

Chicken Tenders

These tenders are not just tasty; they're a breeze to prepare, too. Instead of using the traditional method of dipping the chicken in beaten eggs before breading, they're marinated in olive oil and garlic, then breaded.

Makes approx. 16 chicken tenders

To prepare marinade, combine the following in a small bowl and mix together well:

¼ cup **olive oil**
4 **cloves of garlic,** minced

Pour the marinade into a zippered gallon-sized plastic bag and then add:

2 pounds of **chicken tenders**

Refrigerate for 30 minutes or longer.

Meanwhile, fill a shallow dish with:

1½ cups **gluten-free bread crumbs** (see page 181) or *Celeste's Best Baking Mix* (see page 212)

After tenders have marinated, preheat oven to 400 degrees. Line a large cookie sheet with parchment paper. Dredge each piece of the marinated chicken in the bread crumbs, then place on the baking sheet. Mist tops of tenders with spray oil. Bake for 20 minutes, then turn the chicken pieces over and again mist tops with oil spray. Then bake an additional 20 minutes or until completely cooked and chicken is no longer pink inside.

- Our favorite way to eat these is by adding ¼ teaspoon of both **cayenne** and **black pepper** to the marinade. Gives them just the right amount of kick!

- Make larger batches and store leftovers in the freezer. Great as a quick protein snack, too.

Chicken with 40 Cloves of Garlic

I had often come across this recipe in cookbooks and online before trying it. Even though I admit I am a total garlic lover, I thought that chicken made with forty cloves of garlic would have an overwhelming taste of garlic that would ruin the meal. Boy, was I wrong. The next time I made it, I wanted to add forty more cloves!

Serves 4 – 6

Peel and cut hard end off:

40 **cloves of garlic** (cut in half very large cloves)

In a large skillet over medium heat, add:

3 tablespoons **olive oil**

Season on both sides with **sea salt** and **pepper** and place in heated skillet:

6 skinless, boneless chicken breast halves
40 **cloves of garlic**

Brown chicken well on both sides. (If pan dries out, add a few tablespoons of **chicken stock** to pan to help prevent the chicken from sticking to the pan.)

When chicken is well browned, add to skillet:

3½ cups **chicken stock**
¼ cup **lemon juice**
1 tablespoon **dried basil**
2 teaspoons **dried oregano**

Bring mixture to a boil, then reduce heat and simmer for 10 minutes or until chicken is completely cooked. Meanwhile, in a small bowl or measuring cup whisk together:

½ cup **chicken stock**
2 tablespoons *Celeste's Best Gluten-Free Flour Mix*

Add the chicken stock/flour slurry to skillet and stir together until sauce thickens. Serve over gluten-free pasta, rice or even a bed of freshly steamed vegetables.

Chicken with Fresh Herb Sauce

There may be many who would never imagine adding fresh mint to a sauce for chicken, but you'll be more than pleasantly surprised by the incredible taste of this dish. The mint adds just a little something special to this recipe.

Serves 4 – 6

Preheat oven to 400 degrees. Grease a 13 x 9 x 2-inch baking dish. In a large skillet over medium heat, add:

3 tablespoons **olive oil**

Season with sea salt and fresh pepper the tops of:

6 **skinless, boneless chicken breast halves**

Place in skillet, seasoned side down and cook until well browned about 5 – 7 minutes, then season the other side, flip and cook until also golden brown.

Remove chicken from pan and place in baking dish and continue cooking for 20 – 30 minutes (depending on the thickness of the meat) or until chicken is no longer pink inside and fully cooked.

Meanwhile, prepare sauce by adding to a food processor:

1 cup **chopped fresh parsley**
⅓ cup **chopped fresh mint**
1½ teaspoons **fresh black pepper**
½ teaspoon **sea salt**
the **juice** and **zest** of **2 lemons**
3 **cloves of garlic**, minced

Process for 10 seconds until all ingredients are well combined, then while processor is still running, drizzle in very, very slowly:

⅔ cup **olive oil**

Remove fully cooked chicken from oven. Place on serving plates. Pour sauce over chicken and serve.

*Please see following page for cooking notes and suggestions.

- Variation: The sauce can be placed in the skillet and heated and served hot.

- This sauce makes an excellent topping to freshly steamed vegetables.

- This recipe can also be prepared using 1½ cups fresh parsley and eliminating the mint.

- If you like this recipe, be sure to try the Chimichurri Sauce (see page 358) over steak.

Chicken with Mushroom Sauce

Chicken breasts topped with a creamy mushroom sauce.

Serves 4 – 6

Preheat oven to 350 degrees. In a large non-stick skillet on medium heat, add:

3 tablespoons **olive oil**

Then add:

6 **skinless, boneless chicken breast halves**

Drizzle over both sides of each breast while cooking:

1 tablespoon **extra light olive oil**
1 tablespoon **lemon juice**

Continue to pan sauté the chicken until almost completely cooked. Remove chicken from pan. Grease a large baking dish and arrange chicken in it. Top each breast with:

a slice of lemon

Place pan in oven while preparing sauce. Using the same large skillet again on medium heat, add:

¼ cup **extra light olive oil**
2 **cloves of garlic**, minced

When oil is heated, add:

4 cups **fresh sliced mushrooms**

Sauté mushrooms until tender, about 5 – 7 minutes. Add, stirring until well incorporated with a spatula:

¼ cup *Celeste's Best Gluten-Free Flour Mix*

(continued)

Then add:

4 cups chicken stock

Stir until sauce thickens about 3 – 5 minutes. Chicken is done when juices run clear.
Remove completely cooked chicken from oven and pour a few tablespoons of sauce
over each breast. Place remaining sauce in a serving vessel to accompany meal. Season
with **sea salt** and **pepper** to taste.

Grilled Chicken

A Moroccan inspired rub that adds a little spice to grilled chicken.

Serves 4 – 6

In a small bowl, stir together the following with a fork until well blended:

3 tablespoons **olive oil**
4 cloves of **garlic**, minced
1 tablespoon **paprika**
1½ tablespoons **turmeric**
1½ teaspoons **sea salt**
1 teaspoon **cumin**
¼ teaspoon **allspice**

Trim excess fat off:

8 skinless, boneless chicken breast halves

Carefully score the meat, by cutting small crosswise slits down the length of each chicken breast, without cutting all the way through. This helps the marinade penetrate the meat better and also helps the chicken cook more evenly. Rub spice mixture on both sides of chicken breasts. Place chicken in a large bowl or container and refrigerate for at least an hour.

Grill chicken on medium heat 6 – 8 minutes per side, or until no longer pink in center and juices run clear. Chicken should feel firm to the touch, but not hard, when it's done.

- Grilling chicken on too low a heat can often dry chicken out.

- Avoid using a fork to turn the chicken when grilling. The piercing causes the juices to escape.

Grilled Sweet and Sour Chicken

A delicious combination – the sweet taste of pineapple and brown sugar paired with the tanginess of lemon and ketchup. My daughter loves this meal.

Serves 4 – 6

Drain and reserve both juice and pineapple from:

2 (15¼ ounce) cans **crushed pineapple in its own juice**

Whisk together the following in a bowl then place in a gallon sized resealable plastic food storage bag:

2 cups **reserved pineapple juice**
1 cup **ketchup** (see page 360)
⅓ cup **brown sugar**
2 tablespoons **lemon juice**
1 tablespoon grated **lemon rind**

Add:

6 **skinless, boneless chicken breast halves**

Marinate chicken in refrigerator for 3 hours or longer. Place chicken over medium heat on hot grill and cook 20 minutes on each side or until no longer pink inside. Meanwhile in large saucepan on stove, prepare sweet and sour sauce by combining the following:

reserved crushed pineapple
1 cup **ketchup** (see page 360)
⅓ cup **brown sugar**
2 tablespoons **lemon juice**
1 tablespoon grated **lemon rind**
1 tablespoon **sweet rice flour**

Bring mixture to a boil, then simmer and cook for 5 – 7 minutes until sauce thickens. When chicken is almost fully cooked, pour ½ cup of sauce into a small dish and baste chicken while it grills. Remove fully cooked breasts from heat and place on serving dish. Pour remaining sauce over chicken.

- ▪ This meal can also be prepared in a skillet over medium heat. Brown and cook the chicken with ½ cup of sauce and then pour the remaining sauce over the chicken when serving.

Kelly's Garlic Chicken

This is my daughter Kelly's signature dish. She started making it one night when there was total chaos in the house and I had no idea what to make for dinner. Kelly came to the rescue with this recipe. We often double the sauce and pour half over the chicken before baking and the remaining sauce over the chicken before serving.

Serves 4 – 6

Preheat oven to 425 degrees. Line a large baking dish with parchment paper.

In a small pan, sauté on low heat:

2 tablespoons **olive oil**
4 **cloves of garlic**, minced

Cook garlic until soft and fragrant. Remove from heat and stir in:

¼ cup **brown sugar**
1½ cups **chicken stock**

Return pan to heat. In a small bowl, whisk together:

1 tablespoon **sweet rice flour**
2 tablespoons **water**

Add to pan and continue cooking on low heat until sauce thickens about 3 – 5 minutes.

Place in prepared baking dish:

6 **skinless, boneless chicken breast halves**

Pour brown sugar garlic sauce over chicken and bake for 40 – 45 minutes or until done.

Seasoned Chicken

This chicken is seasoned with an oil based rub of spices and herbs. The first night I made this, my daughter liked it so much she told me, "Mom, this absolutely has to go in the cookbook."

Serves 4 – 6

Preheat oven to 350 degrees. Spread 2 tablespoons of extra virgin olive oil in the bottom of a 13 x 9 x 2-inch baking dish. Place in dish:

6 skinless, boneless chicken breast halves

In a small bowl, thoroughly combine:

¼ cup **extra virgin olive oil**
3 tablespoons **fresh chopped parsley**
2 tablespoons **grated onion**
2 teaspoons **dried thyme**
1 teaspoon **black pepper**
1 teaspoon **dried rosemary**
1 teaspoon **sea salt**
½ teaspoon **rubbed sage**
¼ teaspoon **dried marjoram**

Evenly spread a few teaspoons of spice mixture over the top of each chicken breast. Place pan in oven. Bake for 30 – 40 minutes depending on thickness of breast or until juices run clear and chicken is no longer pink inside.

> ▪ Variation: Add 4 cloves of garlic, minced, to the above recipe before rubbing it on chicken.

Sesame Chicken

A sweet and tangy chicken dish, especially tasty served over a bed of rice.

Serves 4 – 6

In a large skillet on medium heat, add:

2 tablespoons **olive oil**

Then add:

6 **chicken breasts**

Sauté chicken in pan until brown on one side and then turn chicken over and brown other side, cooking chicken until just about done, as chicken will continue cooking in the oven.

Heat oven to 350 degrees and grease a 13 x 9 x 2-inch baking dish. Arrange chicken in greased baking dish and place in oven. (It is intentional here not to preheat the oven, so as not to overcook the chicken while the sauce is prepared.)

Place pan back on stove without rinsing it out and again add 2 tablespoons **olive oil**. Return heat to medium, then add:

1 **onion**, chopped
1 **clove of garlic**, minced

Sauté until onion and garlic are soft and translucent. Then add:

1 cup **water**
¾ cup **brown sugar**
¾ cup **ketchup** (see page 360)

Cook for 1 – 2 minutes on medium heat, then reduce to low and simmer for 5 – 7 minutes. Pour ¼ cup of sauce over each breast, then sprinkle with **toasted sesame seeds**. Bake for 10 minutes. Serve with remaining sauce.

- I cook with stainless steel pans and I often have to add ¼ cup water or more while the chicken is cooking to help prevent it from sticking to the pan.

- This sauce also freezes well.

Turkey Burgers

Low-fat turkey burgers simmered in a mushroom chicken stock. We usually double this recipe and have enough for dinner and also leftovers for lunch the following day.

Serves 2 – 4

In a large bowl, combine:

1 pound **ground turkey**
2 **cloves of garlic**, minced
1 teaspoon **paprika**
½ teaspoon **ground black pepper**

When the ingredients are well combined, shape into 4 patties, each ¾-inch thick and place in a greased, large non-stick skillet on medium heat. Add the patties and cook 5 minutes. Turn patties over and cook 5 more minutes on the other side or until burgers are no longer pink inside.

Remove the burgers to a plate and cover to keep warm. Add to the skillet:

2 tablespoons **extra light olive oil**

Then add:

2 cups **sliced mushrooms**

Sauté mushrooms over medium heat for 5 minutes until soft and tender. Then add:

2 cups (32 ounces) **chicken stock**

Continue to cook on medium heat for 3 minutes, then return burgers to skillet. Reduce heat to low and simmer for an additional 5 minutes.

May be served over a plate of gluten-free fettuccini.

Turkey Sausage Patties

By adding a few carefully chosen spices to ground turkey you can make your own sausage patties. This recipe also works well with ground chicken. My husband loves these and will sometimes heat them up as a snack.

Makes 8 patties

In a large bowl, whisk together the following spices:

¾ teaspoon **ground ginger**
1 teaspoon **sea salt**
1½ teaspoons **freshly ground black pepper**
1 teaspoon **dried sage**
¼ teaspoon **cayenne pepper**

Then add and mix together with your hands until well combined:

1 pound **ground turkey** (with at least 7% fat content)

In a large skillet over medium heat, add:

2 tablespoons **extra light olive oil**

Shape the sausage meat with your hands into ¼–inch thick and 2-inch round patties and place in skillet. Cook until well browned, then flip and cook on alternate side until browned. Cook patties until they are no longer pink inside when cut with a knife, approximately 15 minutes total cooking time. (Can also be baked in 350 degree oven for 20 minutes for each side.)

- Add half an apple, grated, to the turkey before forming into patties.

- Prepare all the patties, then place on a tray and freeze until solid. Remove from tray and place in freezer bag. To use, simply heat up in a pan when needed.

- If you prefer a milder sausage, only use half the amount of spices in patties.

- Combine the ground turkey with the spices the night before cooking the patties and the spices will have a better chance to fully blend in with the meat.

FISH AND SHELLFISH

Stuffed Flounder Roll-ups

Breaded Cod

This is such a simple recipe with just a handful of ingredients, but it tastes like something you might find in a restaurant.

Makes 8 fillets

Preheat oven to 350 degrees. Grease a 13 x 9 x 2-inch baking dish.

Place in dish:

8 cod fish fillets

In a medium size bowl, combine with a fork:

¼ cup chopped **fresh parsley** (see note box below)
3 **cloves of garlic**, minced
zest of 2 **lemons**
¾ teaspoon **sea salt**

Then add:

1 cup **gluten-free bread crumbs** (see page 181)

Drizzle tops of fillets with **olive oil**.

Then top each fillet with about 2 tablespoons of bread crumb mixture. Gently press bread crumbs into fillets. Drizzle again with **olive oil**. Bake for 25 – 30 minutes or until fish flakes easily with fork. Serve with **lemon wedges**.

> - This recipe works best with fresh parsley and not dried. Buy fresh parsley, wash it, chop it up and store it in a plastic bag or container in the freezer. Cilantro is another herb you can buy fresh and store in freezer until needed.

Cod Topped with Tomato and Bread Crumbs

We try to eat fish at least once a week. I usually serve fish on Mondays because that's my busiest day and most of the recipes in this chapter can be prepared and cooked in 40 minutes or less.

Makes 8 fillets

Preheat oven to 350 degrees. Grease a 13 x 9 x 2-inch baking dish**.**

Place in dish:

8 cod fish fillets

Sprinkle over each fillet:

1 teaspoon **lemon juice**
freshly ground black pepper

Cut into slices, ¼-inch thick:

2 large **tomatoes**

Place 2 tomato slices on each fillet. Then in a small bowl, mix together:

½ cup **gluten-free bread crumbs** (see page 181)
3 tablespoons **olive oil**
2 tablespoons finely chopped **scallions** or **onions**
1½ teaspoons **dried basil**

Top each fillet with about 2 tablespoons of bread crumb mixture. Gently press bread crumbs into fillets. Drizzle again with **olive oil**.

Bake for 25 – 30 minutes or until fish flakes easily with fork. Serve with **lemon wedges**.

Lemon Baked Cod

Cod is a mild-tasting, lean white fish that is extremely versatile and lends itself to many recipes.

Makes 8 fillets

Preheat oven to 350 degrees. Grease a 13 x 9 x 2-inch baking dish.

In a shallow dish, whisk together:

¾ cup ***Celeste's Best Gluten-Free Flour Mix***
½ teaspoon **sea salt**
½ teaspoon **freshly ground black pepper**

Dredge into seasoned flour:

8 pieces **cod**, fully defrosted

Place floured fillets in prepared baking dish. Top each fillet with:

a **drizzle of olive oil**
1 tablespoon **lemon juice**
1 teaspoon **lemon zest**

Place baking dish in oven and bake for approximately 30 – 35 minutes. Cod fish is done as soon as it starts to flake.

Crab Cakes

We lived on the Eastern Shore of Virginia near the Chesapeake Bay for many years. It's a beautiful place and crab cakes are often on the menu of most restaurants. This recipe is for the Boardwalk style crab cake which in this particular version is stuffed with bread crumbs.

Makes 8 crab cakes

Preheat oven to 400 degrees. Grease a 13 x 9 x 2-inch baking dish.

Mix together in a large bowl:

4 (6 ounce) cans **crab meat**, drained
¾ cup **gluten-free bread crumbs** (see page 181)
⅓ cup **milk** or **non-dairy milk substitute**

In a separate bowl, combine:

1 **egg** or equivalent substitute
¼ cup **mayonnaise** (see page 362)
2 teaspoons **green onions**, minced
2 teaspoons chopped **fresh parsley**
½ teaspoon **sea salt**
¼ teaspoon **pepper**
½ teaspoon **cream of tartar**
¼ teaspoon **baking soda**

Pour mixture over crab meat and mix until well blended. Form into ⅓ cup patties and place in baking dish. (If time allows, refrigerate crab cakes for one hour.)

Bake for 15 – 20 minutes in preheated oven, or until golden brown, then gently flip over and bake for 10 – 15 minutes longer.

- Use a measuring cup that is the same shape as crab cakes and simply scoop the crab mixture up, compress it into the cup, scrape away any excess and flip the cakes right into the pan. Simple and easy, and all your cakes will be uniform in size and cook more evenly.

- Crab cakes can also be pan fried. Before frying, dust each cake with a light coating of *Celeste's Best Gluten-Free Flour Mix*.

Seasoned Flounder with Lemon Dressing

This is a flounder recipe you can quickly bake up for dinner.

Makes 8 fillets

Preheat oven to 375 degrees. In a small bowl, combine the following:

1 teaspoon **sea salt**
1 teaspoon **dried thyme**
1 teaspoon **dried basil**
1 teaspoon **black pepper**
½ teaspoon **dried crushed rosemary**

Grease two 13 x 9 x 2-inch baking dishes. Arrange in dishes:

8 flounder fillets

Season the tops of the fillets with the prepared seasoning mix.

Mince:

3 cloves of garlic

Thinly slice:

2 lemons

Distribute the garlic evenly over the surface of each fillet and then top each fillet with 2 lemon slices. Place baking dishes in oven and cook for 20 – 25 minutes or until done.

Meanwhile, prepare lemon dressing by whisking together the following in a small bowl or measuring cup:

¼ cup **olive oil**
1½ tablespoons **lemon juice**
½ teaspoon **grated lemon rind** (you'll need 2 medium sized lemons)
¼ teaspoon **sea salt**
¼ teaspoon **pepper**

Place cooked fish on plates and then drizzle dressing over each fillet and serve.

Stuffed Flounder Roll-ups

This was one of my favorite meals growing up. My mother would often make this recipe substituting fillet of sole when available instead of flounder.

Makes 8 fillets

Preheat oven to 375 degrees. Grease a 13 x 9 x 2-inch baking dish.

In a small bowl, combine the following and mix well:

1 cup **gluten-free bread crumbs** (see page 181)
2 tablespoons **fresh parsley**
2 tablespoons **olive oil**
2 **cloves of garlic**, minced
3 tablespoons **lemon juice**

Spread 2 tablespoons of bread crumb mixture evenly across the top of:

8 **flounder** or **sole fillets**

Roll each fillet and secure with **toothpicks**. Place in baking dish. Drizzle a small amount of additional **olive oil** and **lemon juice** on top of each fillet.

Bake for 25 – 30 minutes or until done.

> ▪ The other day I was in a rush, so instead of rolling up the fish, I simply prepared the topping and then spread it across each fillet and baked. Slightly crunchier topping, but still delicious!

Baked Salmon

This is a very simple recipe and one we use quite often because the oil, lemon juice and herbs are truly a perfect complement to the salmon.

Makes 6 fillets

Preheat oven to 375 degrees. Grease a 13 x 9 x 2-inch baking dish. Place in the baking dish, skin side down:

6 (approx. 6 ounce) **salmon fillets**

Mix the following together in a small bowl and drizzle on top of fillets:

¼ cup of **olive oil**
1½ tablespoons **lemon juice**
2 **cloves of garlic**, minced

Meanwhile in another small bowl, combine:

1 teaspoon **dried basil**
1 teaspoon **sea salt**
1 teaspoon **pepper**

Sprinkle herb mixture over top of fillets. Then also season with:

1 tablespoon **fresh parsley**, chopped

Place baking dish in oven and bake fish for 20 – 25 minutes.   The salmon is cooked when the fish flakes apart easily when tested with a fork.   The salmon will continue to cook for another 5 minutes once it's out of the oven, so you want it to be slightly underdone when you remove it from the oven.

> - You can also take all the ingredients and mix them together to create a marinade for the salmon.
>
> - Super-fast method: Spread olive oil on the bottom of baking dish. Place fillets in pan. Drizzle oil and lemon juice on each, then sprinkle with spices and herbs.

Herb Topped Salmon

Even though fish is not one of my husband's favorite meals, the first night I prepared this recipe he ate four bites, smiled and said, "You can make this again." This easy to prepare dish marries the spicy taste of dried herbs with the sweet touch of sugar.

Makes 8 fillets

Preheat oven to 375 degrees. Grease a 13 x 9 x 2-inch baking dish.

For this recipe, you'll need:

8 salmon fillets

In a shallow dish large enough to fit a fillet, whisk together:

2 tablespoons **sugar**
1 tablespoon **chili powder**
1 tablespoon **paprika**
1 tablespoon **cumin**
1 tablespoon **sea salt**
2 teaspoons **black pepper**
1½ teaspoons **dry mustard**
⅛ teaspoon **cinnamon**

Heat 2 tablespoons **olive oil** over medium heat in large skillet.

Dip each fillet into seasonings and coat heavily on one side only. Place fillet seasoned side down in hot skillet and sear for 2 minutes. Turn fish over and cook for 2 minutes on alternate side.

Place seared fish in baking dish and cook in preheated oven for ten minutes or until fish flakes apart easily when tested with a fork.

Salmon with Dill Seasoning

This is a wonderful salmon recipe that can be quickly prepared. The dill seasoning blend adds just the right touch to the salmon.

Makes 6 fillets

Preheat oven to 375 degrees and grease a 13 x 9 x 2-inch baking dish.

Place in baking dish:

6 salmon fillets

In a small bowl, whisk together the following:

2 teaspoons **onion powder**
2 teaspoons **dried dill weed**
1 teaspoon **pepper**
½ teaspoon **sea salt**

Sprinkle mixed seasonings evenly over each fillet. Drizzle **extra light olive oil** over tops of each fillet.

Bake in preheated oven for 20 – 25 minutes. The salmon is cooked when the fish flakes apart easily when tested with a fork. The salmon will continue to cook for another 5 minutes once it's out of the oven, so you want it to be slightly underdone when you remove it from the oven.

Salmon Provencal

This dish can be served as a hot dish, but the leftovers can also be served the following day as a cold salad. It's also great when you are having guests over for dinner and don't want to spend all your time in the kitchen. Make the salad ahead of time, and then just pop the salmon in the oven and bake.

Makes 6 salmon fillets

Preheat oven to 375 degrees. Grease a 13 x 9 x 2-inch baking dish.

Fill a medium sized saucepan with **water** and bring to a boil. While the water is boiling, fill a large bowl with **ice water**.

When the water has come to a boil, place into the water for only 15 seconds:

3 **tomatoes**

Quickly remove tomatoes and place in bowl of ice water for 1 minute. Remove tomatoes from water and allow to dry. Then core them and peel off skin. The blanching should have made this extremely easy to do. Cut the tomatoes into bite sized pieces and place in a large bowl.

Add to the tomatoes and mix well:

3 **shallots**, chopped (see note box on following page)
1 tablespoon chopped **fresh basil**
1 tablespoon chopped **fresh chives**
1 tablespoon chopped **fresh tarragon**
½ teaspoon **sea salt**

In a small bowl, whisk together:

2 tablespoons **lemon juice**
2 tablespoons **olive oil**

Pour olive oil mixture over the tomato salad and mix well. Chill in refrigerator.

Place:

6 **salmon fillets**

in baking dish and drizzle **olive oil** on top. Lightly season with **salt** and **pepper**.

(continued)

Place salmon in oven and bake for 20 – 25 minutes. The salmon is cooked when the fish flakes apart easily when tested with a fork. The salmon will continue to cook for another 5 minutes once it's out of the oven, so you want it to be slightly underdone when you remove it from the oven.

Place salmon fillets on serving plate and spoon tomato salad mixture on top of each fillet.

- Sometimes shallots can be somewhat mild in flavor and other times they can be too intense and overwhelming. If the shallots are strongly flavored, use only one or use green onions instead.

- Break up leftover pieces of salmon and mix together with tomatoes and serve over lettuce the following day for lunch.

- Substitute dried herbs in place of fresh: 1 teaspoon dried tarragon, 1 teaspoon dried basil, but still use the 1 tablespoon of dried chives.

Baked Swai

Swai is a fish that is becoming more popular these days. It's a very mild, white fish, even milder than tilapia. Like other white fishes, Swai can be baked, fried, grilled or poached.

Makes 6 fillets

Preheat oven to 350 degrees. Grease a 13 x 9 x 2-inch baking dish.

Rinse and pat dry:

6 Swai fillets

Place fillets in baking dish and season with **sea salt**.

Meanwhile, prepare the following toppings:

3 **medium tomatoes**, roughly chopped
4 **scallions**, chopped
4 **cloves of garlic**, sliced

Divide the toppings equally among all fillets, then sprinkle over each fillet:

¼ teaspoon **dried dill**

Drizzle over each fillet:

1 teaspoon **olive oil**

Place in oven and bake for 40 – 45 minutes or until fish flakes easily with fork.

Seasoned Tilapia

Tilapia is a mild, light tasting fish. Its fillets are usually thin and cook up quickly. In less than a half-an-hour from start to finish, you can have this meal prepared.

Makes 8 fillets

Preheat oven to 425 degrees. Grease two 13 x 9 x 2-inch baking dishes.

In a small bowl, combine the following spices:

2 teaspoons **chili powder**
1 teaspoon **dried oregano**
½ teaspoon **sea salt**
¼ teaspoon **cayenne pepper**

Place in baking dishes:

8 tilapia fillets

Lightly sprinkle seasoning mix over both sides of fillets.

In another small bowl, whisk together:

3 tablespoons **lemon juice**
2 tablespoons **extra light olive oil**

Pour two teaspoons of oil mixture over each fillet. Then place in oven and bake for 20 – 25 minutes or until done.

- If you prefer a mild seasoning, reduce amount of chili powder to only 1½ teaspoons or omit cayenne pepper.

Spicy Baked Tilapia

This is a meal that I often serve when we have guests over for dinner. There are quite a few spices which all come together along with bread crumbs to perfectly accompany the fillets.

Makes 8 fillets

Preheat oven to 425 degrees. Grease two 13 x 9 x 2-inch baking dishes.

In a small bowl, combine:

2 teaspoons **sea salt**
1½ teaspoons **dry mustard**
1½ teaspoons **Italian seasoning**
1½ teaspoons **onion powder**
1½ teaspoons **paprika**
1 teaspoon **dried basil**
1 teaspoon **ground cumin**
1 teaspoon **garlic powder**
1 teaspoon **black pepper**

Place in a baking dish:

8 tilapia fillets

Season the tops of the fillets with half of the spice mix – approximately 2 tablespoons. Place the remainder of the spices in a shallow dish. Add to the spices in the dish:

2 tablespoons **dried parsley**
1 cup **gluten-free bread crumbs** (see page 181)
2 tablespoons **olive oil**

Mix bread crumb mixture well, then sprinkle evenly over all the fillets. Mist across the tops of fillets with oil spray or drizzle with a small amount of **olive oil**.

Place dishes in oven and bake for 20 – 25 minutes. Fish is done when it becomes flaky. Squeeze **fresh lemon juice** on top of fillets or serve with Tartar Sauce (see page 370).

Tilapia with Lemon and Garlic

Another very simple tilapia recipe.

Makes 8 fillets

Preheat oven to 425 degrees. Grease two 13 x 9 x 2-inch baking dishes.

In a small bowl, combine:

Place in a baking dish:

8 tilapia fillets

Drizzle over each fillet:

2 teaspoons of **lemon juice**
1 teaspoon **olive oil**

Finely chop:

2 **cloves of garlic**

Place a few pieces of chopped garlic over each fillet. Then sprinkle over each fillet:

1 teaspoon **fresh parsley**, chopped

Season fillets lightly with **fresh ground pepper**.

Place dishes in oven and bake for 20 – 25 minutes or until fish flakes when pulled apart with a fork.

Grilled Tuna

Due to the high mercury content in tuna we don't eat it too often. This recipe is easily prepared and the mayonnaise based topping creates a wonderfully moist and well-seasoned piece of fish.

Serves 4 – 6

Preheat outdoor grill to medium high heat.

Meanwhile in a small bowl, combine:

1 cup **mayonnaise** (see page 362)
2 tablespoons **lemon juice**
4 **cloves of garlic**, minced
½ teaspoon **cayenne powder**
½ teaspoon **ground cumin**

Reserve ⅔ of mayonnaise mixture in a separate bowl. Using the remaining ⅓ of mixture, brush the tops and bottoms of:

6 tuna steaks

Preheat grill to medium hot. Place steaks on preheated grill. Grilling will take a total of 4 – 6 minutes on each side depending on thickness and taste. Steaks that are one inch thick should take a total of approximately 8 minutes to cook. Tuna should still be slightly pink inside when done.

Serve with reserved seasoned mayonnaise.

BREAD AND PIZZA

Gluten-Free, Yeast-Free Multi-Grain Bread

Gluten-Free, Yeast-Free Breads

A recent study found that three-quarters of those tested for gluten sensitivity were also sensitive to yeast. My daughter, my sister-in-law and I are all sensitive to yeast.

When I first began developing a gluten-free, yeast-free bread I had no idea how difficult it would be to create a recipe that would be able to do all I had hoped it could do.

I wanted bread that:

> was light and airy
> could be sliced very thin
> tasted good toasted or untoasted
> had the taste and texture of "real" bread
> produced a loaf with a crunchy, golden crust

I knew I was asking for a lot, but I have a hard time settling for less. So with these goals in mind, I began my trials. I had made one bread recipe when our family wasn't sensitive to almond flour and that had worked out well for us for many years. But when we found ourselves sensitive to almonds and I had to eliminate the almond flour in the mix, I was faced with developing another recipe.

I am not understating it when I say it is a great challenge to create a yeast-free loaf. At times it seemed like an absolutely impossible challenge, but luckily I love to prove the impossible possible. So I set out testing and retesting. Most days I baked between four and eight loaves a day. I was so close so many times, but often the bread would be slightly moist or not rise quite high enough.

Some of the many, many test loaves I baked. (The stockpot is full of loaves, too!)

I tried everything I could possibly think of that could yield the best loaf possible. It didn't matter if it the idea was crazy, half-baked (a little bread baking humor) or too far out there to even make any sense. I tried it all.

There were close to two thousand loaves of bread baked that helped lead to the development of these bread recipes. Throughout this time, I had come to several big discoveries.

Konjac powder or xanthan gum will create those wonderful, airy holes in bread that give the bread a better rise. Certain mixes of gluten-free flours will create lighter, softer loaves. And changing one flour measurement by as little as a ¼ cup can turn a flop into a success or vice versa. Mixing the dough on low speed produced the greatest rise in the bread – a rise that didn't collapse as the bread cooled. Sweet potato flour is an essential ingredient for gluten-free bread baking that helps prevent loaves from being too moist. And finally, that without the arrowroot starch/flour and sweet potato flour, my bread didn't rise as much.

When I began this testing, I believed and knew that it had to be possible to bake a great tasting loaf of bread without gluten, dairy or yeast. But six months of trying had proved unsuccessful. I had started doubting myself. And quite frankly, thinking about bread all the time had worn me out - mentally. So upon the encouragement of my husband and daughter, I decided to take a break.

At first, I enjoyed this momentary lapse in baking. I came to see that I had been totally consumed with figuring out how to make a gluten-free, yeast-free loaf of bread. But then as the second week went by, I realized something that really surprised me. I was starting to miss all the researching and tests and trials that went into developing the recipes. I really had been enjoying all that.

So after a two-week break, I went back to the test kitchen. Renewed. Refreshed. I began baking just a loaf a day. "For fun." That week, I developed the basic principles for three of the bread recipes. There's a lesson in all that.

Throughout all this time, a little voice in my head had kept nagging me to try something that didn't seem like it should make that big of a difference. But at this point, as I mentioned earlier, no idea was too far-fetched for me to try.

That nagging thought was to try emulsifying the eggs or egg replacers and oil with an immersion or stick blender before adding them to the flour mix. I had already tried whipping the eggs in the mixer but that didn't produce the desired effect.

But this persistent and determined little thought of emulsifying the eggs kept repeating in my mind, so I decided to give it a try. And much to my surprise - success!! This simple trick of using the immersion blended turned out to be the key to a great loaf of gluten-free, yeast-free, dairy-free bread and eventually even the egg-free bread.

My sister-in-law Susan and her family were the first to test the bread. Anthony, now sixteen, said it was the best gluten-free bread he ever had. Twenty-one year old Joseph, who was recently diagnosed with celiac disease, said it was delicious and went back for seconds at dinner and then thirds later! He marveled at the consistency - it doesn't break when you put butter on it! (And actually, they all walked around their kitchen holding a piece of bread and swinging it back and forth.) My brother Tony and his wife both liked the soft middle and crusty outside. And my sister-in-law's comment after trying it toasted for breakfast, "Yum!"

To have another family enjoying the bread as much as we were made every bit of the testing and retesting so worth it. The funny thing is I have photos of many of my earlier loaves - some barely two inches tall in height. Many so dense. So very dense. And yet at the time, they all seemed like they could be contenders because initially I'd never imagined I'd be able to create a yeast-free loaf that could rise as high as these loaves do. And another great feature of these loaves is that they stay fresh for a couple days in a conventional bread box. Or make a loaf, slice it and freeze it. Toast them or eat them untoasted. Yes, you read that right. This is a gluten-free loaf of bread that does not need to be toasted to taste great.

Another funny thing is that through all of this testing and retesting my own family was so "breaded out" that they couldn't stand to try even one more test loaf. But the week after I had finished all my testing and began work on something new my daughter walked into the kitchen, pulled up the drawer on the bread box and had a look of total shock on her face. She then turned to me and said, "I never thought I'd say this but I can't believe there's not bread in here!" Even my husband does the same thing when he realizes there's no bread left. Gives me the sad face and usually says something like, "Can't believe I'm married to Celeste's Best and still can't get any gluten-free bread." (He thinks he's very funny.)

So I guess I'll still be baking bread for a long while to come!

Gluten-Free, Yeast-Free Bread

This loaf of bread does not require kneading like traditional bread dough. Instead, the ingredients form a batter that is similar to a thick muffin batter. Simply mix the ingredients and pour in a loaf pan and bake for 45 minutes. That's all it takes to enjoy light, airy gluten-free, yeast-free bread.

Makes one loaf

Preheat oven to 425 degrees. Heavily grease a glass 8½ x 4½ x 2½-inch loaf pan.

In a large mixing bowl, briskly whisk together:

1 cup **arrowroot starch/flour**
¾ cup **sweet potato flour**
¾ cup **white rice flour**
¼ cup **tapioca flour**
2 tablespoons **golden flaxseed meal**

3 tablespoons **sugar**
1 tablespoon **konjac powder** or **xanthan gum**
1 tablespoon **cream of tartar**
1½ teaspoons **baking soda**
1 teaspoon **sea salt**

In a 2 cup measuring cup or medium sized bowl, add:

2 **egg whites** (⅓ cup)
1 **egg**
3 tablespoons **extra light olive oil**

Pulse liquid ingredients with **immersion** or **stick blender** on high for 30 seconds or until frothy and thickened slightly but not stiff.

Then add:

1⅓ cups **water**
2 tablespoons **lemon juice**

Pulse again briefly and add to mixing bowl. Beat on low for only 45 seconds (use a timer for accuracy to ensure best rise). Batter will resemble a thick muffin batter. Immediately fold into greased loaf pan. Batter will fill up three quarters of the pan.

Place loaf pan in oven. **(Loaf should be placed in oven soon after liquid has been added to dry ingredients to ensure the greatest rise.)**   (continued)

Bake for 45 minutes. Remove from oven. Slide a dull knife between bread and pan to loosen loaf if necessary. Remove loaf from pan and place on wire rack to finish cooling. (Leaving bread in the pan can cause the bottom crust to become soggy from condensation.)   Allow bread to cool at least an hour for ease in slicing. When completely cool, loosely wrap loaf with plastic wrap and store at room temperature. Bread stays soft and fresh for several days.

Or if desired when it's completely cool, slice and freeze it. Lay slices on a baking sheet that will fit in your freezer. Once frozen, remove bread from tray and place in a resealable bag in your freezer. Or simply separate slices with freezer paper before storing in a resealable bag in freezer. You can then remove as many slices as you need later, and it thaws quickly at room temperature. If you're making sandwiches for school lunches or to take to work and eat later, don't bother to thaw the bread first, as it will be defrosted by the time it's eaten.

- Every ingredient and cooking instruction is important in this recipe in creating the best possible loaf of bread. I do not recommend substituting ingredients in this recipe until you've made it a few times as written.

- My sister-in-law Susan doubles this recipe and then divides the batter into two loaf pans.

Gluten-Free, Yeast-Free French Bread

This loaf is based on the original loaf of bread. It has additional tapioca flour and less water and leavening so that the loaves can be formed and hold their shape.

Makes two loaves

Preheat oven to 425 degrees. Heavily grease both sides of a French loaf pan.

In a large mixing bowl, briskly whisk together:

1 cup **arrowroot starch/flour**
¾ cup **sweet potato flour**
¾ cup **white rice flour**
½ cup **tapioca flour**
2 tablespoons **golden flaxseed meal**

3 tablespoons **sugar**
1 tablespoon **konjac powder** or **xanthan gum**
2 teaspoons **cream of tartar**
1 teaspoon **baking soda**
1 teaspoon **sea salt**

In a 2 cup measuring cup or medium sized bowl, add:

2 **egg whites** (⅓ cup)
1 **egg**
3 tablespoons **extra light olive oil**

Pulse liquid ingredients with **immersion** or **stick blender** on high for 30 seconds or until frothy and thickened slightly, but not stiff.

Then add:

1¼ cups **water**
1 tablespoon **lemon juice**

Pulse again briefly and add to mixing bowl. Beat on low for only 45 seconds (use a timer for accuracy to ensure best rise). Batter will resemble a thick muffin batter.

Immediately fold batter into greased loaf pan, dividing the dough equally between the two loaves. (Best when placed in each side of pan as one uniform lump of dough.)

To shape loaf, fill measuring cup with a small amount of additional water and dip spatula into water (letting excess water drip off) repeatedly. Smooth surface to form loaf, being careful not to press down and compress the loaf too much. With a very sharp knife, score the top by making 3 or 4 diagonal cuts about ¼-inch deep across top of each loaf. Place loaf pan in oven. **(Loaf should be placed in oven soon after liquid has been added to dry ingredients to ensure the greatest rise.)**

Bake for 30 – 35 minutes. Remove from oven. Slide a dull knife between bread and pan to loosen loaf if necessary. Remove loaf from pan and place on wire rack to finish cooling. (Leaving bread in the pan can cause the bottom crust to become soggy from condensation.) When completely cool, loosely wrap loaf with plastic wrap and store at room temperature. Bread stays soft and fresh for several days.

Or if desired when it's completely cool, slice and freeze it. Lay slices on a baking sheet that will fit in your freezer. Once frozen, remove bread from tray and place in a resealable bag in your freezer. Or simply separate slices with freezer paper before storing in a resealable bag in freezer. You can then remove as many slices as you need later, and it thaws quickly at room temperature. If you're making sandwiches for school lunches or to take to work and eat later, don't bother to thaw the bread first, as it will be defrosted by the time it's eaten.

- Every ingredient and cooking instruction is important in this recipe in creating the best possible loaf of bread. I do not recommend substituting ingredients in this recipe until you've made it a few times as written.

- Slicing yeast-free bread on a slight angle will create larger slices.

Gluten-Free, Yeast-Free Multi-Grain Bread

Don't let the amount of ingredients in this loaf intimidate you. The small amounts needed for the amaranth, teff and quinoa flour can be quickly thrown together. Using these nutrient rich grains creates a wonderfully healthy multi-grain loaf of bread packed with protein and fiber. And our whole family loves the taste!

*The trick to getting the greatest rise out of this bread is emulsifying the eggs with an **immersion** or **stick blender** before adding them to the remaining ingredients.*

(For those who need an egg-free version try the Gluten-Free, Yeast-Free, Egg-Free, Multi-Grain Bread recipe instead.)

Makes one loaf

Preheat oven to 425 degrees. Heavily grease a glass 8½ x 4½ x 2½-inch loaf pan.

In a large mixing bowl, briskly whisk together:

1 cup **sweet potato flour**
¾ cup **arrowroot starch/flour**
¼ cup **amaranth flour**
¼ cup **ivory teff flour** (see note box on following page)
¼ cup **quinoa flour**
¼ cup **tapioca flour**
2 tablespoons **golden flaxseed meal**

¼ cup **sugar**
1 tablespoon **konjac powder** or **xanthan gum**
1 tablespoon **cream of tartar**
1½ teaspoons **baking soda**
1 teaspoon **sea salt**

In a 2 cup measuring cup or medium sized bowl, add:

2 **egg whites** (⅓ cup)
1 **egg**
3 tablespoons **extra light olive oil**

Pulse liquid ingredients with **immersion** or **stick blender** on high for 30 seconds or until frothy and thickened slightly, but not stiff.

(continued)

Then add:

1⅓ cups **water**
2 tablespoons **lemon juice**

Pulse again briefly and add to mixing bowl. Beat on low for only 45 seconds (use a timer for accuracy to ensure best rise). Batter will resemble a thick muffin batter. Immediately fold into greased loaf pan. Batter will fill up three quarters of the pan.

Place loaf pan in oven. **(Loaf should be placed in oven soon after liquid has been added to dry ingredients to ensure the greatest rise.)**

Bake for 60 minutes. Remove from oven. Slide a dull knife between bread and pan to loosen loaf if necessary. Remove loaf from pan and place on wire rack to finish cooling. (Leaving bread in the pan can cause the bottom crust to become soggy from condensation.)   Allow bread to cool at least an hour for ease in slicing. When completely cool, loosely wrap loaf with plastic wrap and store at room temperature. Bread stays soft and fresh for several days.

Or if desired when it's completely cool, slice and freeze it. Lay slices on a baking sheet that will fit in your freezer. Once frozen, remove bread from tray and place in a resealable bag in your freezer. Or simply separate slices with freezer paper before storing in a resealable bag in freezer. You can then remove as many slices as you need later, and it thaws quickly at room temperature. If you're making sandwiches for school lunches or to take to work and eat later, don't bother to thaw the bread first, as it will be defrosted by the time it's eaten.

- Every ingredient and cooking instruction is important in this recipe in creating the best possible loaf of bread. I do not recommend substituting ingredients in this recipe until you've made it a few times as written. The arrowroot starch/flour and sweet potato flour are vital ingredients in this recipe and help ensure the greatest rise in this bread.

- If you've made this a few times and you want to experiment with this loaf, you can vary the three flours: amaranth, teff and quinoa. Variations in these three flours doesn't seem to affect the overall consistency of the loaf. Use any combination of flours you prefer equaling a combined ¾ cup.

Gluten-Free, Yeast-Free, Egg-Free Multi-Grain Bread

I can't even begin to tell you how excited I was to develop this recipe. It exceeded all my expectations. This is the loaf we now make on a regular basis rather than the one prepared using eggs.

The amaranth, teff and quinoa are nutrient rich grains. Adding them to the bread creates a wonderfully healthy multi-grain loaf of bread packed with protein and fiber. And this bread tastes so good, too!

*The trick to getting the greatest rise out of this bread is emulsifying the flaxeggs with an **immersion** or **stick blender** before adding them to the remaining ingredients.*

Makes one loaf

Preheat oven to 425 degrees. Heavily grease a glass 8½ x 4½ x 2½-inch loaf pan. In a large mixing bowl, briskly whisk together:

1 cup **sweet potato flour**
¾ cup **arrowroot starch/flour**
¼ cup **amaranth flour**
¼ cup **ivory teff flour** (see note box on following page)
¼ cup **quinoa flour**
¼ cup **tapioca flour**

¼ cup **sugar**
1 tablespoon **konjac powder** or **xanthan gum**
1 tablespoon **cream of tartar**
1½ teaspoons **baking soda**
1 teaspoon **sea salt**

In a small pot, heat to almost boiling:

⅔ cup of **water**

In a 2 cup measuring cup, add:

1 tablespoon **golden flaxseed meal**

Then add to it:

9 tablespoons of the **heated water**   (continued)

Blend with an **immersion** or **stick blender** on high speed for 10 seconds or until mixture becomes bubbly and frothy. Let rest for 1 – 2 minutes, then blend again for 10 seconds or until mixture gels and thickens.

Add to it:

1⅓ cups **water**
3 tablespoons **extra light olive oil**
2 tablespoons **lemon juice**

Pulse again briefly, until all ingredients are blended together, and add to mixing bowl. Beat on low speed (over mixing can create tunnels and cause the top to separate from the rest of loaf after cooking) for only 45 seconds (use a timer for accuracy to ensure best rise). Batter will resemble a thick muffin batter. Immediately fold into greased loaf pan. Batter will fill up three quarters of the pan.

Place loaf pan in oven. **(Loaf should be placed in oven soon after liquid has been added to dry ingredients to ensure the greatest rise.)**

Bake for 45 – 50 minutes. Remove from oven. Slide a dull knife between bread and pan to loosen loaf if necessary. Remove loaf from pan and place on wire rack to finish cooling. (Leaving bread in the pan can cause the bottom crust to become soggy from condensation.) Allow bread to cool at least an hour for ease in slicing. When completely cool, loosely wrap loaf with plastic wrap and store at room temperature. Bread stays soft and fresh for several days.

Or if desired when it's completely cool, slice and freeze it. Lay slices on a baking sheet that will fit in your freezer. Once frozen, remove bread from tray and place in a resealable bag in your freezer. Or simply separate slices with freezer paper before storing in a resealable bag in freezer. You can then remove as many slices as you need later, and it thaws quickly at room temperature. If you're making sandwiches for school lunches or to take to work and eat later, don't bother to thaw the bread first, as it will be defrosted by the time it's eaten.

- Every ingredient and cooking instruction is important in this recipe in creating the best possible loaf of bread. I do not recommend substituting ingredients in this recipe until you've made it a few times as written. The arrowroot starch/flour and sweet potato flour are vital ingredients in this recipe and help ensure the greatest rise in this bread.

- If you've made this a few times and you want to experiment with this loaf, you can vary the three flours: amaranth, teff and quinoa. Variations in these three flours doesn't seem to affect the overall consistency of the loaf. Use any combination of flours you prefer equaling a combined ¾ cup.

Bagels

Nowadays there are a good number of gluten-free bagels on the market, but often they contain yeast. I actually had little hope that these would taste like the bagels I grew up with in New York. I was surprised, but very happy to report, these helped put an end to my craving for a bagel.

Makes 4 bagels

Preheat oven to 375 degrees. Line a medium sized baking sheet with parchment paper.

Fill a large saucepan with at least 3-inch deep water, just enough to cover the bagels, and place on high heat and bring to a boil.

Meanwhile in a large mixing bowl, whisk together the following:

2½ cups *Celeste's Best Gluten-Free Flour Mix* (CBGFFM)
1½ tablespoons **sugar**
2 teaspoons **konjac powder** or **xanthan gum**
1½ teaspoons **cream of tartar**
¾ teaspoon **baking soda**
¼ teaspoon **sea salt**

Add:

1¼ cups **water**

Mix on a low-medium speed for 25 – 30 seconds or until dough is well combined and begins to form a ball. Place 2 teaspoons of **CBGFFM** on a work surface. Scoop dough out of bowl and form a ball. Gently roll dough back and forth until no longer sticky.

Divide dough into 4 equal pieces and shape into balls. Knead each ball of dough in your hands several times. Rinse and dry hands. (Often all the dough needs is kneading in dry hands to achieve correct consistency.) Flatten the ball of dough to ¾-inch thick to form bagel shape. Punch through the center with your thumb (or the handle of a wooden spoon) to make the bagel hole, and then work around the dough to smooth edges around the hole.

Once the water has boiled, lower the heat to medium, and when the water is no longer bubbling, add a few bagels at a time to the pot. The bagels should float. Cook for approximately a minute and a half, then gently flip the bagels over and cook for an additional minute and a half on the other side.

(continued)

Using a slotted spatula, carefully remove partially cooked bagels and while on spatula place desired choice of topping on top of bagel:

coarse sea salt
poppy seeds
minced onion
sesame seeds

Then place on prepared baking tray, topping side down. Sprinkle topping on other side of bagel. Press down lightly to embed toppings into the bagel. Place bagels in oven and bake for 15 minutes. Turn bagels over and cook for an additional 15 minutes or until done.

Cool cooked bagels on wire rack. Best eaten within a day of cooking. Store in a closed paper bag or slice bagels and freeze in plastic bag in the freezer.

- Yeasted bagels were originally boiled many years ago to help preserve them for long journeys by travelers. Even though this recipe contains no yeast, boiling the bagels before baking helps to give the bagels a more authentic taste.

Bread Crumbs

Bread and bread crumbs are definitely two things you may miss when you go gluten-free. You probably never realized how much you used bread crumbs until you've had to remove them from your diet.   The Italian in me has to have them for my meatballs and I also love them sprinkled on baked fish.

Makes approx. 4 cups

Bake **one loaf of any *Celeste's Best* gluten-free, yeast-free bread** (see index for recipes)

Slice the bread into half inch slices. Allow the bread to go stale by placing the slices on a tray and leaving them out overnight.

The bread can also be dried out in a warm oven. Place slices of bread on a baking sheet and put in an oven set at 250 degrees. Bake for 30 minutes or until the bread is fully dry.

Roughly tear apart room temperature slices into small pieces 1-inch square in size (or bigger if your processor can accommodate large pieces) and place in food processor.

Add the following dried spices to the processor:

1 tablespoon **parsley**
½ teaspoon **oregano**
½ teaspoon **basil**
½ teaspoon **garlic**
½ teaspoon **onion powder**

Process on high speed for 3 – 4 minutes until torn bread resembles fine crumbs. Store bread crumbs in a zippered plastic bag in freezer. Defrost and use as needed.

- One loaf of bread can be easily processed into crumbs in a 14-cup processor. For processors with a smaller capacity, divide bread into two batches and add spices to one and then shake all crumbs from both batches together in zippered plastic bag to evenly season them.

- Toasted or thoroughly dried out bread will allow you to process the crumbs very finely. Fresher, softer bread will create large soft bread crumbs.

- The recipes in this cookbook work best with bread crumbs made from the gluten-free, yeast-free breads in this book.

Breadsticks

I had played around with many recipes trying to develop a yeast-free breadstick recipe. Most of the time they wound up being a glorified biscuit and hard and dense, at that. These breadsticks are wonderful. Very quick to prepare and they have just the right texture and consistency.

Makes 6 breadsticks

Preheat oven to 450 degrees.   Spread or brush 2 tablespoons of **olive oil** across the bottom of a large baking tray.

In mixing bowl, whisk together:

⅓ cup **arrowroot starch/flour**
⅓ cup **sweet potato flour**
⅓ cup **white rice flour**
¼ cup **tapioca flour**

Then whisk in:

2 teaspoons **sugar**
1¼ teaspoons **konjac powder** or **xanthan gum**
1 teaspoon **cream of tartar**
½ teaspoon **baking soda**
½ teaspoon **sea salt**

Add:

⅔ cup **milk** or **non-dairy milk substitute**

Beat on low speed for 45 seconds or until dough comes together and pulls away from sides of bowl and forms a ball. Dough will be sticky and tacky.

Divide the dough into 6 equal pieces and form into balls. Take a ball of dough and knead it well in hands. (I place my hands in the oiled tray, so they won't stick to the dough.) Then roll dough into a stick shape roughly 5 inches long by ¾-inch thick.

Place breadsticks on baking sheet and roll in the olive oil on the tray. Sprinkle with **sesame seeds, sea salt** or **Italian seasoning** if desired. Bake for 14 – 18 minutes or until golden. Best served warm from the oven.

- ▪ Variation: Add ¼ teaspoon oregano and garlic powder to flour mixture.

Chapati

Chapati (also known as khakhara) are usually made from chapatti flour (atta), which is a very finely ground whole wheat flour. Chapati is unleavened bread which is cooked on a griddle with no oil or fat and is similar to a tortilla. This flatbread can be used to scoop up other foods eaten with the fingers during a meal and also goes well with curries and other spicy dishes.

This recipe uses a combination of Celeste's Best Gluten-Free Flour Mix along with amaranth, teff and quinoa flour. The addition of these flours helps give the chapati a mild whole wheat taste.

Makes 3 chapati

In mixing bowl, whisk together the following:

½ cup **Celeste's Best Gluten-Free Flour Mix**
¼ cup **quinoa flour**
2 tablespoons **amaranth flour**
2 tablespoons **ivory teff flour**
½ teaspoon **konjac powder** or **xanthan gum**
½ teaspoon **sea salt**

Then add:

1 tablespoon **olive oil**

Beat on medium speed for 30 seconds, then add:

½ cup **water**

Beat on medium speed until mixture comes together in a ball. Divide dough into 3 equal sized pieces and form into balls. Knead each ball by lightly tossing it back and forth in your hands. (If your hands become sticky, rinse and dry them.) You'll be surprised how the consistency of the dough will change by simply kneading gently with dry hands. Take one of the formed balls and press in the center to flatten, then continue to press around the sides until the entire dough ball is flattened.

Place dough on parchment paper and begin rolling. If at any point the dough begins to stick a bit, mist it lightly with oil spray and add a small amount of additional flour if necessary. Also, if your first chapati is sticky, take a moment and knead remaining balls of dough again. You can also roll dough in between two sheets of parchment paper.

Roll dough out to ⅛-inch thick. When you've reached your desired thickness and your griddle is well-heated, place the chapati onto the dry griddle. Cook until "blisters" have formed on the surface, then flip to cook the other side. Then immediately press down on it with a wide spatula, applying gentle but firm pressure all over the top. This will cause the chapati to puff from the steam inside. Blisters will then form over most of this side of the chapati surface as you press down. Turn the chapati again and press the other side until the blisters turn a light golden brown.

Generally cook for about 2 – 3 minutes on the first side. Then flip it over and cook an additional 1 – 2 minutes on the other side, and then a quick minute on the first side again. Place cooked chapati on a plate covered with a clean towel or in a tortilla warmer to stay hot. **This is a very important step, as the steam produced from the hot chapati will help make them soft and pliable.** Chapati taste best served warm. Store completely cooled chapati in a plastic bag in refrigerator. Best when reheated before serving, but may also be eaten cold.

- Variation: Add ¼ teaspoon garlic, turmeric, cumin and basil to the flours before adding the water.

Croutons

There are many ways to make use of leftover bread. You can slice it and freeze it for later, you can process it into gluten-free bread crumbs, and you can also cut it into cubes and freeze to make stuffing. And another absolutely perfect use for any leftover bread is toasting it to use as croutons to top your salads.

Preheat oven to 400 degrees.

Cut into small cubes:

slices of any ***Celeste's Best* gluten-free, yeast-free bread** (see index for recipes)

Arrange cubes in a single layer on a baking sheet. Lightly drizzle over the cubes:

olive oil

Using your hands, lightly toss the cubes around to spread the oil over all the croutons.

Sprinkle the cubes with:

garlic powder
dried basil (freeze dried basil is especially tasty in this recipe)

Place tray in oven and bake for 7 – 10 minutes or until golden brown and toasty.

- Croutons are best served warm from the oven.

- Experiment with different seasonings, or simply enjoy them plain.

- Croutons can also be quickly and lightly toasted in pan.

Hamburger Buns

Imagine being able to eat a hamburger on a bun that actually tastes like a bun, even if it is gluten and yeast free.

Makes 12 hamburger buns

Preheat oven to 400 degrees. Grease twelve 4 x ¾-inch tart or mini quiche pans or 4 x 1¼ inch mini cake pans.

In a medium sized bowl, whisk together the following:

4 **eggs** or equivalent substitute
1½ cups **milk** or **non-dairy milk substitute**
⅔ cup **extra light olive oil**

In mixing bowl, beat together the following for 30 seconds on medium speed:

3 cups *Celeste's Best Gluten-Free Flour Mix*
2 teaspoons **konjac powder** or 1½ teaspoons **xanthan gum**
2 tablespoons **sugar**
2 teaspoons **cream of tartar**
1 teaspoon **baking soda**

Add the wet ingredients to the dry and beat for an additional minute. Batter should have the consistency of a thick cake batter. Place ½ cup batter into each tart pan.

Flatten and shape each top slightly with a wet spatula or wet fingertips. Sprinkle tops with **toasted sesame seeds** if desired.

Place tray in oven and bake for 15 minutes or until lightly browned on top.

> ▪ Instead of tart pans, you can use a jumbo muffin pan.
>
> ▪ You can also make hot dog buns with this recipe by using either an éclair or Twinkie pan (search online) or by free forming the shape on a baking tray.

Italian Flatbread

Traditional Italian flatbread (Piadina) is dough rolled very thin and is more like a large cracker than a bread. I prefer this version which is rolled slightly thicker and is more like a bread.

The first time I made these, they vanished. Makes a hearty addition to any meal.

Makes six, 7-inch flatbreads

If using a cast iron griddle, preheat to medium heat. In a mixing bowl, whisk together:

3 cups **Celeste's Best Gluten-Free Flour Mix**
2 teaspoons **konjac powder** or 1½ teaspoons **xanthan gum**
1½ teaspoons **sea salt**
1 teaspoon **cream of tartar**
½ teaspoon **baking soda**
1 teaspoon **garlic powder**
1 teaspoon **onion powder**

In a small bowl, combine:

1½ cups **water**
3 tablespoons **olive oil**

Add water to mixing bowl. Beat on medium speed until mixture comes together in a ball. Add additional tablespoons of water, if necessary. Dough should form a ball in hand without cracking much at sides when compressed. It should feel like a balloon filled with sand.

This dough should be more on the moist side, than dry. You can also add additional water one tablespoon at a time until desired consistency is reached. (Definitely better to work with a moister dough, than a drier one.)

Divide the dough into 6 equal pieces. Form dough into balls. Knead each ball by lightly tossing it back and forth in your hands. (If your hands become sticky, rinse and dry them.) You'll be surprised how the consistency of the dough will change by simply kneading gently with dry hands. I generally shape all the dough into balls, then rinse my hands and begin kneading the dough again.

Roll each ball of dough out into a 6 or 7-inch circle. Roll it thinner if you prefer it more like a cracker, thicker if you'd like it more like a bread.

(continued)

If using a large skillet heat to medium heat. Take one circle of dough and brush the side that will be heated first with **olive oil**, then place it in the skillet. As it's cooking, lightly prick across the surface 10 times with a fork. Cook until lightly browned. Brush the top again with **olive oil**, then flip over and cook the other side. Best served warm.

- The flatbread can also be used as a crust for mini pizzas.

- Instead of the garlic and onion seasoning, try rosemary and thyme.

- Recipe also tastes good with 1 – 2 cloves of fresh minced garlic in place of the dried garlic.

- Make larger circles of dough to fit the size of a large skillet, cook as instructed above, then divide into slices (like a pizza pie) and serve as wedge-sized pieces.

Baked Stuffing

A moist baked stuffing full of chopped celery, onions and seasoning. Growing up, we used to stuff the turkey, but nowadays due to health concerns, we always bake the stuffing separately. Currently, our favorite way to prepare stuffing is to follow the recipe as instructed and add sautéed mushrooms as suggested in the notes.

Serves 4 – 6

Toast one loaf of sliced **Celeste's Best** **gluten-free, yeast-free bread** (see index for recipes). Cut toasted bread into cubes.

Preheat oven to 350 degrees. Grease an 8 x 8-inch baking dish. In a large skillet heat on medium heat:

½ cup of **extra light olive oil**

Add and cook for 5 – 7 minutes or until softened:

4 **stalks of celery**, chopped
1 **onion**, chopped

Remove from heat and stir in seasonings:

2 teaspoons **poultry seasoning** or **sage**
½ teaspoon **sea salt**
¼ teaspoon **pepper**

Then stir in toasted bread cubes. Add:

2 – 2½ cups **chicken stock**

Mix gently until bread is well moistened. Those who prefer a moister stuffing will need to add the full 2½ cups of stock.

Place stuffing in prepared baking dish and bake uncovered for 35 – 40 minutes.

*Please see following page for cooking notes and suggestions.

- To make your own poultry seasoning, combine: 2 teaspoons ground sage, 1½ teaspoons ground thyme, 1 teaspoon crushed marjoram, ½ teaspoon ground rosemary, ½ teaspoon nutmeg and ½ teaspoon black pepper. Add two teaspoons of seasoning to recipe.

- Sauté 1 cup sliced mushrooms or 1 cup diced granny smith apple along with the onion and celery for a different taste.

- Sprinkle onion and garlic powder on bread before toasting for extra seasoning.

- For an even moister stuffing, cover top of baking dish with a piece of parchment paper while cooking.

- This recipe doubles well. Bake in a 13 x 9 x 2-inch baking dish for 35 – 45 minutes.

Tortillas

I think this is a versatile recipe that lends itself to being used in a variety of ways.

You can roll the dough thin for tortillas. You can also roll it a bit thicker and create wonderful wraps for sandwiches perfect for anything from lunch meat to chicken salad.

Never before with a gf flour mix recipe had I been able to make tortillas so pliable, so thin and so delicious.

Makes 3 – 4 tortillas

The recipe is simple – only six ingredients, but since I think, like our family, you'll be making these often, it has very detailed instructions so you'll achieve the best results possible when preparing the tortillas.

Preheat a griddle or frying pan to a setting just before medium heat. A hot griddle is important.

Prepare your work area.   You'll need parchment paper, a rolling pin and 1 – 2 tablespoons of **Celeste's Best Gluten-Free Flour Mix** to dust the tortilla.

Whisk together in mixing bowl:

1 cup **Celeste's Best Gluten-Free Flour Mix (CBGFFM)**
1 teaspoon **sugar**
¾ teaspoon **konjac powder** or ½ teaspoon **xanthan gum**
½ teaspoon **sea salt**

Beating on medium speed, slowly pour in:

¼ - ½ cup **water (**start with ¼ c. water, then add the remaining water, tablespoon by tablespoon as needed)

Beat on low speed until mixture comes together in a ball — approx. 30 seconds. Add additional tablespoons of water if necessary. Dough should form a soft ball in hand without cracking much at sides when compressed. It should feel like a balloon filled with sand. This dough should be more on the moist side, than dry.

If the ball of dough feels hard when compressed, add additional tablespoons of water until ball feels more elastic. (Always better to work with a slightly moister dough than a drier one.)

Form dough into balls, slightly larger than a ping-pong ball. Knead each ball by lightly tossing it back and forth in your hands. (If your hands become sticky, rinse and dry them.) You'll be surprised how the consistency of the dough will change by simply kneading gently with dry hands.

I generally shape all the dough into balls, then rinse my hands and begin kneading the dough again while I wait for the tortilla pan to heat up.

To roll tortillas:

Take one of the formed balls and press in the center to flatten, then continue to press around the sides until the entire dough ball is flattened.

Place dough on parchment paper or plastic wrap and begin rolling.

If at any point the dough begins to stick, flour the tortilla lightly with a small amount of additional flour. Also, if your first tortilla is sticky, take a moment and knead remaining balls of dough again. You can also roll dough in between two sheets of parchment paper and that makes it a little simpler.

Roll to preferred level of thickness. Very thin for tortillas, and slightly thicker for sandwich wraps. We roll ours out to ⅛-inch or ¼-inch thick.

When you've reached desired thickness and your griddle is well heated, grease it with a small amount of **extra light olive oil**, then pick up your parchment paper with rolled dough and flip your tortilla onto the griddle. Carefully roll back parchment paper and use it again for the next tortilla. As you become accustomed to working with the dough, you'll be able to simply pick the tortilla up off the parchment and place it on the griddle with ease.

When the tortilla has heated well on one side and "blisters" have formed on the surface, flip the tortilla. Then immediately press down on it with a wide spatula, applying gentle but firm pressure all over the top. This will cause the tortilla to puff from the steam inside. Blisters will then form over most of this side of the tortilla surface as you press down. Turn the tortilla again and press the other side until the blisters turn a light golden brown.

Be careful not to overcook, as the tortillas will become tough. Generally cook for about 2 – 3 minutes on the first side. Then flip it over and cook an additional 1 – 2 minutes on the other side. And then briefly on the first side again.

Place cooked tortillas on a plate covered with a clean towel or in a tortilla warmer to stay hot. **This is a very important step, as the steam produced from the hot tortillas will help make them soft and pliable.**

Tortillas taste best served warm. Store completely cooled tortillas in a plastic bag in refrigerator. Best when reheated before serving, but may also be eaten cold. The thicker the wrap the better it will taste unheated.

- We double or sometimes even triple this recipe.

- I make these at least once a week and have now invested in a cast iron tortilla press to form the tortillas (and it's also terrific for empanadas). These presses are readily available online for a nominal price (under $25) and they're a huge timesaver! I line each side of the tortilla press with plastic wrap, place my ball of dough in the press, close, then open it and roll the tortilla out evenly with a mini pastry rolling pin if necessary, pick it up and place on griddle to cook.

Yeast-Free Pizza Crust

This is a great yeast-free pizza crust recipe. This is the recipe we use on a regular basis even though it requires the extra step of mixing the flours. This combination of flours produces a crust closest to one made from wheat flour.

Roll it thick for a Sicilian crust or thinner for a pizza pie. I top this with the Pizza Sauce recipe (see page 363) and goat cheese mozzarella.

Makes one pizza crust

Preheat oven to 425 degrees. Grease a medium sized cookie tray with 2 tablespoons of **olive oil**.

Whisk the following together in a mixing bowl:

1¼ cups **white rice flour**
½ cup **arrowroot starch/flour**
½ cup **sweet potato flour**
¼ cup **tapioca flour**

1½ tablespoons **sugar**
2 teaspoons **cream of tartar**
2 teaspoons **konjac powder** or **xanthan gum**
1 teaspoon **baking soda**
1 teaspoon **sea salt**

In a 2-cup measuring cup, add and process on high speed with an **immersion** or **stick blender** for 10 seconds, let rest for 1 – 2 minutes, then process again for 10 seconds until mixture gels and thickens:

1½ teaspoons **golden flaxseed meal**
¼ cup plus 2 tablespoons **hot water**

Then add and process for 5 more seconds:

¾ cup **water**
2 tablespoons **olive oil**
1 tablespoon **lemon juice**

Using mixer, beat on low speed for only 20 seconds. Dough should be soft, moist, and sticky. (If necessary, add 1 – 2 tablespoons of water to dough to get it to the proper consistency.)

Place 1 – 2 tablespoons of **olive oil** on a work surface and gently roll dough back and forth until no longer sticky. Place ball of dough on baking tray and form a mound by flattening bottom.

Drizzle an additional 1 – 2 teaspoons of **olive oil** over dough. Flatten top of dough and then using a pastry roller or small rolling pin, roll out dough until it fills the pan. Continue rolling over it gently several times in all directions until it takes shape. If dough sticks to the rolling pin add additional oil as needed.

Then smooth around all edges with your fingers. Add toppings and bake for 25 – 30 minutes.

- The other night, I made this dough and maybe I wasn't careful when I measured the water and the dough was extremely wet. At first I thought it might end up in the trash. Nope. Added a bit more flour to it, then placed the dough in the pan and poured a tablespoon or two of olive oil over it and gently spread it around with the palm of my hand, then used a pastry dough roller to even it all out. That night my husband said, "I think this may be the best pizza crust I've ever had."

- Don't have time to make a crust, but have a craving for pizza? Try using large portabella mushroom caps instead of crust. Clean the mushrooms and scrape out the gills and place directly on oven rack upside down in preheated 375 degree oven for 10 – 15 minutes to dry caps out and crisp them up a bit. (Place a tray on the rack underneath them as they tend to drip a bit.) Then remove from oven, turn over and fill with pizza sauce and toppings. Place on baking sheet covered with parchment paper and cook for an additional 15 minutes.

Celeste's Best Pizza Crust

This is another great yeast-free pizza crust recipe that you can cook up in a hurry. From start to finish, you can have pizza on the table in 30 minutes or less. I think the recipe on the previous page makes a crust more like a wheat flour crust, but if you don't have time to mix up the flours or don't have them on hand, this is the recipe we used before I developed the Yeast-Free Pizza Crust.

Makes one 16-inch pizza crust

Preheat oven to 425 degrees. Grease a 16-inch perforated pizza pan. Whisk the following together in a mixing bowl:

1½ cups *Celeste's Best Gluten-Free Flour Mix (CBGFFM)*
1½ tablespoons **sugar**
1½ teaspoons **cream of tartar**
1 teaspoon **konjac powder** or **xanthan gum**
¾ teaspoon **baking soda**
¾ teaspoon **sea salt**

In a 2-cup measuring cup, add and process on high speed with an **immersion** or **stick blender** for 30 seconds:

1½ tablespoons **golden flaxseed meal**
¼ cup plus 2 tablespoons **hot water**

Then add:

½ cup **water**
1½ tablespoons **olive oil**
1 tablespoon **lemon juice**

Using mixer, beat on low speed for only 20 seconds. Dough should be soft, moist, and sticky. (If necessary add 1 – 2 tablespoons of water to dough to get it to the proper consistency.)

Place 1 – 2 tablespoons of **CBGFFM** on a work surface and gently roll dough back and forth until no longer sticky. Place ball of dough on perforated round pizza tray and form a mound by flattening bottom.

Drizzle an additional teaspoon of **olive oil** over dough. Flatten top of dough and then use a pastry roller or small rolling pin to roll out dough until it fills the pan, rolling over it gently several times in all directions until it takes shape. If dough sticks to the rolling pin, add additional oil as needed.

Then smooth around all edges with your fingers. Bake for 7 – 10 minutes, until crust is lightly golden. Remove from oven and add pizza sauce (see page 363) and your favorite toppings. Bake for an additional 7 – 10 minutes.

For a 12-inch crust use the following recipe:

1 cup *Celeste's Best Gluten-Free Flour Mix*
1 tablespoon **sugar**
1 teaspoon **cream of tartar**
¾ teaspoon **konjac powder** or **xanthan gum**
½ teaspoon **baking soda**
½ teaspoon **sea salt**

In a 2-cup measuring cup, add and process on high speed with an **immersion** or **stick blender** for 30 seconds:

3 tablespoons **hot water**
1 tablespoon **golden flaxseed meal**

Then add:

⅓ cup **water**
1 tablespoon **olive oil**
1½ teaspoons **lemon juice**

Using mixer beat on low speed for only 20 seconds. Dough should be soft, moist, and sticky. Then proceed with directions as instructed for the 16-inch crust on the previous page.

Yeast-Free Pizza Crust #2

This is not your usual pizza crust. It's almost like a flat bread crust. You mix up the batter, spread it into a pan and it bakes up into a crust. What I love about this crust is that the crust bakes up soft and fluffy and is similar to a yeast baked pizza dough.

Makes 1 pizza crust

Preheat oven to 400 degrees. Grease a 17 by 11-inch (see note box following recipe) cookie tray well. (Crust has a tendency to stick unless well-greased.)

In a medium sized bowl, whisk together the following:

¾ cup **white rice flour**
¼ cup plus 2 tablespoons **sweet potato flour**
¼ cup **white bean flour**
2 tablespoons **tapioca flour**
1 tablespoon **sweet rice flour**

1½ tablespoons **sugar**
1½ teaspoons **cream of tartar**
1½ teaspoons **konjac powder** or **xanthan gum**
¾ teaspoon **baking soda**
½ teaspoon **sea salt**

In a small bowl or large measuring cup, whisk together the following:

2 **eggs** or equivalent substitute
1 cup **milk** or **non-dairy milk substitute**
2 tablespoons **olive oil**

Add milk mixture to dry ingredients, beating on medium speed for 30 seconds or until well combined.

Batter will resemble a cake batter. Spoon dough across center of pan. Fill a small bowl with water and dip spatula into water (letting excess water drip off) repeatedly. Spread and smooth the surface of the crust into all the corners, filling the tray while being careful not to press down and compress dough too much.

Bake for 15 – 17 minutes. Remove from oven and add pizza sauce and your favorite toppings. Bake for an additional 10 – 12 minutes.

- The size of the pan matters for this recipe. Pans that are too small will produce a crust that is too thick and pizza will be too doughy. Also important to note, do not use perforated pans for this recipe as the batter often seeps through the holes when spreading it across the pan.

- Suggested toppings: sliced tomatoes, sliced peppers, ground beef, grilled chicken, fresh basil, onions, olives and sliced mushrooms.

- If you find your batter too thick to spread adequately around pan, add either ¼ cup more milk or water to thin.

- If you prefer a crispier crust, flip crust into another greased pan that is the same size after the initial 15 minutes of baking and before adding toppings and cook for 5 additional minutes.

PANCAKES AND WAFFLES

Pancakes

Crepes

In France, crepes are made to celebrate renewal, family life, and hope for good fortune and happiness in the months that follow.

These thin pancakes can be filled with just about anything: a sweet filling for a dessert or with a meat-based filling as a main dish. Or they can be served simply with some mixed vegetables as a side dish. And surprisingly, they're very easy to make once you get the hang of them.

Makes 12 crepes

Place the following in food processor:

3 **eggs** (this recipe will not work with flaxeggs or egg replacer)
1¼ cups **water**
1 cup *Celeste's Best Gluten-Free Flour Mix*
2 tablespoons **extra light olive oil**
1 tablespoon **sugar** (optional: best used for dessert crepes)
¼ teaspoon **konjac powder** or **xanthan gum**
½ teaspoon **sea salt**

Process for 30 seconds or until the batter is smooth and there are no visible lumps. The batter should have the consistency of heavy cream. Place batter in refrigerator and chill for at least one hour.

Removed chilled batter from refrigerator. Check consistency. If needed add an additional tablespoon or two of water. Grease a crepe pan or 8-inch fry pan. (Crepes work best with a very good non-stick crepe pan.) Place pan on stove on medium heat.

Note: There are two key points when making crepes. The first is getting your batter to the right consistency. The batter will need to be slightly thick, but yet still thin enough to quickly cover the pan when swirled. Add an additional tablespoon or two of water to batter if necessary to achieve the right consistency. The second key point is maintaining the proper cooking temperature. Your pan should be hot enough that drops of water sizzle in it, but not too hot that the batter bubbles considerably when it is placed in the pan.

Once pan is fully heated, remove it from heat. Pour 3 – 4 tablespoons of batter (a scant ¼ cup or simply fill it only three-quarters full) in the center of the pan and quickly swirl it around to thinly cover its surface. Return pan to heat. Cook on one side until bubbles stop and edges dry, about one minute. Using a spatula, loosen crepe from pan, then flip and continue cooking on the other side until golden brown, approximately 30 seconds.

Gently slide the crepe out of the pan onto a plate. Cooked crepes may be placed on top of each other and will not stick to one another. To keep crepes warm, place in baking dish in oven set to 200 degrees.

Fill your crepes with the filling of your choosing or cover with plastic wrap and store in refrigerator. Crepes can also be frozen. Separate with sheets of parchment or waxed paper and store in a plastic resealable bag. Heat up lightly in pan being serving.

Even great chefs often have to discard their first few crepes. I know I always do, too. So don't be discouraged as you attempt these. It takes some practice to get the batter to the proper consistency and also to gain skill at quickly swirling the batter in the pan.

- Fresh or dried herbs can be added to season the batter.

- If the edges of the crepe brown too much, the batter is being swirled too thin.

French Toast

Use any of the bread recipes in the cookbook to create the most wonderful French toast. And even though this breakfast treat is traditionally made with egg soaked bread, this recipe works just as well with flaxeggs (see page 21) as an egg substitute.

Makes 6 – 8 slices

Coat a frying pan or griddle with a few tablespoons of **extra light olive oil** and heat to medium-low temperature.

Meanwhile in a medium sized bowl, mix together the following:

1 **egg** or equivalent substitute
⅓ cup **milk** or **non-dairy milk substitute**
2 tablespoons *Celeste's Best Gluten-Free Flour Mix*
2 tablespoons **sugar**
½ teaspoon **vanilla extract**
¼ teaspoon **cinnamon**

Cut **one loaf of any of the gluten-free, yeast-free bread recipes** (see index for recipes) into ½-inch thick slices. Dip each slice of bread briefly into the liquid batter, being sure to coat both sides well. Place into preheated pan and cook 2 – 3 minutes on each side until they are lightly browned.

Serve warm with **maple syrup**, **Maple Syrup Substitute** (see page 361) or with additional **sugar** sprinkled on top.

> - Often when I have part of a loaf of bread left over, I cook up some French toast. I let it cool and store the slices separated by parchment paper in a resealable plastic bag in the freezer. Then I simply pop them in a pan on low heat to reheat them as needed.

Pancakes

Pancakes to me are a pure comfort food. Great paired with the Maple Syrup Substitute (see page 361).

Makes fourteen 4-inch pancakes

In a medium sized bowl, briskly whisk together:

2 cups **milk** or **non-dairy milk substitute**
2 **eggs** or equivalent substitute
3 tablespoons **extra light olive oil**
1 teaspoon **vanilla extract**

In another medium sized bowl, briskly whisk together:

2 cups *Celeste's Best Gluten-Free Flour Mix*
3 tablespoons **sugar**
1 tablespoon **cream of tartar**
1 teaspoon **konjac powder** or **xanthan gum**
1½ teaspoons **baking soda**
½ teaspoon **sea salt**

Add flour mixture to wet ingredients and whisk well until batter is free of lumps. For fluffier pancakes, let batter stand for 10 minutes.

Lightly grease a griddle and heat over medium heat.   When griddle is well heated (see note box on following page) pour approximately ¼ – ⅓ cup of batter onto griddle.

Cook until the bottom of pancake has lightly browned. Flip over and cook an additional 1 – 2 minutes, or until both sides are evenly browned.

Serve immediately or keep warm in a 200 degree oven until ready to serve.

Freeze any leftovers in a plastic freezer bag, separating pancakes with sheets of wax or parchment paper between them.

*Please see following page for cooking notes and suggestions.

- You can tell if your griddle is hot enough by flicking a drop or two of water on its surface. The water will dance around and quickly evaporate when ready.

- Griddles are best for pancakes because they don't have sides and you'll be able to maneuver the spatula more easily when flipping the pancakes.

- If you prefer a thinner pancake, add an additional tablespoon or two of milk to the batter.

- Variation: Add one mashed banana to wet ingredients for added flavor. (My personal favorite way to eat pancakes.)

- In a hurry? Try the Baking Mix Pancakes instead (see page 229).

- Prefer a multi-grain pancake? Use only 1¼ cups *Celeste's Best Gluten-Free Flour Mix* and then add ¼ cup of amaranth, ivory teff and quinoa flour. Or you can make up a mix of *Celeste's Best Gluten-Free Flour Mix* with these ratios – 1 cup white rice flour, ½ cup sweet rice flour, ⅓ cup amaranth flour, ⅓ cup quinoa flour, ⅓ cup ivory teff flour and ¼ cup white bean flour. Then measure out the amount needed for this recipe.

Waffles

Along with pancakes, we often eat waffles for dinner as well. This batter bakes up light and crispy waffles.

Makes 8 waffles

Preheat waffle iron.

Combine the following in a large mixing bowl and whisk until mixed:

2 cups **Celeste's Best Gluten-Free Flour Mix**
2 tablespoons **sugar**
1½ teaspoons **cream of tartar**
1 teaspoon **konjac powder** or **xanthan gum**
¾ teaspoon **baking soda**
½ teaspoon **sea salt**

In another bowl, whisk together:

2 cups **milk** or **non-dairy milk substitute**
2 **eggs** or equivalent substitute
⅓ cup **extra light olive oil**
1½ teaspoons **vanilla extract**

Add wet ingredients to dry and mix with a spatula just until blended, being careful not to over mix. Cook following your waffle maker instructions.

- Freeze any leftover waffles. Place waffles in a single layer on a baking sheet that will fit in your freezer and freeze just until waffles harden. Then remove and store in a plastic bag in freezer.

- When we first found out we had celiac disease, we needed to replace our waffle iron with a new one since it's almost impossible to get all the gluten out of a waffle maker. I absolutely love the waffle maker we are currently using. Visit my website at www.celestesbest.com or www.CBglutenfree.com for more information.

Chocolate Heaven Pancakes

We enjoy eating pancakes for dinner instead of breakfast. We've found pancakes are somewhat heavy and can slow down a morning, soon leaving you longing for your warm bed and fluffy pillow again. We tried these pancakes one night after seeing a recipe in a magazine. At first I laughed at the idea of Chocolate Pancakes. It was almost like eating dessert for dinner, but my husband's mind was set on having these and I'm glad because these were absolute heaven!

Makes approx. 15 – 17 pancakes

In a medium sized bowl, combine the following:

2 **very ripe bananas,** mashed
2 cups **milk** or **non-dairy milk substitute**
2 **eggs** or equivalent substitute
¼ cup natural **unsweetened applesauce**

In another larger bowl, combine:

2 cups *Celeste's Best Gluten-Free Flour Mix*
⅔ cup **unsweetened cocoa powder**
½ cup **sugar**
1 teaspoon **baking soda**
1 teaspoon **konjac powder** or **xanthan gum**
1 teaspoon **sea salt**

Add milk mixture to dry mix whisking until dry ingredients are moistened. The batter will be slightly lumpy. (Optional: Add ¼ cup **mini chocolate chips** to the mixed batter.)

Lightly grease a griddle and warm to medium heat. Pour approximately ¼ cup batter for each pancake. Because the pancakes are chocolate and dark in color, it is a little more difficult to tell when they're ready to be flipped. Generally cook 1 – 2 minutes each side.

Top finished pancakes with **maple syrup** (often contains corn), **Maple Syrup Substitute** (see page 361) or sprinkle with **powdered sugar** and serve with **sliced strawberries**. Or if you're really feeling decadent, top with **melted allergen-free chocolate!**

Chocolate Waffles with Chocolate Sauce

A wonderful treat. This recipe bakes up light cake-like waffles. Either for breakfast or as a dessert topped with a sweet chocolate sauce.

Makes 8 waffles

Preheat waffle iron. Combine the following in a large mixing bowl and whisk until mixed:

1½ cups *Celeste's Best Gluten-Free Flour Mix*
¾ cup **sugar**
½ cup **unsweetened cocoa powder**
1 teaspoon **baking soda**
1 teaspoon **cream of tartar**
¾ teaspoon **konjac powder** or **xanthan gum**
½ teaspoon **sea salt**

In another bowl, whisk together:

1¾ cups **water**
2 **eggs** or equivalent substitute
¼ cup plus 2 tablespoons **extra light olive oil**
1 teaspoon **vanilla extract**

Add wet ingredients to dry and mix with a spatula just until combined, being careful not to over mix.

Optional: Fold into batter:

½ cup **mini chocolate chips**

Pour mixture into a hot waffle iron and bake. For my waffle iron I found ½ cup for each waffle was just enough mix for a nice, thick waffle. My baking time was approximately 6 minutes each. You may need to adjust cooking times and amount of mix based on your particular waffle maker.

To prepare the **Chocolate Sauce Topping**: Place the following in a small saucepan and bring to a boil:

2 cups **water**

(continued)

In a small bowl, whisk together:

1 cup **sugar**
½ cup **unsweetened cocoa powder**
2 tablespoons **sweet rice flour**
1 teaspoon **sea salt**

Add sugar mixture to boiling water and continue to cook over medium heat, stirring often until mixture returns to a boil. Cook for 1 minute, stirring constantly as mixture thickens. Remove from heat and add:

1½ tablespoons **extra light olive oil**
2 teaspoons **vanilla extract**

Drizzle topping over waffles before serving.

BAKING MIX RECIPES

Baking Mix Banana Cake with Crumb Topping

Celeste's Best Baking Mix

*Start with **Celeste's Best Gluten-Free Flour Mix** and add a few ingredients to create a convenient pre-mixed baking mix to quickly prepare all the recipes in this chapter.*

*Whenever I make **Celeste's Best Gluten-Free Flour Mix,** I make a little extra so that I can create a bag or two of this mix to have on hand. Definitely comes in handy for those days when you're running a bit short on time.*

Makes approx. 3½ cups

In mixing bowl using whisk attachment, whisk on medium speed for 1 minute:

2½ cups *Celeste's Best Gluten-Free Flour Mix*
1 tablespoon **cream of tartar**
1 tablespoon **sugar**
1½ teaspoons **baking soda**
1¼ teaspoons **konjac powder** or **xanthan gum**
¼ teaspoon **sea salt**

When well mixed, add:

¼ cup plus 1 tablespoon **extra light olive oil**

Beat on medium speed for 1 minute until small, fine crumbs form.

Store in an airtight container or resealable plastic bag in refrigerator.

> - I usually double this recipe so that I always have some on hand.

Baking Mix Biscuits

Keep some of the baking mix on hand to quickly enjoy biscuits at any meal.

Makes 6 biscuits

Preheat oven to 450 degrees. Grease an 8 or 9-inch round pan.

In a large bowl, add:

2 cups **Celeste's Best Baking Mix**

In a small bowl or measuring cup, whisk together:

⅔ cup **milk** or **non-dairy milk substitute**
2 teaspoons **lemon juice**

Gradually add the milk to the baking mix and use a fork to gently incorporate the liquid into the mix.

Form the dough into a ball and place it on a lightly floured surface and roll it in the flour gently until it no longer feels tacky.

Pat down the dough with a very light touch until it is ½-inch thick. Dip a biscuit cutter in flour, then cut into the patted dough.

Place biscuits in the greased pan and cook until the tops have browned slightly, approximately 15 – 17 minutes. Remove from oven and serve warm.

- Instead of rolling dough out, you can simply scoop up dough with an ice cream scoop or large cookie scoop, press down gently on tops to flatten to ½-inch thick and place in pan and bake.

- Have a little extra time? Try the biscuits made from scratch on page 235.

Baking Mix Apple Muffins

Muffins filled with applesauce.

Makes 12 muffins

Preheat oven to 425 degrees. Grease muffin tins well.

In mixing bowl, combine:

2 cups *Celeste's Best Baking Mix*
⅓ cup **sugar**
1 teaspoon **cinnamon**

In a small bowl, whisk together:

⅔ cup **milk** or **non-dairy milk substitute**
½ cup **unsweetened applesauce**
1 **egg** or equivalent substitute
2 tablespoons **extra light olive oil**

Add liquid to dry ingredients using a wooden spoon or spatula stirring just until mixed, about 20 – 25 light strokes. Be sure to scrape the bottom of bowl to ensure that all the flour has been incorporated.

Prepare topping by combining with a fork in a small bowl:

2 tablespoons *Celeste's Best Baking Mix*
1½ tablespoons **extra light olive oil**
¼ cup **brown sugar**

Sprinkle topping evenly across each muffin. Bake for 8 minutes. Then reduce temperature to 375 degrees and bake for an additional 7 – 10 minutes. Bake until muffins are golden brown.

Muffins are done when toothpick or tester inserted into the center comes out clean. Set muffins on wire rack to cool for 5 minutes. Remove muffins from tin and serve slightly warm or continue cooling on wire rack.

Baking Mix Banana Bread

This recipe only requires 3 ingredients other than the baking mix, but still delivers some of the best tasting banana bread I've ever had.

Makes 1 loaf

Preheat oven to 350 degrees. Grease an 8½ x 4½ x 2½ -inch loaf pan.

Add to mixing bowl:

3 **over-ripe medium sized bananas**, mashed (1 cup)
2 **eggs** or equivalent substitute

Beat for 30 seconds on medium speed. Then add and beat for 30 more seconds:

1 cup **sugar**

Add in and beat for another 30 seconds on medium speed:

2 cups *Celeste's Best Baking Mix*

Pour into the greased loaf pan and bake for 50 – 60 minutes. Bread is done when toothpick inserted in center comes out clean. Remove loaf from oven and place on wire rack to cool for 5 minutes. (Leaving in the pan any longer can cause the bottom crust to become soggy from condensation.) Run a knife between bread and pan to loosen loaf if necessary. Remove loaf from pan and place on wire rack.

Once bread has completely cooled, loosely wrap with plastic wrap and store at room temperature. Bread will stay soft and fresh for several days.

Bread is also delicious served chilled.

Baking Mix Banana Cake with Crumb Topping

Whether you decide to make banana bread or banana cake, they're both great ways to make use of a bunch of overly ripened bananas. This cake is one of my husband's favorites and it's absolutely scrumptious!

Makes one 13 x 9-inch cake

Preheat oven to 350 degrees and grease a 13 x 9 x 2-inch baking dish. In a mixing bowl mix together well:

2½ cups *Celeste's Best Baking Mix*
¾ cup **brown sugar**
1½ teaspoons **cinnamon**

In a medium sized bowl, combine until well blended:

1½ cups **ripe bananas**, mashed (about 3 bananas)
¾ cup **milk** or **non-dairy milk substitute**
1 **egg** or equivalent substitute
¼ cup **extra light olive oil**

Add wet ingredients to dry. Beat on medium-high speed for 30 seconds. Pour into prepared pan. Prepare topping by combining with a fork in a small bowl:

2 tablespoons *Celeste's Best Baking Mix*
1½ tablespoons **extra light olive oil**
¼ cup **brown sugar**

Sprinkle topping evenly across cake batter. Bake for 25 – 30 minutes. Cake is done when toothpick inserted in center comes out clean. Serve warm from the oven or refrigerate and serve cool.

Baking Mix Blueberry Muffins

Using the baking mix, you can have muffins mixed up in a jiffy! My daughter doesn't particularly like blueberry muffins, but she loves these.

Makes 9 muffins

Preheat oven to 425 degrees. Grease muffin tins well. In mixing bowl combine:

2 cups *Celeste's Best Baking Mix*

In a strainer, rinse:

1 cup **blueberries**

Remove 1 tablespoon of flour from mixing bowl and sprinkle it over the blueberries to lightly coat them. Place floured blueberries to the side. Meanwhile, add to mixing bowl and whisk together until well combined:

¾ cup **sugar**

In a small bowl, whisk together:

⅔ cup **milk** or **non-dairy milk substitute**
1 **egg** or equivalent substitute
2 tablespoons **extra light olive oil**
½ teaspoon **vanilla extract**

Add liquid to dry ingredients using a wooden spoon or spatula stirring until just mixed, about 20 – 25 light strokes. Be sure to scrape the bottom of bowl to ensure that all the flour has been incorporated.   Add blueberries, then spoon into muffins tins nearly filling the muffin tin. Place in oven.

Bake for 8 minutes. Then reduce temperature to 375 degrees and bake for an additional 8 – 10 minutes. Bake until muffins are golden brown. Muffins are done when toothpick or tester inserted into the center comes out clean.

Set muffins on wire rack to cool for 5 minutes. Remove muffins from tin and serve slightly warm or continue cooling on wire rack.

Baking Mix Brownies

These fudgy brownies taste as rich as those made completely from scratch.

Makes 9 brownies

Preheat oven to 350 degrees. Grease an 8-inch square baking dish.

In mixing bowl, beat for 30 seconds on medium high speed:

¾ cup **sugar**
¼ cup plus 1 tablespoon **extra light olive oil**

Then add and beat for another 30 seconds on medium speed:

1 **egg** or equivalent substitute
1 teaspoon **vanilla extract**
1 tablespoon **water**

In a small bowl, whisk together the dry ingredients:

⅔ cup *Celeste's Best Baking Mix*
⅜ cup (6 tablespoons) **unsweetened cocoa**

Add the dry ingredients to the mixing bowl and beat on medium speed for 30 seconds or until well moistened. Stir in:

⅓ cup **mini chocolate chips**

Using a spatula spread batter in pan. Place pan in oven. Bake for 18 – 22 minutes or until edges begin to pull away from sides of pan. Place cake on wire rack to cool before serving. Brownies are also delicious served chilled.

Baking Mix Chocolate Cake

Using the baking mix, you can quickly bake up a chocolate cake filled with chocolate chips.

Makes one 8-inch cake

Preheat oven to 375 degrees. Grease an 8-inch square baking dish.

In mixing bowl, whisk together:

1¾ cups ***Celeste's Best Baking Mix***
1 cup **sugar**
¼ cup **unsweetened cocoa**

In a small bowl, whisk together:

1 cup **milk** or **non-dairy milk substitute**
1 **egg** or equivalent substitute
1½ tablespoons **extra light olive oil**
1 teaspoon **vanilla extract**

Add the wet ingredients to the dry and beat on medium speed for 30 seconds or until moistened.

Spread batter into pan with spatula. Then sprinkle over top:

½ cup **mini chocolate chips**

Place pan in oven. Bake for 30 – 35 minutes or until toothpick or tester inserted into center of cake comes out clean. Place cake on wire rack to cool before serving.

Baking Mix Chocolate Chip Banana Muffins

Bananas and chocolate come together in perfect harmony for these muffins.

Makes 12 muffins

Preheat oven to 400 degrees. Grease a muffin tray well or line with paper liners. These muffins tend to stick to the liners.

In mixing bowl, beat for 1 minute on medium high speed until pureed:

3 **medium sized bananas**, sliced (producing 1⅓ cups puree)

Then add and beat for 20 – 30 seconds on medium speed:

1 **egg** or equivalent substitute
3 tablespoons **extra light olive oil**

In a small bowl, whisk together:

2 cups *Celeste's Best Baking Mix*
⅓ cup **sugar**

Add liquid to dry ingredients using a wooden spoon or spatula stirring just until mixed, about 20 – 25 light strokes. Be sure to scrape the bottom of bowl to ensure that all the flour has been incorporated.

Then stir in:

⅓ cup **mini chocolate chips**

Spoon into baking cups, filling two-thirds full and bake for 15 – 17 minutes. Remove from oven and cool on wire rack for 5 minutes. When cool enough to handle, remove muffins from pan and place on rack to continue cooling.

> - I sometimes puree the bananas with an immersion blender instead of using the mixer. It almost completely purees the bananas as opposed to beating in the mixer which often can leave small chunks.

Baking Mix Chocolate Chip Brownies

It's hard to tell whether these are brownies that want to be chocolate chip cookies or cookies that want to be brownies. Either way, they're a winner!

Makes 9 brownies

Preheat oven to 350 degrees. Grease an 8-inch square baking dish.

In mixing bowl, whisk together:

1¼ cups **Celeste's Best Baking Mix**
½ cup plus 2 tablespoons **brown sugar**

In a small bowl, whisk together:

1 **egg** or equivalent substitute
2 tablespoons **extra light olive oil**
¼ cup **water**
1 teaspoon **vanilla extract**

Add the wet ingredients to the dry and beat on medium speed for 30 seconds or until moistened. Then stir in:

½ cup **mini chocolate chips**

Pour into prepared baking dish. Smooth batter with spatula dipped in a small amount of water until level. Bake for 20 – 22 minutes. Remove from oven and cool on a wire rack.

Baking Mix Chocolate Chip Cookies

Great to have a mix ready on hand that allows you to bake up chocolate chip cookies when you're aiming to fill your chocolate fix.

Makes 24 cookies

Preheat oven to 350 degrees. Grease two large cookie sheets.

In mixing bowl, beat on medium speed for 1 minute:

¼ cup **extra light olive oil**
½ cup **brown sugar**
½ cup **sugar**
1 **egg** or equivalent substitute
2 teaspoons **vanilla extract**

Then add and beat on medium speed for 30 seconds or until dough comes together and forms a ball:

2¼ cups *Celeste's Best Baking Mix*

Stir in:

⅔ cup **mini chocolate chips**

Form dough into 1-inch balls. (If dough is too sticky, add an additional *Celeste's Best Baking Mix* tablespoon by tablespoon until dough is workable.) Place balls of dough on greased cookie trays 2 inches apart. Press down on tops to flatten so they are ¼-inch thick.

Place trays in center of oven and bake for 9 – 11 minutes, rotating trays from front to back and top to bottom halfway through cooking time so cookies will bake evenly.

Bake until cookies are golden brown. Remove cookies from oven and place trays on wire racks for 2 minutes. Then transfer cookies to wire rack to completely cool.

> • If you only have one tray, run it under cool water before beginning second set of cookies so that the heated tray doesn't cause your cookies to prematurely cook.

Baking Mix Coffee Cake

A quick cake to bake to accompany a hot cup of coffee!

Makes one 8-inch cake

Preheat oven to 350 degrees. Grease an 8-inch square baking dish.

Add the following to a mixing bowl and beat for 30 seconds on low:

2 cups *Celeste's Best Baking Mix*
1 cup **milk** or **non-dairy milk substitute**
3 tablespoons **sugar**
1 **egg** or equivalent substitute

Pour batter into prepared baking dish. Then in a small bowl, whisk together the topping:

⅓ cup **brown sugar**
⅓ cup *Celeste's Best Baking Mix*
½ teaspoon **ground cinnamon**
1½ tablespoons **extra light olive oil**

Sprinkle topping lightly over batter. Place pan in oven. Bake for 27 – 30 minutes or until toothpick or tester inserted into center of cake comes out clean.

Place cake on wire rack to cool before serving.

Baking Mix Doughnut Holes

In the time it takes to heat the oil, you can prepare the dough and then within minutes have a very tasty treat.

Makes 8 doughnut holes

Place 1½ inches of **frying oil** (see note box on following page) in a pan. Oil will bubble and splatter when hot and pot should not be filled more than half full. Set on medium heat.

Check temperature using a **deep fry thermometer** as a guide. Doughnuts cook best between 345 and 365 degrees. A temperature lower than 345 degrees will cause the doughnuts to absorb too much oil and you'll wind up with heavy, greasy doughnut holes.

Oils begin to burn at 400 degrees and can catch fire at 500 degrees so it's important to use extreme caution when deep-frying. Always monitor temperature with a thermometer.

In a small bowl, whisk together:

1 cup *Celeste's Best Baking Mix*
2 tablespoons **sugar**
¼ teaspoon **cinnamon**
⅛ teaspoon **nutmeg**
⅛ teaspoon **mace**

Then add:

⅓ cup **milk** or **non-dairy milk substitute**
1 teaspoon **vanilla extract**

Mix dough together with a fork and then knead gently into one large ball with your hands. Tear off a small piece of dough and form it into a 1-inch ball. Continue until all the dough has been formed into smaller balls.

Once oil has reached desired temperature, begin frying doughnut holes 4 or 5 at a time. Turn doughnut holes over at least once during frying to evenly brown.

Depending on the temperature of the oil, the doughnut holes should take between 30 seconds to a minute to cook. Remove doughnuts with tongs or slotted spoon to paper towel lined plate.

While doughnut holes are still warm, yet cool enough to handle, roll doughnuts in either:

confectioners powdered sugar (see page 23)

or into cinnamon sugar by whisking together the following in a small bowl:

¼ cup **sugar**
1 teaspoon **cinnamon**

Store any leftover doughnuts in a brown paper bag. Storing doughnuts in a sealed container will cause the doughnuts to become overly moist.

- If you don't plan on topping the doughnut holes with the powdered or cinnamon sugar, add ¼ cup sugar to dough instead.

- Test to see if oil is the right temperature by dropping a small amount of batter in hot oil. It should turn golden brown quickly.

- Rice bran oil is an excellent choice for frying. It's a light, very healthy oil that is gluten-free and trans fat free and it also has a very high smoke point which makes it perfect for frying.

Baking Mix Lemon Sesame Chicken

This recipe quickly became a staple in our house. The baking mix adds an incredible crispy coating to the chicken.

Serves 4 – 6

Using a sharp knife, carefully cut in half horizontally into two thin breasts each:

6 skinless, boneless chicken breast halves

Combine the following in a shallow dish:

2 **eggs** or equivalent substitute
¼ cup **lemon juice**

Whisk together the following in a dish or bowl:

1 cup *Celeste's Best Baking Mix*
¼ cup **toasted sesame seeds** (see note box on following page)
1 tablespoon **paprika**

In a large skillet, heat over medium heat:

3 tablespoons **olive oil**

Place chicken breasts one at a time into egg mixture then into dish with baking mix. Coat each breast well, then add chicken to the pan.

Cook chicken for 4 – 5 minutes on each side, adding additional oil to pan as needed. Cook until golden on the outside and no longer pink inside. Place cooked chicken in 300 degree oven to keep warm.

Meanwhile as chicken is cooking, prepare sauce by combining the following in a 1½ quart saucepan:

2 cups **chicken stock**
⅔ cup **sugar**
¼ cup **lemon juice**
2 tablespoons **sweet rice flour**
1 medium **lemon**, grated

Cook over medium heat. Stir occasionally with a whisk until sauce thickens slightly approximately 5 – 7 minutes.

Place lemon sesame chicken on serving dish and spoon sauce over the top of each breast. Then sprinkle over each:

2 **green onions**, thinly sliced

Serve.

- To toast sesame seeds: Place seeds in a dry pan over medium heat, stirring occasionally and toast until golden.

- Variation: Often we simply dredge chicken in the baking mix and sauté until golden in a pan of oil olive and serve. The baking mix produces a wonderful, crispy coating on the chicken.

Baking Mix Little Danish Cookies

This is a great treat when you're short on time and you need a dessert in a hurry.

Makes 18 cookies

Preheat oven to 450 degrees. Grease 2 large cookie sheets.

In mixing bowl beat, on medium speed for 30 seconds until crumbs form:

2 cups *Celeste's Best Baking Mix*
2 tablespoons **sugar**
3 tablespoons **extra light olive oil**

Then stir in just until dough comes together:

⅔ cup **milk** or **non-dairy milk substitute**

Drop rounded tablespoons of dough onto prepared cookie sheets, roughly 9 to each tray. Flatten each cookie to ½-inch thickness. Then press into the top of each cookie with a rounded ½ teaspoon measuring spoon to create a small well.

Fill the well with:

½ teaspoon **raspberry** or **fig preserves**

Bake in preheated oven for 12 – 17 minutes or until golden. Meanwhile, prepare glaze by whisking together until smooth:

⅓ cup **confectioners powdered sugar** (see page 23)
½ tablespoon **water**
¼ teaspoon **vanilla**

When cookies are done, remove from oven and drizzle sugar glaze over them. Store leftovers in sealed container in refrigerator.

> - You can use any flavor preserves. Our family found the cookies tasted best with raspberry or fig. And we also recently tried kumquat preserves and really liked them, too.

Baking Mix Pancakes

Pancakes in a hurry. Just add the liquid ingredients and a few tablespoons of sugar.

Makes twelve 4-inch pancakes

Grease a griddle and heat over medium heat.

In a medium sized bowl, whisk together:

1¾ cups *Celeste's Best Baking Mix*
1½ cups **milk** or **non-dairy milk substitute**
2 tablespoons **sugar**
1 **egg** or equivalent substitute
1 teaspoon **vanilla extract**

When griddle is well heated, pour approximately ¼ cup of batter onto it. Cook until you notice bubbles appearing across the battered surface and bottom of pancake has lightly browned. Flip over and cook an additional 1 – 2 minutes, or until both sides are evenly browned.

Serve immediately or keep warm in a 200 degree oven until ready to serve.

> ▪ For thinner pancakes, add an additional ¼ of milk or water when preparing the batter.

Baking Mix Pineapple Upside Down Cake

*Using **Celeste's Best Baking Mix** you can prepare this cake in under ten minutes and yet it still has the same delectable taste of a traditionally prepared Upside Down Cake.*

Makes one 8-inch square or round cake

Preheat oven to 375 degrees. Grease an 8-inch square or round baking dish. Spread evenly across bottom of dish:

3 tablespoons **extra light olive oil**

Then sprinkle across oil:

¼ cup **brown sugar**

Drain (reserving juice):

1 (10 ounce) can **pineapple slices, in its own juice**

Place one slice of pineapple in center of pan on top of sugar. Place a slice in each corner. Then cut 2 slices in half and place in between the five slices over sugar mixture.

Meanwhile in mixing bowl, whisk together:

1½ cups *Celeste's Best Baking Mix*
½ cup **sugar**

Whisk together the following, then add to the mixing bowl and beat for 30 seconds on medium speed:

1 cup **reserved pineapple juice** (add water if necessary to equal 1 cup liquid)
1 **egg** or equivalent substitute
2 tablespoons **extra light olive oil**
1 teaspoon **vanilla extract**

Pour cake batter over pineapples. Smooth batter with spatula dipped in pineapple juice or water until level. Bake in preheated oven for 30 – 35 minutes. As soon as cake is done, place a plate over the cake and turn upside down and carefully remove pan.   If you wait too long, the sugar will harden and the cake will be difficult to remove.

> ▪   Instead of pineapple, try sliced peaches.

Baking Mix Pumpkin Cake

An extremely moist pumpkin cake with just a touch of spice and raisins.

Makes one 8-inch cake

Preheat oven to 350 degrees. Grease an 8-inch square pan.

Whisk together the following in a medium sized bowl:

1 cup *Celeste's Best Baking Mix*
1 teaspoon **cinnamon** or **pumpkin pie spice**
½ teaspoon **baking soda**

Place the following in mixing bowl and beat for 30 seconds on low:

1 cup **canned pumpkin**
1 cup **sugar**
¼ cup **extra light olive oil**

Then add and beat an additional 30 seconds:

2 **eggs** or equivalent substitute

Add dry ingredients to mixing bowl and beat for 30 seconds longer on low.

Then stir in:

¼ cup **raisins** (optional)

Pour into prepared pan and bake for 30 – 33 minutes or until toothpick inserted into center of cake comes out clean. Remove from oven and cool on wire rack.

Baking Mix Waffles

Keep **Celeste's Best Baking Mix** on hand to quickly whip up a batch of waffles.

Makes 8 waffles

Preheat waffle iron.

In a medium sized bowl whisk together:

2 cups **milk** or **non-dairy milk substitute**
2 **eggs** or equivalent substitute
1 tablespoon **extra light olive oil**
1 teaspoon **vanilla extract**

Then add, stirring in just until moistened:

2¼ cups **Celeste's Best Baking Mix**

Pour mixture into a hot waffle iron and bake. For my waffle iron I found ½ cup for each waffle was just enough mix for a nice, thick waffle. My baking time was approximately 6 minutes each. You may need to adjust cooking times and amount of mix based on your particular waffle maker.

> - We often substitute the eggs in this recipe with flaxeggs to add a bit more fiber to the waffles.

QUICK BREADS AND MUFFINS

Chocolate Bread

Banana Bread

One of my favorite desserts is Banana Bread. There are an abundance of Banana Bread recipes out there, but I prefer this one because it is a bit lower in fat than some of the more traditional versions.

Makes 2 loaves

Preheat oven to 350 degrees. Grease two 8½ x 4½ x 2½-inch loaf pans.

Mash in mixing bowl or beat on medium speed for 1 minute:

4 over-ripe, medium sized bananas

Add the following ingredients and beat on medium speed for 1 minute or until well blended:

1½ cups ***Celeste's Best Gluten-Free Flour Mix***
1 cup **sugar**
1 **egg** or equivalent substitute
2 tablespoons **unsweetened applesauce**
1½ tablespoons **extra light olive oil**
1⅛ teaspoons **baking soda**
1 teaspoon **vanilla extract**
¾ teaspoon **konjac powder** or **xanthan gum**
¼ teaspoon **cream of tartar**

Pour into the greased loaf pans and bake for 50 – 60 minutes. Bread is done when toothpick inserted in center comes out clean. Remove loaf from oven and place on wire rack to cool for 5 minutes. (Leaving in the pan any longer can cause the bottom crust to become soggy from condensation.)

Run a knife between bread and pan to loosen loaf if necessary. Remove loaf from pan and place on wire rack. Once bread has completely cooled, loosely wrap with plastic wrap and store at room temperature. Bread stays soft and fresh for several days.

> - The key to making great tasting banana bread is using over-ripe bananas that are still slightly firm. And as an added bonus, they'll sweeten the bread naturally.
>
> - In a hurry? Try the Baking Mix Banana Bread recipe (see page 215) that uses the baking mix instead of preparing the entire recipe from scratch.

Biscuits

A light, high rising biscuit recipe. This was the final recipe I developed for the cookbook. Most gluten-free biscuits are more akin to hockey pucks, but these will be a welcome change. And you'll be surprised to find that just a few tablespoons of oil could produce such a great tasting biscuit versus the traditional butter or shortening versions.

Makes 12 biscuits

Preheat oven to 450 degrees. Grease a 9-inch round pan.

Whisk together the following in mixing bowl:

1 cup plus 2 tablespoons **white rice flour**
⅓ cup **arrowroot starch/flour**
⅓ cup **sweet potato flour**
¼ cup **tapioca flour**
1½ teaspoons **cream of tartar**
1½ teaspoons **konjac powder** or **xanthan gum**
1 teaspoon **sea salt**
¾ teaspoon **baking soda**

Then whisk together:

1 cup **milk** or **non-dairy milk substitute**
2 tablespoons **extra light olive oil**
1 tablespoon **lemon juice**

Add milk mixture to flour mixture and stir just until moistened and mixture comes together. (For this dough, I prefer to mix this using the electric mixer on stir speed for 20 seconds.) Roll dough on a lightly floured surface and knead it gently a few times. Pat the dough down to ¾-inch thickness.

Cut into circles with biscuit cutter or rim of glass. Or simply cut the biscuits in square shapes. Place on baking sheet and bake for 20 – 25 minutes or until golden brown.

Chocolate Bread

This is a moist, cake-like bread that is similar to a chocolate pound cake.

Makes 1 loaf

Preheat oven to 350 degrees. Grease an 8½ x 4½ x 2½-inch loaf pan. In a medium sized bowl, whisk together:

1½ cups *Celeste's Best Gluten-Free Flour Mix*
½ cup **unsweetened cocoa**
¾ teaspoon **konjac powder** or **xanthan gum**
¾ teaspoon **baking soda**
½ teaspoon **cream of tartar**

In a 2 cup measuring cup, whisk together:

1 cup **milk** or **non-dairy milk substitute**
1 tablespoon **lemon juice**

Place the following in mixing bowl and beat on medium speed for 30 seconds:

1 cup **sugar**
3 tablespoons **extra light olive oil**
3 tablespoons **unsweetened applesauce**

Then add and beat for another 30 seconds:

2 eggs or equivalent substitute
1 teaspoon **vanilla extract**

Beating on low speed add the flour mixture to the mixing bowl alternating with the soured milk. Continue to beat for 30 seconds. Stir in:

½ cup **mini chocolate chips**

Pour into the greased loaf pan and bake for 55 – 60 minutes or until a toothpick inserted in center comes out clean. Remove loaf from oven and place on wire rack to cool for 5 minutes. Remove loaf from pan and place on wire rack. Once bread has completely cooled, loosely wrap with plastic wrap and store at room temperature or refrigerate.

Cinnamon Buns

Many cinnamon bun recipes use yeast as the leavening agent. This recipe does not, but the dough still puffs up and expands into the most delicious buns.

Makes 8

Preheat oven to 425 degrees. Grease an 8-inch or 9-inch round pan.

In a small bowl, mix together the filling for the buns with a fork:

¼ cup plus 2 tablespoons **brown sugar**
2 tablespoons **sugar**
1 tablespoon **extra light olive oil**
2 teaspoons **ground cinnamon**
⅛ teaspoon **ground cloves**
⅛ teaspoon **sea salt**

In a two-cup measuring cup, add:

1½ cups **milk** or **non-dairy milk substitute**
1½ tablespoons **lemon juice**

Allow milk mixture to sour while preparing the dough by whisking together the following in a mixing bowl:

2½ cups *Celeste's Best Gluten-Free Flour Mix*
3 tablespoons **sugar**
1¼ teaspoons **konjac powder** or **xanthan gum**
¾ teaspoon **cream of tartar**
¾ teaspoon **baking soda**
½ teaspoon **sea salt**

Add to the dry ingredients the soured milk and:

1½ tablespoons **extra light olive oil**

Beat on medium speed for 30 seconds, or until the dry ingredients are well moistened. Mixture will appear almost too wet to work with at this point.

Tear off a piece of parchment paper at least 12 by 17-inches. Sprinkle 1 – 2 tablespoons of flour across it, spreading it around with your hand to cover the entire working surface. Drop dough onto floured piece of parchment paper and gently knead, covering it lightly with flour until no longer sticky. Add more flour if necessary.

(continued)

Then use the palms of your hands to shape dough into a 9 by 12-inch rectangle. Dough should be roughly ¼-inch thick. Lightly roll over dough with rolling pin if needed to form rectangle, sprinkling additional flour on surface of dough if necessary before rolling to prevent sticking.

Brush the formed rectangle with:

2 tablespoons **extra light olive oil**

Then sprinkle sugar filling across surface evenly, leaving ½–inch border along edges. Using the palm of your hand, press filling firmly into dough. Beginning on the longer side, carefully begin to roll up the dough, using the parchment paper to help lift it and maneuver it. Seal seam where ends meet by pressing along edge with fingers.

Divide and cut the dough into 8 even slices. I use a length of unwaxed dental floss. Slide the floss under the dough, then gently slice through the dough. The floss will cleanly and smoothly slice through the dough. And on the plus side, it's kind of fun to do!

Brush over slices with an additional:

2 tablespoons **extra light olive oil**

Then, using a spatula pick up each slice and place it in the prepared pan. If you have any difficulty removing the dough from the parchment paper, mist the spatula with some cooking oil first then slide it under the dough.

Bake for 22 – 27 minutes or until edges of the bun have turned golden brown.

Remove from oven and place on a wire rack to cool.

> - A plastic school ruler that can be easily washed comes in handy for this recipe, but you don't need to worry if the rectangle shape you roll the dough into isn't exactly the right size. Just be sure to evenly slice the roll.

Irish Soda Cake

According to the Society for the Preservation of Irish Soda Bread (and, yes, there really is such a society) traditional soda bread doesn't contain any sugar, shortening, baking powder, fruit or eggs and if the recipe calls for these ingredients you're baking Irish soda cake and not bread. Although this recipe isn't the traditional Irish soda bread, I have to say the addition of these few ingredients makes this recipe one of my favorites.

Makes one 8-inch cake

Preheat oven to 350 degrees. Grease an 8-inch round cake pan.

In a mixing bowl, mix together:

3 cups **Celeste's Best Gluten-Free Flour Mix**
¼ cup **sugar**
2 teaspoons **cream of tartar**
1½ teaspoons **konjac powder** or **xanthan gum**
1 teaspoon **baking soda**

When above ingredients are well mixed, add:

2 cups **milk** or **non-dairy milk substitute**
2 **eggs** or equivalent substitute
1 tablespoon **extra light olive oil**

Fold in:

1 cup **raisins**

Pour batter into cake pan. Brush top with:

1 tablespoon **extra light olive oil**

Bake for 55 – 60 minutes. Cake is done when top is golden brown and a toothpick inserted in center comes out clean.

Pumpkin Bread

This recipe only uses two tablespoons of oil per loaf. It also uses less sugar than more traditional loaves, making the bread a bit healthier, without skimping at all on taste.

Makes 2 loaves

Preheat oven to 350 degrees. Grease two 8½ x 4½ x 2½-inch loaf pans.

Add the following to mixing bowl and beat on medium speed for 30 seconds:

4 **eggs** or equivalent substitute
1¼ cups **brown sugar**
1¼ cups **sugar**
1 (15 ounce) can **solid pack pumpkin**
¾ cup **unsweetened applesauce**
¼ cup **extra light olive oil**

Whisk together in a medium sized bowl:

3 cups *Celeste's Best Gluten-Free Flour Mix*
2¼ teaspoons **baking soda**
1½ teaspoons **ground cinnamon**
1½ teaspoons **konjac powder** or **xanthan gum**
½ teaspoon **cream of tartar**
½ teaspoon (scant) **ground ginger**
½ teaspoon **nutmeg**
½ teaspoon **sea salt**
¼ teaspoon **ground cloves**

Add the dry ingredients to the mixing bowl and beat on medium speed for 20 seconds or until smooth and well combined. Pour into the greased loaf pans and bake for 50 – 55 minutes.

Bread is done when toothpick inserted in center comes out clean. Remove loaf from oven and place on wire rack to cool for 5 minutes. (Leaving in the pan any longer can cause the bottom crust to become soggy from condensation.)

Run a knife between bread and pan to loosen loaf if necessary. Remove loaf from pan and place on wire rack.

Once bread has completely cooled, loosely wrap with plastic wrap and store at room temperature. Bread stays soft and fresh for several days.

- Scant means "just barely". Use slightly less than the required amount in a recipe.

- This same recipe also can be used to make delicious pumpkin pancakes.

- A quick substitute for any recipe that calls for 1 tablespoon of Pumpkin Pie Spice = 1½ teaspoons ground cinnamon, ½ teaspoon ground nutmeg, ½ teaspoon (scant) ground ginger and ¼ teaspoon ground cloves.

Soft Pretzel Sticks

I have to say since going gf, there were really only 3 things I really truly missed: bagels, matzos and my favorite - soft pretzels. I loved the taste of a hot, steamy, salty, soft pretzel. But developing a recipe for pretzels that was both gluten-free and yeast-free proved to be more of a challenge than I had anticipated.

Finally one night, I tried dipping the pretzel sticks in a baking soda/boiling water bath for a little more than a minute. Such a simple act that made a huge difference in taste and appearance. I have to say this recipe comes pretty close to a real pretzel, minus the butter, gluten and yeast.

Makes 6 pretzels

Preheat oven to 475 degrees. Line a large baking sheet with parchment paper.

In a mixing bowl, add the following:

1½ cups **Celeste's Best Gluten-Free Flour Mix (CBGFFM)**
2 tablespoons **sugar**
1 teaspoon **cream of tartar**
¾ teaspoon **konjac powder** or **xanthan gum**
½ teaspoon **baking soda**
½ teaspoon **sea salt**

Mix on medium speed for 30 seconds until well blended, then add:

½ cup plus 2 tablespoons **water**
1 tablespoon **extra light olive oil**

Beat for an additional 30 seconds – 1 minute on medium-high until mixture becomes uniform in an almost ball-like state.

In a medium sized saucepan, add and whisk together:

6 cups of **water**
2 tablespoons **baking soda**

Bring water to a boil as you form the pretzels. Sprinkle a tablespoon of **CBGFFM** on a working surface. Tear off a ball of dough and form into a 2-inch ball. Toss it back and forth in your hands, kneading it, until it is no longer sticky. (If your hands become too sticky, rinse hands and dry them and then continue kneading.)

Roll dough out with slightly floured hands into a 5-inch long rope that's ¾-inch thick. (Sometimes the sticks will become hollow inside, simply pinch the dough together and reroll. But even the hollow sticks will bake up into pretzels.)

Roll out the remainder of the dough and form into pretzel sticks. When water is boiling, reduce heat until bubbling ceases slightly, then add a few sticks at a time. Resist the urge to place too many sticks in at once. Boil for approximately one minute and fifteen seconds a piece. Boiling for too long creates hard pretzels.

Remove sticks with a slotted spoon or spatula and place on baking sheet. Once all the sticks have been gone through the baking soda bath, place on the cooking tray and sprinkle each with **coarse kosher sea salt**.

Bake for 12 – 15 minutes, until pretzels turn golden brown. Pretzels are best served warm. Store any leftovers in a paper lunch bag.

- My husband likes his pretzels with extra light olive oil brushed on top before baking for a buttery taste.

- My daughter likes her pretzels rolled in cinnamon and sugar before baking and we omit the kosher sea salt.

- The baking soda/boiling water bath gives the pretzels that authentic pretzel taste and also helps with browning. Be sure that most of the water from the bath has drained off the pretzels before placing on the baking sheet.

- Pretzels taste best hot from the oven. To enjoy the pretzels the following day an easy trick is to hold the sticks quickly under tap water, just to wet them slightly, then place them in a 425 degree oven for a few minutes. You can also freeze them after the baking soda bath and then when needed bake them in the oven for 15 – 17 minutes.

Zucchini Bread

Never again will you have to wonder what to do with a garden full of zucchini in the summer months. This recipe produces a moist loaf that is a bit lower in fat than some of the more traditional versions.

Makes 2 loaves

Preheat oven to 350 degrees. Grease two 8½ x 4½ x 2½-inch loaf pans.

Wash and grate:

3 **medium sized unpeeled zucchini** (3½ cups)

Add the following ingredients to mixing bowl and beat on medium speed for 30 seconds:

3 **eggs** or equivalent substitute
¾ cup **unsweetened applesauce**
¼ cup **extra light olive oil**

Add and beat for 20 seconds:

1 cup **brown sugar**
¾ cup **sugar**
1 tablespoon **vanilla extract**

Whisk together in a medium sized bowl:

3 cups *Celeste's Best Gluten-Free Flour Mix*
1 tablespoon **cinnamon**
1½ teaspoons **baking soda**
1½ teaspoons **konjac powder** or **xanthan gum**
1 teaspoon **cream of tartar**

Add flour mixture to mixing bowl and beat for 30 seconds on medium speed, then add the grated zucchini and beat on low for 20 seconds.

Pour into the greased loaf pans and bake for 50 – 55 minutes. Bread is done when toothpick inserted in center comes out clean. Remove loaves from oven and place on wire rack to cool for 5 minutes. (Leaving in the pan any longer can cause the bottom crust to become soggy from condensation.) Run a knife between bread and pan to loosen loaf if necessary. Remove loaf from pan and place on wire rack.

Once bread has completely cooled loosely wrap with plastic wrap and store at room temperature. Bread stays soft and fresh for several days.

- Variations: Add 8 ounces of crushed pineapple or 1 cup mini chocolate chips to the batter.

- Instead of 3 eggs, use 2 egg whites and 2 mashed bananas.

- Make a crumb topping by whisking together 3 tablespoons extra light olive oil, ½ cup brown sugar, ½ cup *Celeste's Best Gluten-Free Flour Mix* and ¼ teaspoon cinnamon. Sprinkle over loaves before baking.

- Bake as muffins and cook for only 17 – 20 minutes. Makes 24 muffins.

Apple Muffins

This recipe is a favorite at brunches, for snacks, or for a quick dessert. Can be prepared as mini-muffins and also as regular sized muffins.

Makes 12 regular or 24 mini muffins

Preheat oven to 375 degrees. Liberally grease a 12 cup muffin tin.

In a large bowl, whisk together:

2¼ cups **Celeste's Best Gluten-Free Flour Mix**
1 teaspoon **baking soda**
½ teaspoon **konjac powder** or **xanthan gum**
½ teaspoon **sea salt**
½ teaspoon **cinnamon**

In a medium sized bowl or 4 cup measuring cup, whisk together:

1 cup **milk** or **non-dairy milk substitute**
1 tablespoon **lemon juice**

Then briskly whisk in:

1 **egg** or equivalent substitute
¼ cup plus 2 tablespoons **extra light olive oil**
1 teaspoon **vanilla**

And stir in until dissolved:

1½ cups packed **brown sugar**

Then add:

2 cups **peeled and diced** (into ¼-inch pieces) **apples** (roughly 2 medium sized apples)

Add liquid to dry ingredients using a wooden spoon or spatula stirring just until mixed, about 20 – 25 light strokes. Be sure to scrape the bottom of bowl to ensure that all the flour has been incorporated. Mixture will be lumpy. Spoon into muffin tins, filling ⅔ full.

Prepare topping by whisking together the following in a small bowl:

½ cup **brown sugar**
⅓ cup ***Celeste's Best Gluten-Free Flour Mix***
½ teaspoon **cinnamon**

Then with a fork stir in until small crumbs form:

2 tablespoons **extra light olive oil**

Sprinkle cinnamon sugar mix on top of muffins. Bake for 23 – 27 minutes or until light brown. For mini muffins, bake only 12 – 15 minutes. Test by inserting toothpick in center. Muffins are done when toothpick comes out clean.

Basic Muffins

This is a basic muffin recipe. Serve them plain or add the desired filling of your choice.

Makes 12 muffins

Preheat oven to 400 degrees. Grease a muffin tin. In a large bowl, whisk together:

2 cups **Celeste's Best Gluten-Free Flour Mix**
¾ cup **sugar**
1½ teaspoons **cream of tartar**
1½ teaspoons **konjac powder** or 1 teaspoon **xanthan gum**
¾ teaspoon **baking soda**
½ teaspoon **salt**

In a medium sized bowl or 4 cup measuring cup, briskly whisk together:

1½ cups **milk** or **non-dairy milk substitute**
1 **egg** or equivalent substitute
¼ cup **extra light olive oil**

Add liquid to dry ingredients using a wooden spoon or spatula stirring just until mixed, about 20 – 25 light strokes. Be sure to scrape the bottom of bowl to ensure that all the flour has been incorporated. The key to great muffins is not to over mix the batter. A lumpy batter produces a tender muffin.

Fill muffin tins ¾ full with equal amounts of batter. Place in preheated oven and bake for 22 – 25 minutes or until golden brown and tester inserted in center comes out clean. Remove from oven and place muffin tin on wire rack for 10 minutes. Remove muffins from tins and allow them to continue cooling on rack.

Variations: Add any of the following to the batter after wet ingredients have been added.

1 cup **blueberries**
1 cup chopped **dried apricots**
1 cup chopped, peeled **apples**
¾ cup **chopped dates**, pitted and chopped
1 cup mashed **banana**
½ cup canned **pumpkin**
1 cup **flaked coconut**
1 cup **chocolate chips** and 1 teaspoon **vanilla extract**
1 cup **raisins**
1 cup **shredded carrot**
1 cup **pineapple tidbits,** drained

Blueberry Muffins

These muffins should help put an end to lusting after those delectable treats you see in bakery store windows.

Make 6 jumbo muffins

Preheat oven to 375 degrees. Grease a jumbo muffin tin.

In a large mixing bowl, add:

2 cups *Celeste's Best Gluten-Free Flour Mix* **(CBGFFM)**
1 cup **sugar**
½ teaspoon **konjac powder** or **xanthan gum**
½ teaspoon **sea salt**

Whisk the above ingredients until well combined, then add:

3 tablespoons **extra light olive oil**

Beat on medium speed until mixture resembles fine crumbs. **Reserve ¼ cup of mixture for topping.**

In a small bowl, combine:

¾ teaspoon **cream of tartar**
½ teaspoon plus ⅛ teaspoon **baking soda**
½ tablespoon **lemon zest**
½ teaspoon **ground cinnamon**

Add above ingredients to larger flour mixture and beat on medium speed for 30 seconds. Using the same small bowl from previous step if possible, whisk together the following:

1 cup **milk** or **non-dairy milk substitute**
1 tablespoon **lemon juice**
1 egg or equivalent substitute
½ tablespoon **vanilla extract**

Add liquid to dry ingredients using a wooden spoon or spatula stirring just until mixed, about 20 – 25 light strokes. Be sure to scrape the bottom of bowl to ensure that all the flour has been incorporated.

(continued)

Then fold in:

1 cup **fresh blueberries** (see note box below)

Fill muffin tins two-thirds full. Then top with reserved topping, spreading 2 teaspoons of mix on each muffin. Mist each muffin top with spray oil.

Bake for 25 – 28 minutes, or until golden and toothpick inserted in center comes out clean.

Remove from oven and place on wire rack for 5 minutes. Then remove muffins from tins and continue cooling on rack.

- Toss rinsed, clean blueberries with 1 tablespoon of **CBGFFM** before adding to batter to help prevent the blueberries from sinking to the bottom of the muffin.

- If your blueberries are very sweet, you may wish to add less sugar, but if they are very tart, you may need to add more.

- To replace the eggs in this recipe, it's best to use the egg replacer substitute to obtain the greatest rise.

- Instead of blueberries, try strawberries, chocolate chips or even dried fruit.

Bran Muffins

Most people following a gluten-free diet could use a little more fiber in their diet. Rice bran contains 29% of natural dietary fiber. These muffins are made with rice bran and are an excellent way to add that extra fiber. If you thought Bran Muffins were dry and heavy, you'll be pleasantly surprised by this recipe as it produces a very light, tasty muffin.

Makes 12 muffins

Preheat oven to 400 degrees. Grease a muffin tin.

In a medium sized bowl, whisk together:

1 cup *Celeste's Best Gluten-Free Flour Mix*
1 cup **rice bran**
½ teaspoon **konjac powder** or **xanthan gum**
½ cup **sugar**
2 teaspoons **cream of tartar**
1 teaspoon **baking soda**

In a large bowl, whisk together:

2 **bananas**, mashed
2 **eggs** or equivalent substitute
½ cup **milk** or **non-dairy milk substitute**
⅓ cup **extra light olive oil**
1 teaspoon **vanilla extract**

Add liquid to dry ingredients using a wooden spoon or spatula stirring just until mixed, about 20 – 25 light strokes. Be sure to scrape the bottom of bowl to ensure that all the flour has been incorporated. The key to great muffins is not to over mix the batter. A lumpy batter produces a tender muffin. Fill muffin tins ¾ full with equal amounts of batter.

Place in preheated oven and bake for 17 – 20 minutes or until golden brown and tester inserted in center comes out clean. Remove from oven and place muffin tin on wire rack for 10 minutes. Remove muffins from tins and allow them to continue cooling on rack.

> ▪ If you are just starting to add bran to your diet, **start off slowly**. Allow your body's digestive system time to adapt. Adding too much too quickly may result in bloating and discomfort.

Carrot-Raisin Muffins

This is one of the most time-consuming recipes in the book, but still only takes about 30 minutes to prepare. This recipe bakes up low-fat, yet delicious muffins. My husband grabbed another muffin as soon as he took his second bite, then later went back for a third. Replacing the oil in this recipe with applesauce helps cut down on the fat without sacrificing an ounce of taste!

Makes 12 muffins

Preheat oven to 350 degrees. Grease a muffin tin.

In a large bowl, combine:

2 cups *Celeste's Best Gluten-Free Flour Mix*
¾ cup **sugar** (see note box on following page)
2 teaspoons **cinnamon**
1 teaspoon **baking soda**
1 teaspoon **cream of tartar**
1 teaspoon **konjac powder** or **xanthan gum**
½ teaspoon **sea salt**

Meanwhile in a separate bowl, mix together:

3 **eggs** or equivalent substitute
½ cup **milk** or **non-dairy milk substitute**
⅓ cup **unsweetened applesauce**
2 teaspoons **vanilla extract**

Add liquid to dry ingredients using a wooden spoon or spatula stirring just until mixed, about 20 – 25 light strokes. Be sure to scrape the bottom of bowl to ensure that all the flour has been incorporated.

Lastly, stir in until blended:

2 cups **grated carrots**
1 medium **apple**, peeled and grated (see note box on following page)
½ cup **raisins**

Fill muffin cups three-quarters full. Bake for 25 – 30 minutes or until a toothpick inserted into tops comes out clean.

- If using a Granny Smith apple for this recipe or another variety that is tart, increase the amount of sugar by ¼ cup or to taste.

- If batter seems dry, add milk by tablespoons until desired consistency is reached.

- The purpose of konjac powder or xanthan gum is to stabilize and thicken a batter. Keeping that in mind in this recipe, it's best to add the liquid to the dry only after you've prepared and grated the carrots and apples, as the added fiber can often thicken up the batter quickly once it comes in contact with the liquid.

Chocolate Chip Banana Muffins

It's hard to believe these muffins are low fat. They're easy to prepare, too.

Makes 12 muffins

Preheat oven to 350 degrees. Grease a regular sized muffin pan. In your mixing bowl, beat until mashed:

3 medium **ripe bananas**

Add to mixing bowl, whisking until well blended:

1 **egg** or equivalent substitute
½ cup **brown sugar**
½ cup **sugar**
⅓ cup **milk** or **non-dairy milk substitute**
⅓ cup **unsweetened applesauce**

Meanwhile in a small bowl, combine:

1½ cups *Celeste's Best Gluten-Free Flour Mix*
1 teaspoon **baking soda**
1 teaspoon **sea salt**
½ teaspoon **konjac powder** or **xanthan gum**

Add liquid to dry ingredients using a wooden spoon or spatula stirring just until mixed, about 20 – 25 light strokes. Be sure to scrape the bottom of bowl to ensure that all the flour has been incorporated. The key to great muffins is not to over mix the batter. A lumpy batter produces a tender muffin. Add to batter:

¼ cup **mini chocolate chips**

Gently fold the chips into the batter with spatula. Fill muffin tins ¾ full with equal amounts of batter. Place in preheated oven and bake for 25 – 28 minutes or until golden brown and tester inserted in center comes out clean. Cool on wire rack for 10 minutes, then remove muffins from tins and allow them to continue cooling on rack.

> - Instead of regular sized muffin, make mini-muffins. Bake for 15 – 17 minutes. Makes 24 mini-muffins.

Coffee Cake Muffins

Pour yourself a hot cup of Joe and enjoy these moist and flavorful sweet delights!

Makes 12 muffins

Preheat oven to 375 degrees. Grease muffin tins.

In a small bowl, combine:

¼ cup **brown sugar**
1 teaspoon **cinnamon**

In mixing bowl, whisk together the following:

1½ cups *Celeste's Best Gluten-Free Flour Mix*
½ cup **sugar**
1 teaspoon **cream of tartar**
¾ teaspoon **baking soda**
½ teaspoon **konjac powder** or **xanthan gum**
¼ teaspoon **sea salt**

Meanwhile in another small bowl, whisk together:

1 cup **milk** or **non-dairy milk substitute**
1 **egg** or equivalent substitute
⅓ cup **extra light olive oil**

Add liquid to dry ingredients using a wooden spoon or spatula stirring just until mixed, about 20 – 25 light strokes. Be sure to scrape the bottom of bowl to ensure that all the flour has been incorporated.

You'll be layering the batter and the brown sugar mix. Begin by spooning only 2 tablespoons (⅛ cup) of batter into each muffin tin. Then top each muffin with ½ tablespoon of cinnamon sugar mix. Finish off the muffins by spooning an additional tablespoon of batter on each muffin.

Bake for 18 – 21 minutes or until toothpick inserted in center comes out clean. Remove from oven and cool on wire racks.

Garlic Onion Muffins

These muffins are a cross between a muffin and a biscuit.

Makes 12 muffins

Preheat oven to 400 degrees. Grease a muffin tin or line with paper liners.

In mixing bowl, whisk together the following:

2 cups *Celeste's Best Gluten-Free Flour Mix*
2 tablespoons **sugar**
2 teaspoons **cream of tartar**
1 teaspoon **baking soda**
1 teaspoon **konjac powder** or **xanthan gum**
1 teaspoon **sea salt**

In a medium sized bowl, mix together:

1½ cups **milk** or **non-dairy milk substitute**
1 medium **onion**, diced (½ cup)
1 egg or equivalent substitute
3 tablespoons **extra light olive oil**
2 **cloves of garlic**, minced

Add liquid to dry ingredients using a wooden spoon or spatula stirring just until mixed, about 20 – 25 light strokes. Fill muffin cups ⅔ full. Bake for 20 minutes or until a toothpick inserted into tops comes out clean.

Remove muffins from tins and cool on wire racks.

Pecan Pie Mini Muffins

One of two recipes in the book that contain nuts. A very quick, simple recipe that can be pulled together easily. These muffins definitely live up to their name. They taste just like a slice of pecan pie hot out of the oven. When we were able to eat nuts, this was one of our favorite recipes.

Makes approx. 20 – 22 mini muffins

Preheat oven to 425 degrees. **Heavily** grease a mini muffin tray.

In a large mixing bowl, combine:

1 cup **brown sugar**
½ cup *Celeste's Best Gluten-Free Flour Mix*
¼ teaspoon **konjac powder** or **xanthan gum**

Mix the above mixture well to remove any lumps of brown sugar.

In a one-cup measuring cup or small bowl, combine:

2 **eggs** or equivalent substitute
¼ cup plus 2 tablespoons **extra light olive oil**
1 teaspoon **vanilla extract**

Add liquid to dry ingredients. Beat mixture for 1 minute on medium speed, then add and beat an additional 15 – 20 seconds on low:

1 cup **chopped pecans** (see note box on following page)

When batter is well blended, pour into muffin cups, filling to the top of the rim (not the usual ⅔ full as is normally recommended). Place filled tray in preheated oven and bake for approximately 5 minutes only. (The initial higher temperature will help create a taller, higher domed muffin.) **Then reduce heat to 350 degrees** and continue cooking for an additional 6 - 9 minutes or until tops are golden brown and toothpick inserted in center of one muffin comes out clean.

Immediately remove muffins from tray (they have a tendency to stick otherwise) and cool on wire rack. Serve warm or cold.

- This recipe calls for "1 cup chopped pecans" which means to chop your pecans first, then measure out 1 cup.

- These muffins are also terrific to take to gatherings. Expect to take home an empty dish as they'll disappear quickly.

- Muffins freeze well.

- You can also make regular sized muffins with this recipe. Bake these in a very heavily greased tray for 20 – 25 minutes.

- The muffins tend to stick heavily to paper liners, so it's best to bake these directly in the muffin tray.

Pumpkin Chocolate Chip Muffins

I think after baking up a batch of these muffins you will come to the same conclusion that I did — pumpkin and chocolate are two foods that were meant to be together.

Makes 12 muffins

Preheat oven to 400 degrees. Grease a muffin tray.

In a large mixing bowl, beat on medium high speed for 1 minute:

2 **eggs** or equivalent substitute
1 cup **canned pure pumpkin**
¾ cup **sugar**
½ cup **unsweetened applesauce**
¼ cup **extra light olive oil**
¼ cup **water**

In a medium sized bowl, whisk together:

1½ cups *Celeste's Best Gluten-Free Flour Mix*
1¼ teaspoons **baking soda**
1 teaspoon **cinnamon**
½ teaspoon **cream of tartar**
½ teaspoon **konjac powder** or **xanthan gum**
½ teaspoon **sea salt**

Add liquid to dry ingredients using a wooden spoon or spatula stirring just until mixed, about 20 – 25 light strokes. Be sure to scrape the bottom of bowl to ensure that all the flour has been incorporated.

Then stir in:

1 cup **mini chocolate chips**

When batter is well blended, pour into muffin cups filling to the top of the rim. Place filled tray in preheated oven and bake for 15 – 20 minutes or until tops are golden brown and toothpick or tester inserted in center of one muffin comes out clean. Remove muffins from tray and cool on wire rack.

Sweet Potato Muffins

These muffins almost taste like a cross between a pumpkin and a carrot muffin. You may be as surprised as I was by how delicious these muffins are.

Makes 12 muffins

Preheat oven to 350 degrees. Grease a muffin tray.

In a large bowl, combine:

2 cups **Celeste's Best Gluten-Free Flour Mix**
1½ teaspoons **cream of tartar**
1 teaspoon **cinnamon**
1 teaspoon **konjac powder** or **xanthan gum**
¾ teaspoon **baking soda**
½ teaspoon **sea salt**
½ teaspoon **ground allspice**
½ teaspoon **ground nutmeg**

Meanwhile in a medium sized bowl, mix together:

4 cups **shredded raw sweet potato** (about 2 medium sized sweet potatoes)
2 **eggs** or equivalent substitute
1 cup plus 2 tablespoons **brown sugar**
¼ cup **extra light olive oil**
¼ cup **milk** or **non-dairy milk substitute**
¼ cup **unsweetened applesauce**
1 teaspoon **vanilla extract**

Add liquid to dry ingredients using a wooden spoon or spatula stirring just until mixed, about 20 – 25 light strokes. Fill muffin cups full to the rim. Bake for 35 – 40 minutes or until a toothpick inserted into tops comes out clean.

- You can grate the sweet potatoes by using a hand grater or in a food processor.

- If batter seems dry, add milk by tablespoons until desired consistency is reached.

BROWNIES, BARS, COOKIES & CRACKERS

Gingerbread Cookies

Blondies

What is a brownie without chocolate? A blondie or sometimes called a blond brownie.

Makes 9 blondies

Preheat oven to 350 degrees. Grease an 8 x 8-inch baking dish.

In a small bowl, whisk together:

1½ cups ***Celeste's Best Gluten-Free Flour Mix***
½ teaspoon **cream of tartar**
½ teaspoon **konjac powder** or **xanthan gum**
¼ teaspoon **baking soda**
¼ teaspoon **sea salt**

In a mixing bowl, add the following and beat on medium speed for 30 seconds or until well combined:

¾ cup **sugar**
½ cup **brown sugar**
½ cup **extra light olive oil**
2 teaspoons **vanilla extract**

Then beat in:

2 **eggs** or equivalent substitute

Add the flour mix to the wet ingredients and beat on low speed an additional 15 seconds. Then stir in:

½ cup **mini chocolate chips**

Pour into prepared baking dish and bake for 27 – 32 minutes. Cool on wire rack.

Brownies

There are two types of brownies: cake-like and fudgy. Cake-like brownies have a bit of rise in them. This recipe is for the darker, denser, fudge brownies.

Cake-like, fudgy – doesn't matter to me. When it comes to brownies, all I can say is "Yummy, ummy, good!!!!"

Makes 9 brownies

Preheat oven to 350 degrees and grease an 8 x 8-inch baking dish.

In a small bowl, whisk together:

¾ cup *Celeste's Best Gluten-Free Flour Mix*
3 tablespoons **unsweetened cocoa**
2 tablespoons **special dark cocoa**
¼ teaspoon **cream of tartar**
¼ teaspoon **konjac powder** or **xanthan gum**
¼ teaspoon **sea salt**
⅛ teaspoon **baking soda**

Add the following in a mixing bowl:

1 cup **sugar**
¼ cup plus 2 tablespoons **extra light olive oil**

Beat on low speed for 30 seconds or until well combined.

Then beat in:

2 **eggs** or equivalent substitute
1 teaspoon **vanilla extract**

Add the flour and cocoa mix to the wet ingredients and beat on low speed an additional 30 seconds. Scrape down the sides of mixing bowl with a spatula to ensure all cocoa is incorporated. Then, if desired, add:

½ cup **mini chocolate chips**

Mix on low for 10 seconds, just until well combined. Pour into prepared baking dish and bake for 27 – 32 minutes. Serve warm or especially good served chilled.

- This recipe can be easily doubled and baked in a 13 x 9 x 2-inch baking dish, but will need to cook for 32 – 37 minutes.

- If you don't have any special dark cocoa, simply use ⅓ cup unsweetened cocoa instead and omit the dark cocoa.

- It's often difficult to tell when fudge brownies are done. When fully cooked, they begin to pull away slightly from the edges of the pan and you'll also notice a slight change in the appearance on the top surface of the brownie. The edges of the brownies will be slightly firm to the touch and the center will be soft. The brownies will still look slightly under baked in the center, but will firm up as they cool. If the brownies are over baked, they can become hard. In my oven, they bake for 31 minutes, but if you like a moister brownie, you may choose to bake yours for the minimum amount of time.

Chocolate Chip Banana Bars

Any recipe that combines chocolate chips and bananas together has got to be good if you ask me. I mean, how could you possibly go wrong putting chocolate and banana together anyway?

The neat part about this recipe is you divide the original batter in half and add the chocolate to one half and the remaining batter becomes the top of the bars.

Makes 16 bars

Preheat oven to 350 degrees. Grease a 13 x 9 x 2-inch baking dish.

In a mixing bowl, beat on medium speed for 1 minute:

1 cup **sugar**
¼ cup plus two tablespoons **extra light olive oil**

Add to mixing bowl and beat on medium speed for 30 seconds:

1½ cups **mashed ripe bananas** (about 3 medium)

Then add and beat for 30 seconds longer:

1 **egg** or equivalent substitute
1 teaspoon **vanilla extract**

In another bowl, combine:

1½ cups *Celeste's Best Gluten-Free Flour Mix*
1¼ teaspoons **baking soda**
¾ teaspoon **konjac powder** or **xanthan gum**
½ teaspoon **cream of tartar**
½ teaspoon **sea salt**

Add dry ingredients to wet ingredients. Beat on low for an additional 30 seconds or until well combined.

Remove 1½ cups of batter and place in a separate bowl. Add to this portion of batter:

¼ cup **mini chocolate chips**

Mix well and set aside.

(continued)

For the bottom layer of bars, add the following to the remaining batter in mixing bowl and beat on medium speed for 15 seconds:

¼ cup **baking cocoa**

Spread chocolate batter in bottom of baking pan. Top with remaining reserved half of batter.

Bake for 25 minutes or until a toothpick or tested inserted into bars comes out clean. Allow to cool and then place in refrigerator. Best when served chilled (if you can wait that long!) Cut into 16 bars.

> ▪ Variation: Place both the chocolate chips and cocoa powder in the bottom layer.

Dream Bars

This is a fun recipe. A crusted base, topped with a chocolate chip dough, drizzled with chocolate. Hate to admit, it but we ate half of it in one sitting. My husband decided that instead of a birthday cake this year, he'd rather have a whole tray of Dream Bars all to himself.

Makes 16 bars

Preheat oven to 350 degrees. Grease a 13 x 9 x 2-inch baking dish.

In a medium sized bowl, mix:

½ cup **brown sugar**
¼ cup **extra light olive oil**

Stir in and mix until well blended:

1 cup *Celeste's Best Gluten-Free Flour Mix*
½ teaspoon **konjac powder** or **xanthan gum**

Press mixture into bottom of greased baking dish distributing the mixture evenly around the dish to form a crust. Bake for 10 minutes, until slightly golden.

Meanwhile, mix together:

2 **eggs** or equivalent substitute
1 cup **brown sugar**
1 teaspoon **vanilla extract**

Stir in:

1 cup **mini chocolate chips**
2 tablespoons *Celeste's Best Gluten-Free Flour Mix*
½ teaspoon **cream of tartar**
½ teaspoon **sea salt**
¼ teaspoon **baking soda**

Pour topping over baked crust, spreading it evenly across the top with a spatula. Return baking dish to oven for 15 – 20 minutes or until bars are golden brown. It will be bubbly and will settle once removed from the oven as it cools. For this recipe, you have to depend more on cooking time and coloring to tell when it is done.

(continued)

Allow bars to cool completely.

To prepare the chocolate drizzle-topping, place the following ingredients in a **double boiler** until melted, stirring often:

½ cup **mini chocolate chips**
2 teaspoons **extra light olive oil**

Drizzle melted chocolate over cooled bars. Let chocolate cool and harden slightly, then cut into desired size squares. Refrigerate for 30 minutes to an hour before serving.

- To drizzle melted chocolate for the topping, simply dip a spatula or spoon into chocolate and quickly dance it across the top of the bars first horizontally, then vertically.

- To make this egg-free, flaxeggs seem to work best. The topping will rise when baking then settle down as it cools.

Lemon Bars

These bars are almost like lemon pies in cookie form. A crusted bottom layer topped with a tart lemon filling. Incredibly delicious!

Makes 8 bars

Preheat oven to 350 degrees. Grease an 8 x 8-inch baking dish.

In a mixing bowl, whisk together:

¾ cup *Celeste's Best Gluten-Free Flour Mix*
3 tablespoons **sugar**
½ teaspoon **konjac powder** or **xanthan gum**

Then add:

¼ cup **extra light olive oil**

Mix dough on medium speed for 30 seconds or until you have a crumb like mixture. Place dough in baking dish and press to form crust. (You can also gently roll the dough into place using a pastry roller.)

Place baking dish in the oven and cook for only 12 – 15 minutes or until the crust turns slightly golden.

Meanwhile, prepare the filling by whisking together the following in a medium sized bowl:

2 **eggs** or equivalent substitute
⅔ cup **sugar**
2 tablespoons *Celeste's Best Gluten-Free Flour Mix*
2 tablespoons **lemon juice**
1 tablespoon **lemon zest**
1 tablespoon **water**
¼ teaspoon **cream of tartar**
⅛ teaspoon **baking soda**

Pour mixture over the baked crust. Return pan to oven and bake for an additional 20 – 25 minutes or until the lemon topping has set. Allow bars to cool then sprinkle with powdered sugar before serving.

- 1 tablespoon of lemon zest is the zest of one medium sized lemon. Using a micro or fine zester/grater allows you to zest a lemon quickly.

- This recipe can be doubled and baked in 13 x 9 x 2-inch baking dish.

- This recipe can be made using one of egg substitute recipes in the book. It does have a slightly different consistency than when baked with real eggs, but still delicious. The top will rise high when baking, then settle down when cooling.

Quinoa Raisin Bars

Quinoa is a gluten-free, grain-like seed. It's a superfood, packing 8 grams of complete protein containing all nine essential amino acids in each cooked cup. Quinoa is also a very good source of manganese as well as being a source of magnesium, iron, copper and phosphorus. No wonder this ancient grain was once called the "gold of the Incas".

Makes 12 bars

Preheat oven to 350 degrees. Grease an 11 x 7 x 1½-inch baking dish.

Whisk together the following in mixing bowl:

1½ cups **Celeste's Best Gluten-Free Flour Mix**
1 cup **quinoa flakes**
1 teaspoon **baking soda**
1 teaspoon **cinnamon**
1 teaspoon **cream of tartar**
1 teaspoon **konjac powder** or **xanthan gum**
¼ teaspoon **ground nutmeg**

Whisk together the following in a medium sized bowl:

1 cup **brown sugar**
2 **eggs** or equivalent substitute
½ cup **milk** or **non-dairy milk substitute**
⅓ cup **extra light olive oil**
¼ teaspoon **lemon juice**
2 teaspoons **vanilla extract**

Add liquid ingredients to mixing bowl and combine with spatula just until mixed. Then stir in:

1 cup **raisins**

Spoon the batter evenly into the prepared baking dish. Fill measuring cup with a small amount of additional water and smooth and level top of bars by dipping spatula into water repeatedly, letting excess drip off and running it over the surface while being careful not to press down and compress the bars too much.

Place baking dish in oven. Cook for 30 – 35 minutes or until tester or toothpick inserted in center comes out clean.

Chocolate Chip Cookies

I truly think this recipe makes the best soft chocolate chip cookies and no one will be able to tell the difference between this gluten-free version and one made with wheat flour.

Makes eighteen, 3-inch cookies

Place the following in a mixing bowl and beat on medium high speed for 1 minute or until well blended:

¾ cup **brown sugar**
¾ cup **sugar**
½ cup **extra light olive oil**

Then add, beating for 1 minute:

2 **eggs** or equivalent substitution
2 teaspoons **vanilla extract**

Whisk together the dry ingredients in a small bowl:

2 cups *Celeste's Best Gluten-Free Flour Mix*
2 tablespoons **golden flaxseed meal**
1 teaspoon **konjac powder** or **xanthan gum**
¾ teaspoon **baking soda**
½ teaspoon **sea salt**

Add dry ingredients to wet in mixing bowl and beat on low for approximately 1 minute or until well blended.

Remove bowl from mixer and with a spatula stir in:

1 cup **mini chocolate chips**

Refrigerate dough for 1 hour or longer.

Preheat oven to 375 degrees. Grease two large cookie trays. Drop chilled dough by rounded tablespoons full onto trays. Press down on tops to flatten so they are ¼-inch thick. Cookies will not spread much when baking. Place trays in center of oven and bake for 8 – 11 minutes, rotating trays from front to back and top to bottom halfway through cooking time so cookies will bake evenly.

There's a fine line with cookies between well baked and overcooked. Bake until golden brown on top and browned slightly on bottom. Remove cookies from oven. Leave on tray until cool then transfer to wire rack.

- Use a cookie scoop (available at most kitchen stores) to get beautifully, rounded cookies that are uniformly sized and cook more evenly.

- If you only have one tray, run it under cool water before beginning second batch of cookies so that the heated tray doesn't cause your cookies to prematurely cook. It also will be necessary to refrigerate remaining dough between batches. The dough is easier to work with when chilled.

- To make smaller cookies, drop by teaspoonfuls and only bake 7 – 9 minutes.

Chocolate Cream Filled Cookies

Vanilla cream filling sandwiched between dark chocolate cookies. The dark cocoa gives these cookies that wonderful taste and coloring just like the originals. It will definitely "be hard to hide the kid inside" while eating these.

Makes 22 cookies

Place in a covered double boiler over medium heat:

1 ounce (1 square) **unsweetened chocolate**

Stir chocolate occasionally with a spatula until melted. Remove from heat and let cool for 2 – 3 minutes. In a medium sized bowl, whisk together and put aside:

1¼ cups *Celeste's Best Gluten-Free Flour Mix*
3 tablespoons **unsweetened dark cocoa**
¾ teaspoon **konjac powder** or **xanthan gum**
½ teaspoon **baking soda**
⅛ teaspoon **sea salt**

In mixing bowl on medium speed, beat for 30 seconds:

¼ cup **extra light olive oil**
½ cup **sugar**

Then add and beat for 1 minute:

1 **egg** or equivalent substitute
1 teaspoon **vanilla extract**

Add in and beat for 30 seconds:

prepared melted chocolate

Add flour mixture to mixing bowl and beat on low for an additional 30 seconds longer. Chill dough in refrigerator for 20 – 30 minutes. When dough is chilled, preheat oven to 350 degrees.

Roll dough out between two pieces of parchment paper to ⅛-inch thickness. Using a 2-inch round cutter, cut the dough into circles. Place cookies on greased large cookie trays, 1½ inches apart. Bake for 7 – 8 minutes, rotating trays halfway through baking to ensure even cooking. Then remove from oven and cool on wire racks.

Meanwhile, prepare cream filling by placing the following into mixing bowl or mini food processor:

1¼ cups **confectioners powdered sugar** (see page 23)
¼ cup **shortening**

Mix or pulse until shortening is incorporated into the sugar, then add:

1 tablespoon **water**
½ teaspoon **vanilla extract**

Add more water teaspoon by teaspoon until cream is the proper consistency. Place cream filling into a cake-decorating bag fitted with a ½-inch tip. Pipe about ½ tablespoon into the center of each cookie. Top with another cookie and gently press down on the icing and twist slightly until it just reaches the sides, sandwiching the cream inside the cookies.

Store in an airtight container.

> ▪ If you don't have a cake-decorating bag, simply place cream filling into a sandwich size plastic bag. Snip off the bottom corner and squeeze filling onto cookies. Or even simpler – spoon ½ tablespoon into the center of each cookie. (I measure out ½ tablespoon and then form it into a small ball using my hands, then press the ball between the cookies.)

Chocolate Pretzel Cookies

Chocolate cookies twisted into pretzel shapes. Puts two of my favorites together – chocolate and pretzels.

Makes 2 dozen cookies

Preheat oven to 350 degrees. Grease two cookie sheets.

In medium sized bowl, combine:

2½ cups **Celeste's Best Gluten-Free Flour Mix**
½ cup **unsweetened cocoa**
1 teaspoon **konjac powder** or **xanthan gum**
½ teaspoon **baking soda**
¼ teaspoon **sea salt**

In mixing bowl, combine:

2 **eggs** or equivalent substitute
1 cup **sugar**
½ cup **extra light olive oil**

Mix on low speed for one minute. Gradually add flour mixture and beat dough for an additional minute. Remove dough from bowl and knead lightly.

Form dough into 2 balls. Break off a piece of dough from one ball about 1-inch in diameter. Roll out dough into a strip, ¼-inch in diameter and 10-inches long.

Form into pretzel shapes.   Dip top surface of cookie into a bowl of:

¼ cup **sugar**

Place on cookie sheet. Bake for 8 – 10 minutes. Cookie will set and become slightly hard on top when done. Cool cookies on tray on wire rack for 5 minutes. Then remove cookies and set on wire rack.

When cookies have completely cooled, top with Chocolate Glaze (recipe follows) if desired.

Chocolate Glaze

In a small saucepan over low heat, add:

1½ tablespoons **extra light olive oil**
3 tablespoons **unsweetened cocoa**
2 tablespoons **water**

Stir constantly until mixture thickens. (Do not allow mixture to boil.) Remove from heat and stir in:

½ teaspoon **vanilla extract**

Gradually whisk in, beating until smooth:

1 cup **confectioners powdered sugar** (see page 23)

- Use a plastic 12-inch ruler as a guide to aid in measuring out lengths of dough.

- This dough rolls easily without needing any additional flour or sugar on the rolling surface.

Chocolate Roll Out Cookies

These are wonderful, soft cookies that are sturdy enough to be frosted and decorated.

Makes 2 dozen cookies

Preheat oven to 350 degrees. Lightly grease two large cookie sheets. In a mixing bowl beat on medium speed for 30 seconds:

1 cup **sugar**
¼ cup plus 2 tablespoons **extra light olive oil**
1 **egg** or equivalent substitute
1 tablespoon **milk** or **non-dairy milk substitute**
1 teaspoon **vanilla extract**

Meanwhile in small bowl, whisk together the following:

1¾ cups *Celeste's Best Gluten-Free Flour Mix (CBGFFM)*
⅓ cup **unsweetened cocoa**
¾ teaspoon **konjac powder** or **xanthan gum**
½ teaspoon **cream of tartar**
¼ teaspoon **baking soda**
⅛ teaspoon **sea salt**

Add dry ingredients to wet, mixing on low speed for 1 minute or until mixture comes together in a ball. Divide dough into 2 equal sized balls.

Tear off a large sheet of parchment paper and lightly flour surface with *CBGFFM* or **sugar**. Using a rolling pin, roll one ball at a time to ⅛-inch thickness. Cut out shapes in dough with cookie cutters or rim of a drinking glass. Place on cookie sheet 1 inch apart.

Bake for 6 – 8 minutes or until lightly golden on top. Let cookies cool on tray for 5 minutes, then remove cookies from tray and allow them to finish cooling on a wire rack.

Chocolate Wafer Cookies

This recipe not only makes great cookies, but also can be used to make ice cream sandwiches.

Makes eighteen 2¾ inch cookies

Place in a covered double boiler over medium heat:

2 ounces (2 squares) **unsweetened chocolate**

Stir chocolate occasionally with a spatula until melted. Remove from heat and let cool for 2 – 3 minutes.

In a medium sized bowl, whisk together and put aside:

1¼ cups *Celeste's Best Gluten-Free Flour Mix*
½ teaspoon **baking soda**
½ teaspoon **cream of tartar**
½ teaspoon **konjac powder** or **xanthan gum**
⅛ teaspoon **sea salt**

In mixing bowl on medium speed, beat for 30 seconds:

½ cup **sugar**
3 tablespoons **extra light olive oil**

Then add and beat for 1 minute:

1 **egg** or equivalent substitute
1 teaspoon **vanilla extract**
1 tablespoon **milk** or **non-dairy milk substitute**

Add in and beat for 30 seconds:

prepared melted chocolate

Add flour mixture to mixing bowl and beat on low for an additional 30 seconds longer. Chill dough in refrigerator for 20 – 30 minutes.

When dough is chilled, preheat oven to 350 degrees. Then roll dough out between two pieces of parchment paper to ⅛-inch thickness.

Cut into round circle with a cookie cutter. Place cookies on greased large cookie trays, 1½ inches apart. Bake for 7 – 8 minutes, rotating trays halfway through baking to ensure even cooking. Then remove from oven and cool on wire racks.

For ice cream sandwiches: Allow cookies to cool completely, then place softened ice cream on top of one cookie, laying it about 1-inch thick. Top with another chocolate wafer and press down gently. Wrap each sandwich with clear plastic wrap and freeze for at least 2 or more hours.

Double Chocolate Biscotti

The word "biscotti" means twice baked in Italian. Biscotti cookies are crisp cookies perfect for dipping in milk, coffee or tea.

Makes 14 cookies

Preheat oven to 375 degrees. Line a large cookie tray with parchment paper.

In mixing bowl, beat on medium speed for 1 minute:

⅔ cup **sugar**
¼ cup **extra light olive oil**

Then add and beat on medium speed for 30 seconds:

2 **eggs** or equivalent substitute

Mix together in a medium sized bowl:

1¾ cups *Celeste's Best Gluten-Free Flour Mix*
¼ cup **unsweetened cocoa powder**
1 teaspoon **cream of tartar**
½ teaspoon **baking soda**
½ teaspoon **konjac powder** or **xanthan gum**

Add dry ingredients to mixing bowl and beat on low speed for 30 seconds. Then add:

½ cup **mini chocolate chips**

Beat on low for an additional 15 seconds. Divide dough in half. Dough will be wet and sticky.

Wetting your hands a bit, shape each half of dough into a loaf about 7-inches long, by 2-inches wide and 1-inch high.

Place tray in preheated oven and bake for 22 – 25 minutes. Remove from oven and place biscotti on a wire rack to cool for 15 minutes. Reduce oven temperature to 325 degrees.

Once cool, cut loaves into thick slices diagonally. Lay cut side down and bake for an additional 8 minutes. Turn over and bake other side for 8 minutes until dry. Remove from oven and cool cookies on wire rack.

- The longer the cookies are baked the second time, the harder the cookies will be.

- To save time and also create softer cookies, I stand my cookies up on the cookie tray for the second baking, so both sides cook at the same time and only bake them for 8 minutes.

- These cookies also taste good with melted chocolate drizzled over the tops once cooled.

Double Chocolate Chip Minis

Mini chocolate cookies full of chocolaty chips!

Makes 2 dozen cookies

Preheat oven to 350 degrees. Lightly grease two large cookie sheets.

In a mixing bowl, beat on medium high speed for 1 minute:

1¼ cups **brown sugar**
¼ cup plus 2 tablespoons **extra light olive oil**

Then add and beat for an additional minute:

2 **eggs** or equivalent substitute
1½ teaspoons **vanilla extract**

Meanwhile in small bowl, whisk together the following:

1¾ cups *Celeste's Best Gluten-Free Flour Mix*
½ cup **unsweetened cocoa**
¾ teaspoon **konjac powder** or **xanthan gum**
½ teaspoon **baking soda**
⅛ teaspoon **sea salt**

Add dry ingredients to wet in mixing bowl and beat on low for approximately 1 minute or until well blended. Remove bowl from mixer and with a spatula stir in:

½ cup **mini chocolate chips**

Refrigerate dough for 30 minutes or longer. Form chilled dough into 1-inch balls. Place onto greased cookie trays. Press down on tops to flatten so each is ¼-inch thick. Cookies will not spread much when baking.

Place trays in center of oven and bake for 10 – 12 minutes or until done. You may need to rotate trays from front to back and top to bottom halfway through cooking time so cookies will bake evenly. Remove cookies from oven and after 2 minutes transfer to wire rack to cool.

- When replacing eggs in this recipe, flaxeggs are the perfect substitute.

Ginger Cookies

I have to admit, ginger cookies had never been one of my favorites – that is until this recipe. These cookies are amazing! Or as one of my daughter's friends exclaimed after his first bite, "Scrumdiddlyumptious!"

Makes eighteen, 2-inch cookies

Preheat oven to 350 degrees. Grease two large cookie trays.

In a medium sized bowl, whisk together the following:

2 cups **Celeste's Best Gluten-Free Flour Mix**
1¼ teaspoons **ground ginger**
¾ teaspoon **konjac powder** or **xanthan gum**
¾ teaspoon **baking soda**
½ teaspoon **ground cinnamon**
¼ teaspoon **ground cloves**
⅛ teaspoon **sea salt**

In mixing bowl, beat on medium speed for 1 minute:

⅔ cup **sugar**
¼ cup plus 2 tablespoons **extra light olive oil**

Add and beat for 30 seconds:

1 **egg** or equivalent substitute

Then add and beat for an additional 30 seconds:

2 tablespoons **molasses**
1 tablespoon **water**

Gradually stir in the dry ingredients and beat for 30 seconds on low or until dough forms one unified mass. Shape dough into 1½-inch balls. Then roll dough balls in a small bowl filled with a few tablespoons of additional sugar.

Place balls of dough on prepared cookie trays and flatten to ¼-inch thick. Bake for 9 – 11 minutes. Remove from oven and allow cookies to cool on trays for 5 minutes before transferring to wire rack to cool completely.

Gingerbread Cookies

These gingerbread cookies will fill your home with the wonderful aroma of cinnamon, ginger and cloves. The cookies have only a few tablespoons of molasses which adds that distinctive gingerbread taste without imparting any bitterness. And unlike many gingerbread recipes you may have tried in the past, these actually taste good!

Makes eighteen, 2-inch cookies

Preheat oven to 325 degrees. Grease two large cookie trays. In a medium sized bowl, whisk together the following:

3½ cups **Celeste's Best Gluten-Free Flour Mix**
2 teaspoons **ground cinnamon**
1½ teaspoons **konjac powder** or **xanthan gum**
1 teaspoon **ground ginger**
½ teaspoon **ground cloves**
½ teaspoon **sea salt**

In mixing bowl, beat on medium speed for 1 minute:

1½ cups **sugar**
¼ cup plus 2 tablespoons **extra light olive oil**

Add and beat for 30 seconds:

2 **eggs** or equivalent substitute

Then add and beat for an additional 30 seconds:

2 tablespoons **molasses**

Gradually stir in the dry ingredients and beat for 30 seconds or until dough forms one unified mass. Form dough into three balls and chill for 15 – 30 minutes. Remove one ball at a time and place on a sheet of parchment paper. (If dough is sufficiently chilled, it should not stick to the parchment paper.)

Roll dough out to ¼-inch thickness. Cut with cookies cutters. Bake for 9 – 11 minutes, rotating trays half way through. Remove from oven and allow cookies to cool on trays for 2 – 3 minutes before transferring to wire rack to cool completely.

> ▪ If you're looking for a very sturdy gingerbread dough to build a gingerbread house, please visit my website at www.celestesbest.com/recipes.

Graham Crackers

Graham crackers for me were always these dry, unsweetened cookies I never cared for much, except in s'mores! But I find these graham crackers delicious. Normally graham crackers are made with graham flour, but even though this recipe doesn't contain any graham, the crackers still taste as though they do. You can make them plain or add cinnamon sugar to bake up some Cinnamon Graham Crackers.

Makes 22 crackers

Preheat oven to 350 degrees. Grease two large cookie trays. In a medium sized bowl, mix together:

2¾ cups **Celeste's Best Gluten-Free Flour Mix**
1¼ teaspoons **konjac powder** or **xanthan gum**
1 teaspoon **cinnamon**
½ teaspoon **baking soda**
½ teaspoon **sea salt**

Meanwhile place in your mixing bowl:

2 **eggs** or equivalent substitute
½ cup plus 1 tablespoon **extra light olive oil**
⅓ cup **brown sugar**, packed
⅓ cup **sugar**
1 teaspoon **vanilla extract**

Beat for 1 minute on low speed, then add flour mixture to mixing bowl and beat until dough comes together and forms a ball, about another minute.

Roll dough out on top of a sheet of parchment paper to ⅛-inch thickness. Cut with a sharp knife into 2½ x 3-inch rectangle shapes. With a toothpick or fork, prick several holes in tops of each cracker.

(For cinnamon crackers: Whisk together 3 tablespoons **sugar** and 2 teaspoons **cinnamon**. Brush the tops of cookies with **extra light olive oil**, then sprinkle cinnamon sugar mixture on surface.)

Bake in preheated oven for 12 – 15 minutes, or until lightly browned along edges. Remove from the oven and let cool on tray for 10 minutes, then remove from tray and allow to finish cooling on a wire rack.

Lemon Sugar Cookies

Cookies baked with just a sweet touch of lemon.

Makes 2 dozen, 2-inch cookies

Preheat oven to 375 degrees. Lightly grease two large cookie sheets.

In a mixing bowl, beat on medium speed for 30 seconds:

⅔ cup **sugar**
½ cup **extra light olive oil**

Then add, mixing for an additional 30 seconds:

2 **eggs** or equivalent substitute
2 teaspoons **lemon zest**

Meanwhile in small bowl, whisk together the following:

1¾ cups *Celeste's Best Gluten-Free Flour Mix*
1 teaspoon **konjac powder** or **xanthan gum**
¾ teaspoon **cream of tartar**
½ teaspoon **baking soda**
⅛ teaspoon **sea salt**

Add dry ingredients to wet, mixing on low speed for 1 minute. Refrigerate dough for 30 minutes or longer. Form chilled dough into 1½-inch balls. Place onto greased cookie trays. Press down on tops to flatten so each is ¼-inch thick. Cookies will not spread much when baking.

Place trays in center of oven and bake for 10 – 12 minutes or until done. You may need to rotate trays from front to back and top to bottom halfway through cooking time so cookies will bake evenly. Remove cookies from oven and after 2 minutes transfer to wire rack to cool.

Quinoa "Oatmeal" Chocolate Chip Cookies

Organic quinoa flakes are a great substitute for oatmeal in most recipes. These were quickly gobbled up in our house.

Makes 2 dozen, 3-inch cookies

Preheat oven to 350 degrees. Grease two large cookie trays.

In mixing bowl, beat on medium speed for 1 minute:

1 cup **brown sugar**
1 cup **sugar**
¾ cup **extra light olive oil**

Then add, beating for 1 minute:

2 **eggs** or equivalent substitute
1 teaspoon **vanilla extract**

Whisk together the dry ingredients in a small bowl:

2 cups *Celeste's Best Gluten-Free Flour Mix*
2 cups **quinoa flakes**
1¼ teaspoons **baking soda**
1 teaspoon **konjac powder** or **xanthan gum**
½ teaspoon **cream of tartar**
½ teaspoon **sea salt**

Add dry ingredients to wet in mixing bowl and beat on low for approximately 1 minute or until well blended. Remove bowl from mixer and with a spatula, stir in:

2 cups **mini chocolate chips**

Drop dough by rounded tablespoonfuls 2 inches apart onto lightly greased cookie trays. Press down on tops to flatten so they are ¼-inch thick. Cookies will not spread much when baking.

Place trays in center of oven and bake for 12 – 15 minutes or until golden brown on top, rotating trays from front to back and top to bottom halfway through cooking time so cookies will bake evenly. Remove cookies from oven and after 2 minutes transfer to wire rack to cool.

- Use a cookie scoop (available at most kitchen stores) to get beautifully, rounded cookies that are uniformly sized and cook more evenly.

- If you only have one tray, run it under cool water before beginning second set of cookies so that the heated tray doesn't cause your cookies to prematurely cook. It also will be necessary to refrigerate remaining dough between batches. The dough is easier to work with when chilled.

- To make smaller cookies, drop by teaspoonfuls and only bake 9 – 11 minutes.

Quinoa "Oatmeal" Raisin Cookies

Quinoa is one of the best tasting, quick sources of complete protein available in a grain (technically a seed) and quinoa flakes mimic the taste of oatmeal in many recipes.

Makes sixteen, 3-inch cookies

In a small saucepan over medium high heat, bring to a boil for 3 – 4 minutes:

½ cup **water**
1 cup **raisins**

Remove from heat and let cool in pot for 15 – 30 minutes. (This will plump up the raisins and make them soft and juicy when baked.)

Preheat oven to 350 degrees. Grease two large cookie trays.

In mixing bowl, beat on medium speed for 1 minute:

¾ cup **sugar**
¼ cup plus 2 tablespoons **extra light olive oil**
¼ cup **brown sugar**

Then add, beating for 1 minute:

1 **egg** or equivalent substitute
½ teaspoon **vanilla extract**

Whisk together the dry ingredients in a small bowl:

1½ cups **quinoa flakes**
¾ cup *Celeste's Best Gluten-Free Flour Mix*
¾ teaspoon **baking soda**
½ teaspoon **ground cinnamon**
½ teaspoon **cream of tartar**
½ teaspoon **konjac powder** or **xanthan gum**
¼ teaspoon **sea salt**

Add dry ingredients to wet in mixing bowl and beat on low for approximately 1 minute or until well blended. Then using a slotted spoon to drain any remaining water stir in:

boiled raisins

Drop dough by rounded tablespoonfuls, 2 inches apart onto lightly greased cookie trays. Press down on tops to flatten so they are ¼-inch thick. Cookies will spread slightly when baking.

Place trays in center of oven and bake for 12 – 14 minutes or until golden brown on top, rotating trays from front to back and top to bottom halfway through cooking time so cookies will bake evenly.

Remove cookies from oven and after 2 minutes transfer to wire rack to cool.

- Use a cookie scoop (available at most kitchen stores) to get beautifully, rounded cookies that are uniformly sized and cook more evenly.

- If you only have one tray, run it under cool water before beginning second set of cookies so that the heated tray doesn't cause your cookies to prematurely cook. It also will be necessary to refrigerate remaining dough between batches. The dough is easier to work with when chilled.

- To make smaller cookies, drop by teaspoonfuls and only bake 9 – 11 minutes.

Spritz Cookies

The name spritz comes from the German word "spritzen" which means "to squirt or spray." This recipe requires a cookie press or cookie shooter. Every year at Christmastime, we always made several batches of these buttery tasting cookies.

The real trick to spritz cookies is to have just the right consistency for the dough so that it effortlessly comes through the press. These cookies do not use any konjac powder or xanthan gum, which would firm and tighten the dough too much and make it more difficult to press into cookies.

Makes 5 – 6 dozen cookies

Preheat oven to 375 degrees.

In a medium sized bowl, whisk together the following:

1¾ cups **Celeste's Best Gluten-Free Flour Mix**
½ teaspoon **sea salt**
¼ teaspoon **cream of tartar**
⅛ teaspoon **baking soda**

Place the following in mixing bowl and beat on high for 3 minutes:

¾ cup **extra light olive oil**
¾ cup **sugar**

Then add and beat for an additional minute:

1 **egg** or equivalent substitute
2 teaspoons **vanilla extract**

Reduce mixer speed to low and gradually add in flour mixture in three additions, mixing well after each addition. Fill and assemble cookie maker and press cookies onto an **ungreased cookie sheet** and bake for 8 – 10 minutes or until the cookies just start to turn light golden brown.

Sugar Cookies

Even though I've been baking these up for a while now, it's still difficult to believe these sugar cookies were baked with oil instead of butter.

These are wonderful, soft cookies that are sturdy enough to be frosted and decorated.

Makes 2 dozen cookies

Preheat oven to 350 degrees. Lightly grease two large cookie sheets.

In a mixing bowl, add the following and beat on medium speed for 2 minutes:

½ cup **sugar**
⅓ cup **extra light olive oil**

Then add and beat for one minute:

1 **egg** or equivalent substitute
1 teaspoon **vanilla extract**

Meanwhile in small bowl, whisk together the following:

1½ cups *Celeste's Best Gluten-Free Flour Mix (CBGFFM)*
¾ teaspoon **cream of tartar**
¾ teaspoon **konjac powder** or **xanthan gum**
¼ plus ⅛ teaspoon **baking soda**
¼ teaspoon **sea salt**

Add dry ingredients to wet, mixing on low speed for 1 minute or until mixture comes together in a ball. Divide dough into 2 equal sized balls and place in bowl covered with clear plastic wrap. Chill dough in refrigerator for 30 minutes or longer.

Tear off a large sheet of parchment paper and lightly flour surface with a tablespoon of *CBGFFM* or **sugar**. Using a rolling pin, roll one ball at a time to ¼-inch thickness. Cut out shapes in dough with cookie cutters or rim of a drinking glass. Place on cookie sheet.

Bake for 10 minutes (rotating trays halfway through cooking time) or until lightly golden on top. Let cookies cool on tray for 5 minutes, then remove cookies from tray and allow them to finish cooling on a wire rack. (Undercooked cookies may have a slight bean taste.)

Vanilla Treats

These cookies are incredibly easy to throw together and if you love vanilla you're in for a real treat.

Might want to consider doubling the recipe, as these tend to go quickly!

Makes 18 cookies

Preheat oven to 350 degrees. Grease two large cookie sheets.

In a mixing bowl, beat on medium speed for 1 minute:

1 cup **sugar**
¼ cup plus 2 tablespoons **extra light olive oil**

When well mixed, add:

2 **eggs** or equivalent substitute
1 teaspoon **vanilla extract**

In a separate bowl, combine the following:

1½ cups *Celeste's Best Gluten-Free Flour Mix*
1 teaspoon **ground cinnamon**
¾ teaspoon **konjac powder** or **xanthan gum**
½ teaspoon **cream of tartar**
¼ teaspoon **baking soda**
¼ teaspoon **sea salt**

Add the above ingredients to the oil and sugar mixture. Beat on low speed for 1 minute or until well blended. Cover and refrigerate for 20 minutes or until firm.

Remove dough from refrigerator and shape into balls about ¾-inch in size. Then press down lightly with hands or the back of a flat spatula until they are ¼-inch thick. Place on cookie sheet 1-inch apart and bake for 10 – 12 minutes or until lightly browned.

- To create a cinnamon-sugar treat, roll balls in a mixture of ¼ cup sugar and 1 tablespoon of cinnamon before baking.

- Dip flattened cookies in ¼ sugar for a slightly crunchy cookie.

Vanilla Wafers

My recollections of vanilla wafers were these hard cookies that my sister Liz loved. I prefer the cookies made from this recipe which aren't quite as hard, but still just as delicious.

Makes 2 dozen cookies

Preheat oven to 375 degrees. Lightly grease two large cookie sheets.

In small bowl, whisk together the following:

1¾ cups **Celeste's Best Gluten-Free Flour Mix**
¾ teaspoon **konjac powder** or **xanthan gum**
½ teaspoon **cream of tartar**
½ teaspoon **sea salt**
¼ teaspoon **baking soda**

In a mixing bowl, beat on medium speed for 30 seconds:

½ cup plus 2 tablespoons **sugar**
¼ cup plus 2 tablespoons **extra light olive oil**
1 **egg** or equivalent substitute
2 teaspoons **vanilla extract**

Add dry ingredients to mixing bowl, beating on low speed for 1 minute or until mixture comes together and forms a ball. Shape dough into 1-inch balls and place on cooking sheets, 12 cookies per tray. Flatten each ball with the palm of your hand to ⅛-inch thickness.

Bake for 6 – 8 minutes or until lightly golden on top. Let cookies cool on tray for 5 minutes, then remove cookies from tray and allow them to finish cooling on a wire rack.

Crispy Crackers

Light and crunchy crispy crackers perfect with anything.

Makes 50, 1½-inch crackers

Preheat oven to 400 degrees. Line two large cookie trays with parchment paper.

In mixing bowl, briskly whisk together:

1 cup **white rice flour**
¼ cup **amaranth flour**
¼ cup **quinoa flour**
2 tablespoons **golden flaxseed meal**
¾ teaspoon **konjac powder** or **xanthan gum**
½ teaspoon **cream of tartar**
¼ teaspoon **baking soda**

Then combine and add to mixing bowl:

⅔ cup **water**
3 tablespoons **extra light olive oil**
½ teaspoon **sea salt** (dissolve in water before adding to flour)

Beat on medium speed for 30 seconds or until mixture comes together and forms a uniformed mass. Divide dough into 2 pieces. Cut a sheet of parchment paper. Place dough on top. Flatten dough ball and lay another sheet of parchment paper on top. (Parchment paper will prevent the dough from sticking. You can also use plastic wrap.)

Roll dough out to at least $^1/_{16}$-inch thick. Your goal is to roll out the dough to as thin as you can get it without it tearing. The thinner the dough is rolled, the crispier the crackers will taste. Prick tops of cracker with the tines of a fork several times. Place crackers on prepared cooking trays. Sprinkle with sea salt. Bake for 17 – 22 minutes or until golden brown. (Crackers that are undercooked will be chewy.) When done, remove from trays and cool on wire racks. When completely cool, store crackers in a sealed container.

- Just wanted to stress again that the dough has to be rolled very thin for the crackers to be crispy. As thin as you can possibly roll them.

- Try the recipe with just 1½ cups white rice flour instead of the amaranth or quinoa.

Matzo

Matzo (also known as matzah, matza, matzoh, matzo, matsah, matsa, and matze) is a yeast-free bread or cracker. This recipe is for a non-kosher version of matzo. Kosher matzo must be prepared using either wheat, rye, barley, spelt or oat flour and cooked within a specific amount of time.

Matzo dough must be rolled as thin as possible to the point that you can almost see through the dough. That's the key to producing that authentic matzo taste.

Makes 12 matzos

Preheat oven to 500 degrees. Whisk together in a medium sized bowl:

2 cups *Celeste's Best Gluten-Free Flour Mix*
1 teaspoon **konjac powder** or **xanthan gum**
½ teaspoon **sea salt**

In a 2 cup measuring cup or small bowl, combine using an **immersion** or **stick blender** beating on high speed until emulsified:

¾ cup **water**
⅓ cup **extra light olive oil**

Place flour mixture in food processor. Add liquid ingredients and pulse until mixture comes together and forms a uniform mass. Remove from processor and knead in hands or on pastry board. Divide dough into 12 equal pieces and form into small balls. Roll each ball of dough between two sheets of parchment paper until you're unable to roll them any thinner about ($\frac{1}{16}$-inch to $\frac{1}{32}$-inch thin) without dough cracking or tearing.

Prick across each matzo with a fork (see note box below). Place matzo on large ungreased cooking tray. Bake for 3 minutes, flip matzo over with a large spatula and bake for an additional 3 minutes. Remove from oven and cool on wire rack. When completely cool, store in an airtight container.

> - To obtain a crispy matzo, the dough must be rolled as thin as possible.
>
> - I use a comb I purchased just for pricking the holes across the top of the crackers.

Sesame Bran Crackers

You could pay a small fortune for a handful of gluten-free crackers or you can save a few dollars and make them yourself. It only takes a cup of flour and a few other ingredients you might already have on hand. This particular recipe is made with sesame seeds and rice bran. Toasting raw sesame seeds for a few minutes in a dry skillet before adding them to the dough really helps to bring out the flavor in these crackers.

Makes approx. 4½ dozen, 1½-inch crackers

Preheat oven to 350 degrees. In a small pan over medium heat, add:

¼ cup **untoasted sesame seeds**

Continually stir seeds with a spatula until they turn slightly brown in color. Remove from heat.

In mixing bowl, briskly whisk together:

1 cup *Celeste's Best Gluten-Free Flour Mix*
previously **toasted sesame seeds**
2 tablespoons **rice bran**
½ teaspoon **konjac powder** or **xanthan gum**
½ teaspoon **sea salt**

Then combine and add to mixing bowl:

½ cup **water**
2 tablespoons **extra light olive oil**

Beat on medium speed for 30 seconds or until mixture comes together and forms a uniformed mass. Divide dough into 3 pieces. Cut a sheet of parchment paper. Place dough on top. Flatten dough ball and lay another sheet of parchment paper on top. (Parchment paper will prevent the dough from sticking.)

Roll dough out to $\frac{1}{16}$-inch thick. The thinner the dough is rolled, the crispier the crackers will taste. Prick tops of cracker with the tines of a fork several times. Place crackers on ungreased large cookie sheets.

Bake for 25 – 30 minutes or until golden. When done, remove from trays and cool on wire racks. When completely cool, store crackers in a sealed container.

CAKES

White Cake

Carrot Cake

An easy cake to bake. You can grate fresh carrots or buy the pre-grated ones. Either way, you'll bake up one deliciously moist cake. This recipe can also be doubled.

Makes one 9-inch square cake

Preheat oven to 350 degrees. Grease a 9-inch square pan. In a medium sized bowl, whisk together the following:

1¼ cups **Celeste's Best Gluten-Free Flour Mix**
1¼ teaspoons **baking soda**
1 teaspoon **cinnamon**
½ teaspoon **cream of tartar**
½ teaspoon **konjac powder** or **xanthan gum**
¼ teaspoon **nutmeg**
½ teaspoon **sea salt**

Meanwhile in a mixing bowl, combine and beat on medium speed for 1 minute:

½ cup **extra light olive oil**
2 **eggs** or equivalent substitute
½ cup **sugar**
¼ cup plus 2 tablespoons **brown sugar**
¼ cup **milk** or **non-dairy milk substitute** or **water**
1½ teaspoons **vanilla extract**

Add in dry ingredients and beat on medium speed for 30 seconds. Then fold in:

1½ cups **grated carrots**
⅓ cup **raisins**

Pour batter in greased pan and bake for 32 – 37 minutes or until tester inserted into center of cake comes out clean.

> - The fat content can be lowered on this recipe by substituting ¼ cup of the oil with unsweetened applesauce.

Chocolate Cake

This cake is made with cocoa powder instead of unsweetened chocolate and is so moist and delicious, you won't need a drop of frosting on it. For birthday celebrations though, we do like to frost this incredibly light and utterly scrumptious cake with chocolate or vanilla frosting (see pages 314 - 315).

Makes one 13 x 9-inch cake or two 8-inch square cakes or two 8-inch round cakes

Preheat oven to 350 degrees. Grease cake pan/s.

Bring to a boil:

¾ cup **water**

Meanwhile in a large mixing bowl, whisk together:

2 cups **sugar**
1¾ cups *Celeste's Best Gluten-Free Flour Mix*
¾ cup **unsweetened cocoa**
1¾ teaspoons **baking soda**
1 teaspoon **konjac powder** or **xanthan gum**
1 teaspoon **sea salt**
¾ teaspoon **cream of tartar**

In a small bowl, combine:

1 cup **milk** or **non-dairy milk substitute**
2 **eggs** or equivalent substitute
½ cup **extra light olive oil**
2 teaspoons **vanilla extract**

Add wet ingredients to mixing bowl and beat on medium speed for 1 minute. Then stir in boiling water by hand with a spatula.

Pour batter into prepared cake pan/s and bake 30 – 35 minutes for the round or square pans and 35 – 40 minutes for the rectangular pan. Cake is done when toothpick inserted in center comes out clean. Place on wire racks until cooled.

Crumb Cake

This recipe produces an incredibly moist and delicious crumb cake. Great for a Sunday brunch or for dessert. And believe me, you'll want to eat every last crumb of this cake!

Makes one 13 x 9-inch cake

Preheat oven to 350 degrees and grease a 13 x 9 x 2-inch baking dish. In a mixing bowl, mix together well:

2¾ cups **Celeste's Best Gluten-Free Flour Mix**
1 cup **brown sugar**
¾ cup **sugar**
1 teaspoon **sea salt**
1 teaspoon **cinnamon**
¾ teaspoon **konjac powder** or **xanthan gum**

Add, stirring with a fork until blended:

¾ cup **extra light olive oil**

When well-blended, remove 1 cup of mix and place in small bowl. Meanwhile, blend the following together in a 2-cup measuring cup:

1½ cups **milk** or **non-dairy milk substitute**
1 **egg** or equivalent substitute
1½ tablespoons **lemon juice**
1¼ teaspoons **baking soda**
1 teaspoon **vanilla extract**
½ teaspoon **cream of tartar**

Add wet ingredients to dry in mixing bowl and beat on medium speed for 1 minute. Pour batter into baking dish. Lightly sprinkle the reserved flour crumb topping mixture over batter.

Bake for 35 – 40 minutes or until golden brown. Cool cake in pan set on a rack. Wonderful served hot and steamy fresh from the oven, or eaten when cooled.

Double Chocolate Chip Cupcakes

Hard to resist – chocolate cupcakes full of chocolate chips. A chocolate lover's delight. They taste especially good chilled. This recipe can also be made without the chips for a plain chocolate cupcake.

Makes 12 cupcakes

Preheat oven to 350 degrees. Line 12 muffin cups with liners. In a large mixing bowl, whisk together:

1¼ cups **Celeste's Best Gluten-Free Flour Mix**
1 cup **sugar**
⅓ cup **unsweetened cocoa**
1 teaspoon **baking soda**
½ teaspoon **sea salt**
¼ teaspoon **konjac powder** or **xanthan gum**

In a small bowl, whisk together the wet ingredients:

¾ cup **milk** or **non-dairy milk substitute**
½ cup **extra light olive oil**
2 **eggs** or equivalent substitute
1 tablespoon **lemon juice**
1½ teaspoons **vanilla extract**

Add the wet ingredients to the dry and beat on medium speed for 1 minute. Then add:

½ cup **mini chocolate chips**

Stir in the chocolate chips with a spatula, then fill muffin tins three-quarters full with batter. Bake in preheated oven for 17 – 22 minutes.

Cool on wire racks for 5 minutes, then remove from tins and continue cooling on racks.

Doughnuts

Why is it called a doughnut? This deep fried pastry started out as a little ball of dough the size of a nut.

And just like so many of your favorite foods, there's absolutely no reason to give up enjoying this sweet treat every now and then, even when following an allergen-free diet!

Makes 14 – 16 doughnuts

Place the following in a mixing bowl and beat on medium speed for 1 minute:

¾ cup **sugar** (see note box on following page)
1 tablespoon **extra light olive oil**

Then add, beating on medium speed for 45 seconds:

3 **eggs** or equivalent substitute

In a medium sized bowl, combine the dry ingredients:

3 cups *Celeste's Best Gluten-Free Flour Mix*
1½ teaspoons **cream of tartar**
1½ teaspoons **konjac powder** or **xanthan gum**
¾ teaspoon **baking soda**
½ teaspoon **sea salt**
½ teaspoon **cinnamon**
¼ teaspoon **mace**
¼ teaspoon **nutmeg**

Add the dry ingredients to the mixing bowl, alternating with:

⅔ cup **milk** or **non-dairy milk substitute**

Beat on medium speed for 1 minute or until mixture comes together and forms a ball.

Fill a large pot half full with **frying oil** (see note box on following page). Oil will bubble and splatter when hot and should not be filled more than half full. Set on medium heat.

Check temperature using a **deep fry thermometer** as a guide. Doughnuts cook best between 345 and 365 degrees. A temperature lower than 345 degrees will cause the doughnuts to absorb too much oil and you'll wind up with heavy, greasy doughnut holes.

Oils begin to burn at 400 degrees and can catch fire at 500 degrees so it's important to use extreme caution when deep-frying. Always monitor temperature with a thermometer. While oil is heating, roll out the dough to ½-inch thickness on a piece of parchment paper sprinkled with 2 tablespoons **sugar**. Cut into doughnut shapes. Form dough scraps into rolls, 4 inches long by ½-inch thick and twist two together to form a cruller twist.

Place a wire rack on top of large cookie sheet covered with paper towels. Once oil has reached desired temperature, begin frying doughnuts. Turn doughnuts over at least once during frying to evenly brown. Remove doughnuts with tongs or slotted spoon to wire rack to drain. When cool enough to handle, roll doughnuts in either:

confectioners powdered sugar (see page 23)

or into cinnamon sugar by whisking together the following in a small bowl:

¼ cup **sugar**
1 teaspoon **cinnamon**

Store any leftover doughnuts in a brown paper bag. Storing doughnuts in a sealed container will cause the doughnuts to become overly moist.

- If you don't plan on topping the doughnuts with the powdered or cinnamon sugar, increase the amount of sugar in the dough to 1 cup.

- In lieu of a doughnut cutter, use the bottom rim of a cup and cut the center out with an apple corer or hand cut or make them all crullers.

- Use the doughnut holes as your tests to check the temperature of oil.

- Rice bran oil is an excellent choice for frying. It's a light, very healthy oil that is gluten-free and trans fat free. It also has a very high smoke point which makes it perfect for frying.

- Mace isn't a common spice to have on hand, but it helps gives doughnuts that authentic taste.

Dutch Coffee Cake

*I have to tell you, I think I might have gained one or more pounds on this recipe alone.
It was hard to walk by those pie plates without snatching a small sliver each time.
Quickly realized after that to bake these only when I'm expecting company so I wouldn't
be tempted to eat them all myself!*

Makes two 9-inch cakes

Preheat oven to 350 degrees. Grease two 9-inch cake pans or pie plates. In mixing bowl, whisk together:

3 cups **Celeste's Best Gluten-Free Flour Mix**
1½ cups **sugar**
1 teaspoon **baking soda**
1 teaspoon **konjac powder** or **xanthan gum**

Add to mixing bowl and beat on medium speed for 1 minute:

½ cup **extra light olive oil**

Mixture should have the consistency of small peas.

** **Reserve 1½ cups of above mixture for crumb topping.**** Add to reserved crumb topping:

2 tablespoons **extra light olive oil**

Meanwhile, whisk together in a small bowl:

1 cup **milk** or **non-dairy milk substitute**
1 tablespoon **lemon juice**

Then briskly whisk in:

3 **eggs** or equivalent substitute
2 teaspoons **vanilla extract**

Add wet ingredients to mixing bowl and beat on medium speed for 1 minute. Batter will be thick. Pour batter equally into the two prepared pans or pie plates. Sprinkle reserved crumb topping over batter.

Bake for 25 – 30 minutes, or until golden on top and toothpick inserted into center of cake comes out clean.

Egg-Free, Milk-Free Chocolate Cake

A chocolate cake for those who would prefer a cake without any eggs or milk. Even without the addition of these ingredients, this recipe bakes up a light and delicious cake.

Makes one 8 x 8-inch cake

Preheat oven to 350 degrees. Grease an 8 x 8-inch square cake pan.

In a large mixing bowl, whisk together:

1½ cups **Celeste's Best Gluten-Free Flour Mix**
1 cup **sugar**
½ cup **unsweetened cocoa**
1¼ teaspoon **baking soda**
¾ teaspoon **konjac powder** or **xanthan gum**
½ teaspoon **cream of tartar**
½ teaspoon **sea salt**

In a small bowl, briskly whisk together:

1 cup **water**
⅓ cup **extra light olive oil**
1 tablespoon **lemon juice**
1 teaspoon **vanilla extract**

Add wet ingredients to mixing bowl and beat on medium speed for 1 minute.

Pour batter into prepared cake pan and bake 32 – 37 minutes. Cake is done when toothpick inserted in center comes out clean.

Pound Cake

A traditional British pound cake got its name because it was made of a pound each of flour, butter, sugar, fruit and eggs. I particularly like this recipe because it is much lighter than most traditional recipes without sacrificing an ounce of taste. Be sure to try the variation for the Lemon Pound Cake (see note box below).

Makes one cake

Preheat oven to 325 degrees. Grease an 8½ by 4½ by 2½-inch loaf pan. In a large bowl, mix together the following:

1½ cups **Celeste's Best Gluten-Free Flour Mix**
¾ teaspoon **konjac powder** or **xanthan gum**
½ teaspoon **cream of tartar**
¼ teaspoon **baking soda**
¼ teaspoon **sea salt**

In a mixing bowl, beat on medium speed for 1 minute:

1 cup **sugar**
¼ cup plus 2 tablespoons **extra light olive oil**

When well mixed, add:

2 **eggs** or equivalent substitute
½ cup plus 2 tablespoons **milk** or **non-dairy milk substitute**
2 teaspoons **vanilla extract**

Add dry ingredients to oil/sugar mixture until well blended, beating on medium speed for 1 minute. Pour batter into pan. Bake 55 – 60 minutes or until golden brown and toothpick inserted into center comes out clean. Serve warm or cool.

- Variation: Lemon Pound Cake: Follow the recipe as directed, but omit the vanilla extract. Instead of adding 2 extra tablespoons of milk, add 2 tablespoons **lemon juice** and 1 tablespoon **lemon zest**. After cake has baked and cooled, make a glaze of ⅓ cup **lemon juice** and ¼ cup **sugar** and drizzle across the top and serve.

Pumpkin Cake

A light and moist cake spiced with cinnamon, ginger and cloves.

Makes one bundt or one 13 x 9-inch cake

Preheat oven to 350 degrees. Grease a bundt pan or 13 x 9 x 2-inch cake pan. In mixing bowl, combine and beat on medium speed for 30 seconds:

2 cups **sugar**
¾ cup **unsweetened applesauce**
½ cup **extra light olive oil**

Then add, beating for 20 seconds:

4 **eggs** (see note box below)
1 (15 ounce) can **solid pack pumpkin**
1 teaspoon **vanilla extract**

In a medium sized bowl, whisk together:

2 cups *Celeste's Best Gluten-Free Flour Mix*
2¾ teaspoons **baking soda**
2 teaspoons **ground cinnamon**
1½ teaspoons **cream of tartar**
1 teaspoon **konjac powder** or **xanthan gum**
¼ teaspoon **ground ginger**
⅛ teaspoon **ground cloves**

Add flour mixture to mixing bowl and beat on medium speed for 30 seconds. Pour batter into prepared cake pan.

Bake for 40 – 45 minutes for a bundt cake and 30 – 35 minutes for a sheet cake or until toothpick or tester inserted in center comes out clean.

> ▪ Since this recipe requires 4 eggs, those with egg sensitivities and allergies would find this recipe would work best by reducing all ingredients in half and using 2 flaxeggs and then baking in an 8 x 8-inch square baking dish for 25 – 30 minutes.

Spice Cake

Cinnamon, nutmeg, allspice, cloves and ginger help spice up this cake. As this bakes, the whole house will be filled with the wonderfully, aromatic scent of all the spices.

Makes one 9-inch square cake

Preheat oven to 350 degrees. Grease a square 9-inch square baking dish.

In a medium sized bowl, whisk together:

1½ cups **Celeste's Best Gluten-Free Flour Mix**
1 teaspoon **ground cinnamon**
¾ teaspoon **cream of tartar**
¾ teaspoon **nutmeg**
½ teaspoon **konjac powder** or **xanthan gum**
¼ teaspoon plus ⅛ teaspoon **baking soda**
¼ teaspoon **allspice**
¼ teaspoon **ginger**
¼ teaspoon **ground cloves**
¼ teaspoon **sea salt**

In a mixing bowl, beat on medium speed for 1 minute:

1 cup **sugar**
¾ cup **milk** or **non-dairy milk substitute**
¼ cup plus 2 tablespoons **extra light olive oil**
1 **egg** or equivalent substitute
1 teaspoon **vanilla extract**

Add flour mixture to wet ingredients, mixing on low speed for 1 minute or until well blended.

Pour batter into baking dish and bake for 35 – 40 minutes, or until toothpick inserted in center comes out clean.

- Make a glaze by whisking together ½ cup **sugar**, 1½ tablespoons **extra light olive oil**, 2 teaspoons **milk** and ½ teaspoon **vanilla extract** and drizzle over the cake.

Vanilla Cupcakes

Almost any layer cake recipe can often be used to make cupcakes instead.   But certain recipes seem to fair better than others when made into these little "fairy cakes" as they were once called.   This recipe produces a light, airy cupcake with just the right amount of dome shape at the top for frosting.   But I have to tell you, these little cakes taste so good unfrosted, you'll have to frost them quickly before they disappear!

Makes 12 cupcakes

Preheat oven to 325 degrees. (Vanilla cakes need to bake in a slightly cooler oven to avoid browning.) Line a cupcake pan with paper liners or grease tray. In a small bowl or 4 cup measuring cup, briskly whisk together the following:

2 **eggs** or equivalent substitute
¾ cup **milk** or **non-dairy milk substitute**
¼ cup plus 2 tablespoons **extra light olive oil**
½ teaspoon **vanilla extract**

In mixing bowl, whisk together:

1½ cups *Celeste's Best Gluten-Free Flour Mix*
1 cup **sugar**
1½ teaspoons **cream of tartar**
¾ teaspoon **baking soda**
½ teaspoon **konjac powder** or **xanthan gum**
½ teaspoon **sea salt**

Add half the wet ingredients to mixing bowl and beat on medium speed for 30 seconds and then the remainder of the wet ingredients and beat for 1 minute. Scoop batter into cupcake tins with a ¼-cup measuring scoop, filling each liner about two-thirds full.

Bake on center rack for 17 – 21 minutes, or until tops of cake are lightly golden and a toothpick or tester inserted in the center of one comes out clean.

Place cupcake pan on wire rack to cool for at least 5 minutes. Remove cupcakes from the pan and place them back on the rack to further cool. Let cupcakes cool completely before decorating.

Yellow Cake

A light and airy, moist and delicious yellow cake.

Makes one 9-inch square cake

Preheat oven to 325 degrees. Grease an 8-inch square baking dish. In mixing bowl, beat on medium speed for 30 seconds:

1 cup **sugar**
⅓ cup **extra light olive oil**

Meanwhile in a small mixing bowl, whisk together until well blended:

1¾ cups *Celeste's Best Gluten-Free Flour Mix*
1½ teaspoons **cream of tartar**
¾ teaspoon **baking soda**
½ teaspoon **konjac powder** or **xanthan gum**

Add dry ingredients to mixing bowl and beat on medium speed for 30 seconds. In a liquid measuring cup, whisk together:

1 cup **milk** or **non-dairy milk substitute**
1 tablespoon **lemon juice**

Then add:

1½ teaspoons **vanilla extract**

Add liquid ingredients to mixing bowl. Beat on medium speed for only 20 seconds, then immediately pour into prepared pan and place in oven. Bake for 30 – 35 minutes or until toothpick or tester inserted in center comes out clean.

White Cake

A classic white cake recipe. This cake makes a terrific birthday cake, topped with either Vanilla or Chocolate Frosting (recipes at end of this chapter).

Makes one 9-inch round cake

Preheat oven to 350 degrees. Grease a round 9–inch cake pan.

In a mixing bowl, beat on medium speed for 1 minute:

¾ cup **sugar**
½ cup **extra light olive oil**

Meanwhile in a small bowl, whisk together:

1 cup *Celeste's Best Gluten-Free Flour Mix*
2 tablespoons **tapioca flour**
½ teaspoon **konjac powder** or **xanthan gum**
1 teaspoon **cream of tartar**
½ teaspoon **baking soda**

Add flour mixture to mixing bowl and beat on medium speed for 1 minute. Then in a two cup measuring cup, whisk together briskly:

3 **egg whites** ($^3/_8$ cup) or equivalent substitute
½ cup **milk** or **non-dairy milk substitute**
1½ teaspoons **vanilla extract**

Add liquid ingredients to mixing bowl and beat on medium speed for an additional minute. Pour batter into greased baking pan and bake for 30 – 35 minutes, or until toothpick inserted in center comes out clean.

> - This recipe is also great for cupcakes, but reduce cooking time to 20 – 25 minutes.
>
> - Normally I cook white and yellow cakes at 325 degrees, but this cake seems to do better at a slightly higher temperature.
>
> - This cake can easily be doubled.

Chocolate Frosting

A terrific frosting made without any gluten or dairy. If you're sensitive to corn, be sure to make your own confectioners powdered sugar (see page 23).

Makes enough to frost one 13 x 9 x 2-inch layer cake

In a medium sized mixing bowl, combine:

4 cups **confectioners powdered sugar** (see page 23)
½ cup **shortening**
½ cup **unsweetened cocoa**
2 tablespoons **milk** or **non-dairy milk substitute**
1 teaspoon **vanilla extract**

Beat on medium speed for one minute. Add:

4 – 5 additional tablespoons of **milk** or **non-dairy milk substitute**

Add milk tablespoon by tablespoon while continuing to beat on medium speed until frosting is smooth and desired consistency has been reached.

Vanilla Frosting

This frosting works well on cakes and also can be used to decorate cookies. If you're sensitive to corn, be sure to make your own confectioners powdered sugar (see page 23).

Makes enough to frost one 13 x 9 x 2-inch layer cake

In a medium sized mixing bowl, combine:

4 cups **confectioners powdered sugar** (see page 23)
½ cup **shortening**

Beat on medium high speed for 1 minute. Then add:

1 teaspoon **vanilla extract**
3 tablespoons **milk** or **non-dairy milk substitute**
optional: **food coloring**

Beat on medium for an additional minute. Add:

1 – 2 additional tablespoons of **milk** or **non-dairy milk substitute**

Add milk tablespoon by tablespoon while continuing to beat on medium speed until frosting is smooth and desired consistency has been reached.

PIES AND PASTRIES

Apple Pie

Pastry Dough

This is an amazing pastry dough. It produces a pie crust that is both flaky and tender. The dough is easy to work with because it's extremely pliable. It's hard to believe this is a gluten-free pie crust.

Makes one pie crust

Whisk together in mixing bowl:

1½ cups **Celeste's Best Gluten-Free Flour Mix (CBGFFM)**
1 teaspoon **konjac powder** or **xanthan gum**
½ teaspoon **sea salt**

Add:

½ cup **shortening**

Beat on medium speed until dough resembles large crumbs, then slowly add:

½ cup **ice water**

Beat on medium speed for approximately 20 – 30 seconds or until dough forms a ball. The consistency of the dough should be slightly moist. If dough seems dry add additional water tablespoon by tablespoon until desired consistency is reached. The dough is always easier to work with slightly wet. A dry dough that will create a pie pastry that cracks when handled.

Cover work area with a sheet of parchment paper. Lightly flour surface with a teaspoon or two of **CBGFFM,** or for dessert pies, I place a few teaspoons of sugar on the rolling surface. Lay ball of dough on parchment paper and flatten with rolling pin. Place a teaspoon of flour or sugar on top, spreading it around with your hand, then set another sheet of parchment paper on top of dough.

Roll to uniform thickness. Take off the top sheet of parchment paper and carefully transfer to the pan, being sure the pie plate is greased before putting the dough into it. (Can't tell you how many times I've been so busy making the dough, that I forgot to grease the plate.)

My method of transferring the dough to the plate is to place the rolled out dough on top of a thin, glass cutting board and lay the pie plate on top and while carefully holding them together, flip them over. Another way to do this is to lightly wrap the dough around your rolling pin, then unroll it as you transfer it into your pie plate.

To double the recipe and make 2 crusts, follow the instructions above but with the following changes:

Whisk together in mixing bowl:

2½ cups *Celeste's Best Gluten-Free Flour Mix*
2 teaspoons **konjac powder** or **xanthan gum**
1 teaspoon **sea salt**

Add:

1 cup **shortening**

Beat on medium speed until dough resembles large crumbs, then add:

1 cup **ice water**

Prebaking a pie crust:

Preheat oven to 400 degrees. Liberally grease pie plate. Fit the pastry dough into pie pan. Prick over the bottom surface with a fork. Cut out a piece of parchment paper to fit inside of crust, coming up sides slightly. Fill paper insert with pie weights. This helps set the crust by weighing down the dough as it bakes so it doesn't puff and bubble up. Bake for 15 minutes. Then carefully remove liner and weights.

Reduce temperature to 375 degrees and continue to bake for 10 – 12 minutes for a partially baked crust and up to 15 – 17 minutes for a fully baked crust.

Remove from oven and set on wire rack until cool.

- For best results, keep pastry dough chilled until ready to use. Place unfilled pie crusts in refrigerator until ready to fill.

- This is the perfect crust for Chicken Pot Pie (see pages 127 – 128).

Fast and Easy Pie Crust

A fast and easy pie crust that doesn't need to be rolled out and is mixed together right in the pie plate.

Makes one pie crust

Liberally grease a 9-inch pie plate. (If prebaking the pie crust, preheat oven to 375 degrees.)

In a medium sized bowl, whisk together:

2½ cups **Celeste's Best Gluten-Free Flour Mix**
2 teaspoons **sugar**
1½ teaspoons **konjac powder** or **xanthan gum**
1 teaspoon **sea salt**

In a liquid measuring cup, briskly whisk together:

½ cup **extra light olive oil**
¼ cup **milk** or **non-dairy milk substitute**

Place dry ingredients in pie pan. Make a well in the center. Do this by simply pushing away the flour with your spatula, creating a hole in the middle. You will fill this with the wet ingredients.

Next, slowly pour wet ingredients into the well, while stirring with a fork. As you do, pull in some more flour from outside the well and incorporate it into the wet ingredients, bit by bit, until all has been incorporated.

Shape dough in a ball, then flatten and press into the pan to form pie crust. A small pastry roller can be used to smooth bottom.

To prebake crust: Bake at 375 degrees for 10 – 12 minutes or until crust has turned golden brown.

Apple Pie

Never been a big fan of apple pie or any kind of fruit pie, but my husband grew up on them. Thought I would give this one a try, pairing it with the Pastry Dough crust recipe, and was surprised to find I enjoyed it almost as much as my husband did. You'll need to make two pie crusts, one for the bottom and one for the top.

My daughter gave me a great compliment after eating her slice. "Mom, this is the best. No, I mean the best in the whole world!"

Makes one pie

Preheat oven to 425 degrees. Liberally grease one 9-inch pie plate and line with **Pastry Dough** (see pages 318 – 319). Place bottom crust in refrigerator to chill until ready to fill. Place top crust in a cool place until needed. (Refrigerating top crust makes it less flexible and harder to handle.)

Peel:

6 medium sized **granny smith apples**

In a saucepan, combine into a paste the following:

¼ cup plus 2 tablespoons **extra light olive oil**
3 tablespoons *Celeste's Best Gluten-Free Flour Mix*

Add:

½ cup **brown sugar**, packed
½ cup **sugar**
3 tablespoons **water**

Bring ingredients in saucepan to a boil on medium heat (too high a heat will burn the sauce), then reduce heat and simmer for 5 minutes.

While sauce is simmering, core and thinly slice peeled apples. Fill pastry lined pie dish with sliced apples, forming a slight mound in the center of the pan. Filling will be taller than the sides of the pan but will cook down.

Reserve two tablespoons of sauce. Pour remainder over the apples.

Top pie with **second pastry**. Use a fork or your fingers to pinch the edges together. Take a knife and make a few slits in the top to vent the steam.

(continued)

Brush top with reserved two tablespoons of sauce. If sauce hardens, reheat to soften.

Bake in preheated oven 15 minutes, then reduce heat to 350 degrees. Cook an additional 40 – 45 minutes or until crust is golden brown.

- Certain varieties of apples have the right tartness and texture needed to create a great tasting apple pie, such as: Granny Smith, Jonathan, McIntosh, Ida Red, and Northern Spy, to name a few.

- Try using a combination of half McIntosh and half Golden Delicious or half McIntosh and half Granny Smith.

- Reduce the apples down to 5 and add a peach or a pear for a slightly varied taste.

Cherry Pie

A pie that is sweet, thick and full of fresh Bing cherries.

Makes one pie

Preheat oven to 375 degrees. Liberally grease a 9-inch pie plate and line with **Pastry Dough** (see pages 318 – 319) or **Fast and Easy Pie Crust** (see page 320). Place in refrigerator to chill until ready to fill.

Then in a medium sized bowl, pit (see note box) and cut in half:

4 cups **sweet cherries**

Then pour over cherries:

1 tablespoon **lemon juice**

In another medium sized bowl, whisk together:

½ cup **sugar**
¼ cup *Celeste's Best Gluten-Free Flour Mix*
¼ teaspoon **ground cinnamon**
¼ teaspoon **sea salt**

> *A very easy way to pit cherries is to remove the stems, then insert a jumbo paper clip into the stem end until it is underneath the pit, twist it around to grasp the stone center and simply pull it out. Once you do a few, you'll get a knack for this and the pitting goes quickly.*

Add sugar mix to bowl of cherries and toss until all of the fruit is well coated with the mix. Pour cherries into prepared pie crust.

To prepare the topping, whisk together in a medium sized bowl:

½ cup *Celeste's Best Gluten-Free Flour Mix*
½ cup **sugar**
¼ teaspoon **ground cinnamon**
¼ teaspoon **ground nutmeg**

Add, whisking in until coarse crumbs form:

2 tablespoons plus 1 teaspoon **extra light olive oil**

Sprinkle topping over cherry pie filling. Bake in preheated oven for 30 minutes. Then cover top with a piece of parchment paper to prevent the crust from over browning and bake an additional 20 – 30 minutes. Remove from oven and cool on a wire rack. Refrigerate any leftover pie.

Chocolate Chip Pie

Either this is a chocolate chip pie or one giant chocolate chip cookie. Whatever way you slice it – it's yummy!!!

Makes one pie

Preheat oven to 350 degrees. Grease a 9-inch pie pan.

In medium sized bowl, whisk together:

1¼ cups plus 2 tablespoons *Celeste's Best Gluten-Free Flour Mix*
¾ cup **brown sugar**
¼ cup **sugar**
1 teaspoon **konjac powder** or **xanthan gum**
¾ teaspoon **baking soda**
¾ teaspoon **sea salt**
½ teaspoon **cream of tartar**

In mixing bowl, combine the following:

2 **eggs** or equivalent substitute
¼ cup plus 2 tablespoons **extra light olive oil**
1½ teaspoons **vanilla extract**

Beat on medium speed for 30 seconds, then add the dry ingredients in two parts, mixing for about 30 seconds after each addition or until all the flour and other ingredients have been well incorporated. Batter will be thick. Then beat in on stir speed:

1½ cups **mini chocolate chips**

Spoon batter into pie pan with spatula, smoothing the top and making sure the batter has been evenly dispersed. Bake for 27 – 33 minutes or until golden brown. Remove from oven and cool completely on wire rack before slicing and serving.

Chocolate Cream Pie

This is a single crusted pie filled with a thick chocolate pudding.

Makes one pie

Prepare one recipe of pastry dough (see pages 318 – 319) and fully prebake the crust and let it cool for 30 – 60 minutes.

To prepare filling, in a medium sized saucepan combine:

¾ cup **sugar**
⅓ cup *Celeste's Best Gluten-Free Flour Mix*
¼ teaspoon **sea salt**

In a small bowl, whisk together:

2 cups **milk** or **non-dairy milk substitute**
2 **eggs** or equivalent substitute

Add milk to saucepan and whisk together until well combined. Turn heat on to medium. (The pudding will burn and stick to bottom of pot if heat is too high.) Continue to cook for 7 – 10 minutes or until thickened.

Stir in:

½ cup **mini chocolate chips**
1 tablespoon **extra light olive oil**
1 teaspoon **vanilla extract**

Let filling cool slightly then pour into prebaked pie crust. Refrigerate and chill for 2 hours or more before serving.

Cream Puffs

This was one of my mother's signature dishes growing up. I always remember her baking a dozen or more of these whenever we were invited anywhere.

They're especially wonderful filled with Custard Cream Pudding (see page 351).

Makes 12 cream puffs

Preheat oven to 400 degrees. Line a large cookie sheet with parchment paper. In a medium sized saucepan, bring to a boil:

1 cup **water**
¼ cup plus 2 tablespoons **extra light olive oil**

Meanwhile in a small bowl, whisk together:

1 cup *Celeste's Best Gluten-Free Flour Mix*
½ teaspoon **konjac powder** or **xanthan gum**
¼ teaspoon **sea salt**

Add flour mixture to saucepan and stir continually until mixture forms a ball, about 30 seconds. Remove dough from pan and place in mixing bowl. Add all at once:

4 **eggs** (This recipe will only work with real eggs or real egg substitute.)

Beat on low speed for 20 seconds, then medium speed for 1 – 1½ minutes. (Batter will seem too runny, but will thicken as you continue to mix). Drop dough by heaping tablespoons, 2 inches apart, on prepared cookie sheet.

Bake for 35 – 40 minutes. Remove from oven and let cool on wire racks. Create a small slit in the back of each puff with a knife to release steam.

Fill the puffs after they have completely cooled. Using a serrated knife, cut the upper third from each puff and gently scoop out any moist interior. Spoon in filling.

Sprinkle with powdered sugar or drizzle chocolate across the tops.

- For best results, fill cream puffs just before you are going to eat them.

- You can use a cake decorating tube to pipe the filling in through a hole in the back.

Empanadas

An empanada is a stuffed or filled pastry that is baked or fried. The name comes from the Spanish verb, empanar, meaning to wrap or coat in bread.

Personally, I think these are amazing and taste like they were made with a gluten filled dough. One of our favorite fillings is the Beef Empanada Filling (see pages 104 – 105).

Makes 22 – 24 empanadas

Preheat oven to 375 degrees. Line two large cookie sheets with parchment paper.

In mixing bowl, whisk together:

2¼ cups *Celeste's Best Gluten-Free Flour Mix*
1 tablespoon **sugar**
1 teaspoon **konjac powder** or **xanthan gum**
½ teaspoon **cream of tartar**
¼ teaspoon **baking soda**
¼ teaspoon **sea salt**

In a small bowl, briskly whisk together:

¾ cup plus 2 tablespoons **water**
⅓ cup **extra light olive oil**

Add the wet ingredients to the dry and beat on medium speed for 20 – 30 seconds or just until mixture forms a ball and pulls away from the sides of mixing bowl. If dough seems dry, add additional water tablespoon by tablespoon until desired consistency is reached. The dough is always easier to work with slightly wet.

Dough should be able to form a small ball which doesn't crack much at sides when compressed. It should feel like a balloon filled with sand. This dough should be more on the moist side, than dry.

Form dough into balls, 1½-inches in diameter. Knead each ball by lightly tossing back and forth in your hands. (If your hands become sticky, rinse and dry them.) You'll be surprised how the consistency of the dough will change by simply kneading gently with dry hands.

Once all the dough has been formed into small balls, place a ball on a small piece of parchment paper and roll it out to $^1/_{16}$-inch thick with rolling pin or for faster preparation flatten using a tortilla press.

(continued)

Place flattened circles of dough on a plate with small pieces of parchment paper between them to prevent sticking.

Stuff the dough circles with filling of your choosing (only needs 1 teaspoon full per empanada) or follow any of the following recipes which can be found in the index:

Chicken Pot Pie Empanadas (see page 129)
Beef Empanadas (see pages 104 – 105)
Banana Empanadas (see page 340)
Pumpkin Empanadas (see page 340)

Once filled, fold over and pinch around edges with your fingers to seal. If too dry to seal, moisten one side with a small amount of water first.

Place filled empanadas on parchment lined baking trays. Mist tops of empanadas with extra light olive oil spray. Bake for 25 – 30 minutes in a preheated oven or as instructed in recipe.

Remove from oven and cover with a lightweight kitchen towel for several minutes to steam and soften the empanadas before serving.

Pecan Pie

This is one of the few recipes in the book that contains nuts. It's a terrific Pecan Pie recipe. Not only is it simple to follow, but it also doesn't contain any corn syrup. Instead it uses a combination of white and brown sugar, so those who are sensitive to corn but can eat nuts can enjoy.

Makes one pie

Preheat oven to 350 degrees. Liberally grease a 9-inch pie pan.

Fill the bottom of pie pan with either one recipe of **Pastry Dough** (see pages 318 – 319).

Place the following in a large mixing bowl and beat on medium speed for 1 minute:

3 **eggs** or equivalent substitute
1 cup **brown sugar**
1 cup **sugar**
¾ cup **milk** or **non-dairy milk substitute**
¼ cup plus 2 tablespoons **extra light olive oil**
3 tablespoons *Celeste's Best Gluten-Free Flour Mix*
2 teaspoons **vanilla extract**

Then stir in:

2 cups **pecan halves**

Pour into prepared pie shells and bake for 35 – 45 minutes. Remove from oven and place on wire rack to cool.

Toaster Pastries

You will have to forget any dieting when these pastries are around. If you had a hankering for those tart pastries that pop up from the toaster, then you won't be able to resist these.

Makes 6 pastries

Preheat oven to 425 degrees. Grease a large cookie sheet.

Prepare one recipe of **Pastry Dough** (see pages 318 – 319). Divide dough into two even sized balls. Cover work area with a sheet of parchment paper. Lightly flour surface with a teaspoon or two of *CBGFFM* or a few teaspoons of sugar on the rolling surface.

Lay one ball of dough on parchment paper and flatten with rolling pin. Place a teaspoon of flour or sugar on top, spreading it around with your hand, then set another sheet of parchment paper on top of dough.

Roll to ⅛-inch thickness. Take off the top sheet of parchment paper. Cut a template out of paper or an index card in the shape of a rectangle 3½ x 5-inches. Place template on top of dough and cut out shape with pizza cutter or shape knife. Gently pick up the six pastry bottoms and place them on the greased cookie sheet.

Roll out the second ball of dough and again use the template to cut out the pastry tops. Roll over each top with a dough docker or pierce the tops several times with a fork.

Prepare the filling by choosing one of the following:

Fruit Filling

Stir together the following in a small bowl:

½ cup **jam** or **preserves**
½ tablespoon **sweet rice flour**
½ tablespoon **water**

Sugar Cinnamon Filling

½ cup **brown sugar**
½ teaspoon **cinnamon**
1 tablespoon *Celeste's Best Gluten-Free Flour Mix*

Place one tablespoon of desired filling into the center of each pastry on the cookie sheet, leaving ¼ -inch perimeter around the outside of the pastry without filling.

Dip finger into a small bowl of water and wet the perimeter of each pastry, then top with remaining piece of dough. Press along edges with the tines of a fork to crimp dough.

Brush tops lightly with **extra light olive oil**. Then sprinkle with a small amount of **sugar** if desired.

Bake in preheated oven for 15 – 18 minutes or until golden brown. Best served warm. Once cool, store remaining pastries in sealed container or freeze in a zippered plastic bag for up to 3 months. Reheat pastries in toaster.

- Variation: When making fruit filled toaster pastries, try adding some thinly sliced fresh fruit along with the jam or preserves.

Play Dough

I wasn't quite sure where to place this recipe, but thought it might fit nicely in this section with the pastry dough.

When my daughter Kelly was young, I used to make batches of this dough up all the time. It's a great substitute for the commercial, wheat based brand.

Makes 1½ cups

In a medium sized bowl, whisk together:

1½ cups **white rice flour**
¾ cup **sea salt**
1 tablespoon **cream of tartar**

In a 2 cup measuring cup, whisk together:

1½ cups **water**
1½ tablespoons **extra light olive oil**
food coloring (5 – 7 drops) or 1(¼ ounce) package **Kool-Aid drink mix**

Add liquid ingredients to dry and whisk together briskly. Place mixture in non-stick skillet on low heat. Stir often with a spatula for 2 – 3 minutes or until the dough begins to thicken and congeal and resemble the consistency of play dough. (I often flip mine like a giant pancake to cook thoroughly.) Dough will also change to a slightly darker shade when it is done, which helps identify which parts may need to cook longer.

Remove the pan from heat and allow the dough to cool sufficiently for handling. Once slightly cool, knead dough vigorously several times.

Store in an airtight container or resealable zippered bag when not being used.

- For this recipe, use Kool-Aid without any added sugar or sweetener.

- Darker colors of Kool-Aid provide the best shades for play dough. (At the time of this writing, Kool-Aid is gluten-free but is not corn-free.)

- I tried this recipe with several gluten-free flours and found white rice seemed to give the dough the best consistency.

FRUIT DESSERTS, FROZEN DESSERTS AND BEVERAGES

Strawberry Ice Cream

Apple Crisp

My husband's favorite type of dessert would be anything baked with apples. Apple crisp, to me, is like the best part of an apple pie without the effort of having to make pie crust. Just note the crisp needs to cook an hour, to ensure that the apples are tender.

Serves 4 – 6

Preheat oven to 325 degrees. Grease a 13 x 9 x 2–inch baking dish. Prepare the filling by combining the following in a medium sized bowl:

3 tablespoons **sugar**
1 tablespoon *Celeste's Best Gluten-Free Flour Mix*
¼ teaspoon **ground cinnamon**

Whisk above ingredients until well blended, then add:

4 large (or 6 medium) **Granny Smith apples**, peeled, cored, halved and thinly sliced

Toss the apples with the sugar mix until well-coated, then place in bottom of baking dish. In a mixing bowl, prepare the topping by adding:

¾ cup *Celeste's Best Gluten-Free Flour Mix*
½ cup **brown sugar**
½ teaspoon **ground cinnamon**

Then add and mix with a fork until crumbs form:

¼ cup **extra light olive oil**

Sprinkle all of the above mixture over the apples. Place in preheated oven and bake for 55 – 65 minutes. Crisp is done when top begins to golden and the apples have become tender.

> - This recipe would also work well baked in six individual ramekin dishes. Cooking time would then be approximately 45 minutes.

Apple Turnovers

One of our favorite recipes. Just made a batch of these again for Father's Day. My husband loves them.

Makes 6 – 7 turnovers

Preheat oven to 350 degrees. Grease a large cookie tray. Prepare one recipe of the **Pastry Dough** (see pages 318 – 319) and roll dough to ⅛-inch thickness. Cut circles into dough approximately 3 inches in diameter. Each turnover will require two circles, one for the bottom and one for the top.

Prepare the turnover filling by mixing together:

1 large **granny smith apple**, pared and finely chopped into tiny cubes
3 tablespoons **sugar**
½ teaspoon **ground cinnamon**
½ teaspoon **lemon juice**

Place a heaping tablespoon of prepared apple mixture in center of each pastry circle. Drizzle with a small amount of **extra light olive oil** and then also drizzle with approximately ½ tablespoon **honey** or **sugar**.

Top with additional pastry circle, sealing edges together with fork. Take a knife and slit an "X" in the top to vent the steam. Bake in a preheated oven for 25 – 30 minutes.

- An easy way to cut circular shapes in dough is by using a large drinking glass or coffee mug turned upside down and tracing around it.

- Instead of circles, use any shape desired. Squares work well, too, and can be folded diagonally to create triangles.

- If turnover dough seems dry when sealing, use a bit of water to create some additional moisture to join the top to the bottom.

- We also chop up an additional apple and add the sugar, cinnamon and lemon juice to it, then put this in a small baking dish and bake this alongside the turnovers. It makes a tasty accompaniment to the apple turnovers.

Cuccidati (Sicilian Fig Cookies)

I remember these cookies fondly from my childhood. Cuccidati cookies are made from a sweetened pastry dough and then stuffed with a fig and raisin filling. We find the taste of these cookies very similar to the taste of the commercial brand fig cookies.

Makes approx. 2 dozen, 2-inch cookies

Preheat oven to 350 degrees. Grease 2 large cookie trays. Prepare fig filling by adding to greased food processing bowl:

1 (7 ounce) bag **dried figs**, stems removed and sliced
½ cup **raisins**
3 tablespoons **sugar**
1 tablespoon **lemon rind**

Process until mixture is ground and well combined.

To make the pastry dough, whisk together the following in mixing bowl:

2 cups *Celeste's Best Gluten-Free Flour Mix (CBGFFM)*
½ cup **sugar**
2 teaspoons **konjac powder** or **xanthan gum**

Then add:

½ cup **shortening**

Beat on medium speed until dough resembles large crumbs, then add:

½ cup **ice water**

Beat on medium speed for approximately 20 – 30 seconds or until dough forms a ball. The consistency of the dough should be slightly moist. If dough seems dry add additional water tablespoon by tablespoon until desired consistency is reached. The dough is always easier to work with slightly wet. A dry dough will create a pie pastry that cracks when handled. Divide dough into 3 equal sized balls.

Cover work area with a sheet of parchment paper. Lightly flour surface with a teaspoon or two of *CBGFFM* or a few teaspoons of sugar on the rolling surface. Lay a ball of dough on parchment paper and flatten with rolling pin. Place a teaspoon of flour or sugar on top, spreading it around with your hand, then set another sheet of parchment paper on top of dough.

Using a rolling pin, roll to ¼-inch uniform thickness into a rough rectangle shape. Take off the top sheet of parchment paper. Cut dough into strips at least 2½ -inches wide, so that each ball of dough will give you 3 – 4 long strips. (Don't worry if the outside edges of dough are not straight.)

Take ¼ cup of prepared fig filling and spread down the center of each strip of dough. Dip a finger into a small bowl of water and moisture the edge of one side of dough. Roll over one side of dough to cover the filling, then the other and pinch seam slightly or seal with a small amount of additional water. Tuck any overlapping ends under the roll.

Cut cuccidati rolls into 2-inch long pieces. Then carefully with a knife, cut two small slits on top of each piece to vent dough.

Place on cookie sheet and bake for 20 minutes or until cuccidati are golden brown on bottom. Remove and cool on wire rack.

- Drizzle a sugar glaze of 1 cup **confectioners powdered sugar** (see page 23) mixed with 1 – 2 tablespoons of milk if desired over cuccidati.

Fruit Filled Empanadas

Empanadas stuffed with either banana or pumpkin filling.

Makes 22 – 24 empanadas

Prepare the **empanada dough** (see pages 327 – 328) according to recipe instructions.

Preheat oven to 400 degrees. Line two large cookie sheets with parchment paper.

Banana Empanadas

In a small bowl, combine:

3 cups sliced ripe **bananas**
2 tablespoons **brown sugar**
1 teaspoon **ground cinnamon**

Pumpkin Empanadas

In a small bowl, combine:

1 (15 ounce) can **solid pack pumpkin**
¼ cup **brown sugar**
¼ cup **sugar**
½ teaspoon **ground cinnamon**
¼ teaspoon **ground ginger**
⅛ teaspoon **ground cloves**

Place a teaspoon of fruit mixture inside each empanada. Fill a very small bowl with water. Dip finger into water and moisten edges of dough. Seal edges with fingers or by pressing with tines of fork.

Place on baking sheet. Mist tops of empanadas with extra light olive oil spray. Bake for 15 – 20 minutes or until crust has turned golden brown.

Remove from oven and cover with a lightweight kitchen towel for several minutes to steam and soften the empanadas before serving.

- I usually half each recipe and make half a batch of banana and half pumpkin empanadas.

Peach Cobbler

There are two types of cobbler: one where fruit is topped with a biscuit-like topping and this version where a batter is prepared which rises and encases the fruit as it bakes.

Makes one 13 x 9-inch cobbler

Preheat oven to 350 degrees. Grease a 13 x 9 x 2-inch baking dish. Peel, core and slice:

6 medium **peaches** (4 cups sliced)

In mixing bowl, whisk together:

1¼ cups *Celeste's Best Gluten-Free Flour Mix*
1 cup **sugar**
1½ teaspoons **cream of tartar**
¾ teaspoon **baking soda**
½ teaspoon **konjac powder** or **xanthan gum**
¼ teaspoon **sea salt**
½ teaspoon **ground cinnamon**

In a small bowl or 2-cup measuring cup, whisk together:

1¼ cup **milk** or **non-dairy milk substitute**
¼ cup **extra light olive oil**
½ teaspoon **vanilla extract**

Add wet ingredients to mixing bowl and beat on medium speed for 30 seconds or until just combined. Pour batter in prepared baking dish, spreading it across bottom of pan with spatula to fill the corners. Place slice peaches over batter in a single layer.

Top simply with:

2 tablespoons **brown sugar**

Lightly sprinkle sugar over the peaches.

Or for a sugar crumb topping, whisk together in a small bowl:

¾ cup *Celeste's Best Gluten-Free Flour Mix*
½ cup **brown sugar**
½ teaspoon **ground cinnamon**

(continued)

Then add and mix with a fork until crumbs form:

¼ cup **extra light olive oil**

Sprinkle topping across peaches. Bake in preheated oven for 50 – 60 minutes.   Remove from oven and place on a wire rack to cool slightly before scooping onto a plate and serving. Refrigerate leftovers and reheat before serving or serve chilled.

- Try substituting the peaches in this cobbler with plums, pears, blueberries or apples or even a mix of different fruit. We just made this recipe with raspberries and it was delicious.

- This recipe does not contain any eggs. Thought I'd add that as I just baked up a cobbler and wondered if I had mistakenly omitted the eggs when I wrote the recipe. Some traditional versions of this recipe do contain eggs, but this one does not.

Fruit Sorbet

Sorbet is one dessert we enjoy all year long. It naturally contains no gluten, dairy or yeast and is just about fat free. There are a variety of fruits you can use to make this iced treat: mangos, strawberries, pineapple, peaches and bananas to name just a few. Our family's personal favorite is a mixture of bananas, peaches and pineapple chunks.

Makes eight, ½ cup servings

Slice or cut up in small pieces 4 cups of fruit or any combination of the fruits of your choice:

Ripe Bananas
Strawberries
Pineapple
Peaches
Melon
Mangos
Apricots
Raspberries

Place cut fruit on a cookie sheet or plate and place in freezer until frozen, preferably overnight.

When ready to process the sorbet, remove the four cups of fruit from freezer and place in food processor and allow fruit to sit for 15 minutes until slightly thawed.

After fruit has thawed slightly, begin to puree it in the processor. You may have to stop from time to time to scrape the blade with a spatula as the frozen fruit pieces can often become stuck.

Add the juice of:

½ **lemon** or **lime**

Continue to process for 2 – 3 minutes until fruit reaches the consistency of sorbet, a soft, very smooth consistency with no individual chunks of fruit visible.

Sweeten to taste with:

2 – 4 tablespoons **sugar**

Process for 30 seconds longer after the addition of the sugar and then spoon into eight ½-cup covered storage containers.

Return fruit to freezer and allow it to harden again before serving.

- You can also use a bag of frozen fruit for this recipe. Since the fruit will be full sized, I often let it sit for almost 30 minutes in the processor before I begin processing. Adding a frozen ripe banana to the mix will help sweeten the sorbet.

- Keep bananas that have ripened in the freezer. You can peel them and slice them or chop them into pieces and place them in a plastic bag until needed.

- Using sweet, ripe fruit will produce a better tasting sorbet.

Chocolate Ice Cream

I scream, you scream, you'll all be screaming for this delicious, soft, creamy, dairy-free chocolate ice cream!

Serves 4 – 6

Pulse the following with an **immersion** or **stick blender** on high for 5 – 10 seconds in a medium sized bowl or 4-cup measuring cup:

2 cups **milk** or **non-dairy milk substitute**
⅔ cup plus 2 tablespoons **sugar**
¼ cup **crushed ice**
⅔ cup **extra light olive oil**
⅓ cup **unsweetened cocoa**
2 teaspoons **vanilla extract**
¼ teaspoon **konjac powder** or **xanthan gum**

If needed, place ice cream mixture in measuring cup in an ice bath for 30 minutes or in freezer for 5 – 10 minutes or until well chilled.

Place liquid mixture in ice cream maker canister and process for 20 – 25 minutes or until mixture reaches desired thickness and creaminess. Spoon mixture into paper containers and place in freezer for several hours to chill and harden. Let the ice cream stand at room temperature for 5 – 10 minutes to soften before serving.

- Add ¼ cup of mini chocolate chips to mixture in the last 5 minutes of processing.

- The ¼ cup of crushed ice is needed to chill the mixture sufficiently before processing.

- The oil helps to keep the ice cream soft and creamy.

- **Important Note:** It's best to store ice cream in hot and cold paper food containers that are suitable for foods stored in the freezer. Visit www.celestesbest.com or www.CBglutenfree.com to find sources for the containers.

- For more delicious ice cream recipes, see my eBook, ***Celeste's Best Gluten-Free, Dairy-Free Ice Cream & Frozen Desserts.***

Strawberry Ice Cream

Once I had developed the vanilla and chocolate recipes, I started playing around with other flavors. Use organic strawberries as conventionally grown berries carry high pesticide residues.

Serves 4 – 6

Pulse the following with an **immersion** or **stick blender** on high for 5 – 10 seconds in a medium sized bowl or 4-cup measuring cup:

2 cups **milk** or **non-dairy milk substitute**
1 cup **organic strawberries**, hulls removed and roughly sliced
¼ cup **crushed ice**
⅔ cup **extra light olive oil**
½ cup plus 2 tablespoons **sugar**
1½ teaspoons **vanilla extract**
¼ teaspoon **konjac powder** or **xanthan gum**

If needed, place ice cream mixture in measuring cup in an ice bath for 30 minutes or in freezer for 5 – 10 minutes or until well chilled.

Place liquid mixture in ice cream maker canister and process for 20 – 25 minutes or until mixture reaches desired thickness and creaminess. Spoon mixture into paper containers and place in freezer for several hours to chill and harden. Let the ice cream stand at room temperature for 5 – 10 minutes to soften before serving.

- The ¼ cup of crushed ice is needed to chill the mixture sufficiently before processing.

- **Important Note:** It's best to store ice cream in hot and cold paper food containers that are suitable for foods stored in the freezer. Visit www.celestesbest.com or www.CBglutenfree.com to find sources for the containers.

- For more delicious ice cream recipes, see my eBook, *Celeste's Best Gluten-Free, Dairy-Free Ice Cream & Frozen Desserts.*

Vanilla Ice Cream

I attempted many times to make non-dairy ice cream. More often than not, we usually wound up with bowls of "ice milk." While this recipe was churning away in the ice cream maker, I dipped a spoon in and sampled it. My face lit up. It tasted just like ice cream made with cream, due to the combination of the milk and the oil.

I placed it in the freezer and waited. Most of my previous attempts never fared too well in this step. But adding oil to the recipe did the trick and keeps the ice cream soft and prevents ice from forming into the usual "ice milk" we normally experienced.

Serves 4 – 6

Pulse the following with an **immersion** or **stick blender** on high for 5 – 10 seconds in a medium sized bowl or 4-cup measuring cup:

2 cups **milk** or **non-dairy milk substitute**
¼ cup **crushed ice**
⅔ cup **extra light olive oil**
½ cup plus 2 tablespoons **sugar**
1½ teaspoons **vanilla extract**
¼ teaspoon **konjac powder** or **xanthan gum**

If needed, place ice cream mixture in measuring cup in an ice bath for 30 minutes or in freezer for 5 – 10 minutes or until well chilled.

Place liquid mixture in ice cream maker canister and process for 20 – 25 minutes or until mixture reaches desired thickness and creaminess. Spoon mixture into paper containers and place in freezer for several hours to chill and harden. Let the ice cream stand at room temperature for 5 – 10 minutes to soften before serving.

- Add ¼ cup of mini chocolate chips to mixture in the last 5 minutes of processing.

- The ¼ cup of crushed ice is needed to chill the mixture sufficiently before processing.

- **Important Note:** It's best to store ice cream in hot and cold paper food containers that are suitable for foods stored in the freezer. Visit www.celestesbest.com or www.CBglutenfree.com to find sources for the containers at the best price.

- For more delicious ice cream recipes, see my eBook, *Celeste's Best Gluten-Free, Dairy-Free Ice Cream & Frozen Desserts.*

Chocolate Protein Shake

A quick, energizing way to start the day. Like having dessert for breakfast!

Makes one 24 ounce shake

In blender (or if using an **immersion blender**, a large glass) add:

1 cup **chopped ice**
1½ cups **milk** or **non-dairy milk substitute**
1 **ripe banana**, broken into 2-inch pieces
2 tablespoons **chocolate gluten-free protein powder**
1 tablespoon **unsweetened cocoa powder** (optional)
Sweeten to taste with **stevia** or **sugar**

Blend until smooth and creamy.

- ▪ Variation: For a vanilla shake, follow the recipe above but omit the cocoa powder and replace the chocolate protein powder with vanilla.

- ▪ I also add ½ teaspoon **konjac powder** for a little extra fiber.

PUDDINGS AND CUSTARDS

Chocolate Pudding

Chocolate Pudding

For me, this is as close as you can get to one of those boxed pudding mixes, but even better!

Makes 3 cups

Whisk together the following in medium sized saucepan:

¾ cup **brown sugar**
2 tablespoons **special dark cocoa**
2 tablespoons **unsweetened cocoa**
3 tablespoons **sweet rice flour**
2 tablespoons **tapioca flour**
⅛ teaspoon **sea salt**

Turn heat to medium while gradually stirring in:

2¾ cups **milk** or **non-dairy milk substitute**

Whisk briskly to separate any lumps until mixture is smooth. Scrape bottom with spatula to make sure all of the dry ingredients have been incorporated into the milk. (Try a spoonful of mixture to ascertain if mixture is sweetened sufficiently.) Continue to cook on medium heat, 6 – 8 minutes, stirring often, just until mixture begins lightly boiling and has thickened slightly.

Once pudding boils, cook for only 1 – 2 additional minutes, stirring often. Then remove pan from heat and add, stirring well:

1½ teaspoons **extra light olive oil** (optional)
1 teaspoon **vanilla extract** or **mint extract**

Pour into serving dishes and refrigerate for 2 – 3 hours to allow pudding to set. Serve chilled.

- Special dark cocoa or black cocoa is actually "super alkalized" or Dutch processed more than most other cocoas and gives baked foods a darker color and intensified chocolate flavor. Use a combination of both the dark and regular unsweetened cocoa for best results.

- One of our favorite ways to serve chocolate pudding is frozen as pops. The pudding freezes very well.

Custard Cream Pudding

This recipe creates a custard cream that is suitable as a pudding or as a filling for desserts such as Cream Puffs (see page 326).

To create that true custard taste, it's best to use real eggs or real egg substitute for this recipe.

Makes 2½ cups

In a medium sized saucepan, pour:

2 cups **milk** or **non-dairy milk substitute**

Cook on medium heat, until almost boiling.

Meanwhile in a small bowl, whisk together:

⅔ cup **sugar**
¼ cup **sweet rice flour**
a pinch **sea salt**

Then when well mixed, add:

2 **eggs**

Beat well and add to milk, stirring constantly as pudding thickens, 2 – 3 minutes.

Remove pan from heat and whisk in:

1 teaspoon **vanilla extract**
1 tablespoon **extra light olive oil**

Pour into serving dishes, refrigerate and serve chilled.

Rice Pudding

My husband will often make more rice than we need for a meal "by mistake" so that I'll make rice pudding. This recipe uses cooked rice and makes an incredibly, creamy pudding.

Makes six ½ cup servings

In a medium sized saucepan, whisk together:

½ cup plus 2 tablespoons **sugar**
1½ tablespoons **sweet rice flour**
¼ teaspoon **sea salt**

Then add:

2 cups **milk** or **non-dairy milk substitute**

Cook above mixture over medium heat, stirring often, for ten minutes until it becomes bubbly and thickens. Meanwhile, place in a 2 cup measuring cup:

2 **eggs** or equivalent substitute

If using eggs, temper the eggs by adding the heated milk mixture to them very slowly, ¼ cup at a time, as you continually stir until you have 1½ cups of milk mixture and egg in measuring cup. Whisk the egg mixture into the remaining milk in the pan.

Then add:

2 cups **cooked rice**
½ cup **raisins** (optional)
1 tablespoon **extra light olive oil**
1 teaspoon **vanilla extract**

Stir well to break up any rice clumps. A whisk works well for this. Turn off stove and allow rice to remain on heated burner for 10 minutes, stirring occasionally. Pour into serving dishes and serve warm or refrigerate and serve chilled.

> - When adding real eggs to liquid ingredients that are already hot, you'll need to temper the eggs by adding a small amount of the hot liquid to the eggs while continually stirring. This will raise the temperature of the eggs and dilute them so that their proteins won't coagulate when you add them to the rest of the hot liquid.

Vanilla Pudding

A good vanilla pudding like many puddings, begins with milk. It's the foundation of the pudding and the taste of the pudding heavily depends on the taste of the milk. Using some milk substitutes can throw off the taste quite a bit. Choose a substitute that closely resembles real milk in color and taste to create the best vanilla pudding.

Makes four ½ cup servings

In a medium sized saucepan, pour:

2 cups **milk** or **non-dairy milk substitute**
⅓ cup **sugar**
pinch of **sea salt**

Cook on medium heat, until mixture begins to steam.

Meanwhile in a small bowl, whisk together until smooth and free of lumps:

½ cup **milk** or **non-dairy milk substitute**
3 tablespoons **sweet rice flour**

Beat well and add to milk, stirring often as pudding thickens and just comes to a boil. Then reduce heat to low, again stirring often, for 5 – 7 minutes or until pudding has thickened.

Remove pan from heat and whisk in:

1 teaspoon **vanilla extract**

Pour into serving dishes, refrigerate and serve chilled.

> - My new favorite way to make this pudding is to warm ½ cup of milk and add 2 tablespoons of golden flaxseed meal to it. Process that for 15 seconds with an immersion blender. Add the additional 2 cups milk, ⅓ cup sugar, ¼ cup sweet rice flour and pinch of sea salt and cook on medium low heat until thickened. Then whisk in 1 teaspoon vanilla.

SAUCES, CONDIMENTS AND SEASONINGS

Chimichurri Sauce

Barbeque Sauce

It can be a challenge to find a barbeque sauce that doesn't contain vinegar but still retains that barbeque flavor. This recipe fits the bill perfectly.

Makes 1¾ cups

Combine the following in a medium sized saucepan:

1¼ cups **brown sugar**
1 cup **unsweetened applesauce**
½ cup **ketchup** (see page 360)
¼ cup plus 2 tablespoons **lemon juice**
½ teaspoon **cinnamon**
½ teaspoon **garlic salt**
½ teaspoon **paprika**
sea salt and **pepper** to taste

Stir the above ingredients with a whisk or spatula until well mixed. Heat on medium heat and bring to a boil. Allow to boil for 4 – 5 minutes, stirring often. Then turn heat down to low and simmer without stirring for an additional 15 minutes.

> ▪ This barbeque sauce tastes especially good on chicken on the grill.

Burrito Sauce

The perfect accompaniment to Beef and Bean Burritos (see page 357).

Makes about 2 cups

In a skillet over medium heat add:

2 tablespoons **extra light olive oil**

When slightly heated, add:

1 **onion, chopped**

With a spatula or whisk, blend in:

2 tablespoons *Celeste's Best Gluten-Free Flour Mix*

Then add:

1 cup **chicken stock**

Whisk constantly until smooth, then stir in:

1 cup **tomato sauce**
2 tablespoons **canned** or **fresh chopped green chili peppers**
½ teaspoon **garlic salt**

Cover and reduce heat to simmer. Continue to cook for 20 minutes. Place your favorite filling in tortilla, roll and place seam side down on plate. Spoon burrito sauce on top.

- This recipe can easily be doubled or tripled.

Chimichurri

Chimichurri is an Argentinean sauce similar to a pesto. This sauce tastes absolutely incredible spread across freshly grilled steak. I sometimes serve this to company. Also goes well with tilapia.

Makes 1¼ cups

Wash well and trim off thick bottom stems of:

1 bunch of **flat leaf parsley**, cut into 2-inch pieces

Place parsley in **food processor** and pulse several times to finely chop. Then add:

8 **cloves of garlic**, minced
1 **shallot**, sliced
1 teaspoon **dried basil** or **dried oregano**
1 teaspoon **black pepper**
1 teaspoon **sea salt**
½ teaspoon **red pepper flakes**

Pulse several times, until finely chopped and well blended, then add:

1 cup **olive oil**
¼ cup **lemon juice**

Pulse again quickly, then serve. Store in a covered container for up to a week in the refrigerator. Allow sauce to return to room temperature before serving.

- This sauce can also be used to baste your meat before cooking.

Cocktail Sauce

A very simple sauce with only four ingredients.

Makes 2¼ cups

Whisk together the following in a small bowl:

2 cups **ketchup** (see page 360)
¼ cup freshly grated **horseradish**
2 tablespoons **lemon juice**
1 teaspoon **black pepper**

Serve immediately or store in sealed container in refrigerator.

- Add additional horseradish for a spicier sauce.

- Keep horseradish root in a plastic bag in the freezer until needed. Then peel and grate with a micro or fine zester/grater when needed, being sure not to breath in the fumes while grating as they can be quite strong. (These fine zester/graters are wonderful kitchen gadgets and are available at most kitchen stores and online shops.)

Ketchup

For some on a vinegar restricted diet, finding a suitable ketchup is not the easiest thing to do. Many recipes require cooking the tomatoes first but this recipe is much quicker and all the ingredients are simply whisked together. Especially good with sweet potato cubes and fries (see pages 81 – 82) and also chicken tenders (see page 135).

Makes approx. 3 cups

Meanwhile in medium sized bowl, combine the following:

2 (6 ounce) cans **tomato paste**
1 (15 ounce) can **tomato sauce**
¾ cup **lemon juice**
⅓ cup **sugar**
1 teaspoon **sea salt**
½ teaspoon **onion powder**
scant ⅛ teaspoon **allspice**
scant ⅛ teaspoon **cloves**
⅛ teaspoon **cinnamon**
⅛ teaspoon **garlic powder**

Whisk ingredients together. Store in a sealed container in refrigerate for up to one week.

> ▪ If ketchup thickens when chilled, simply add ¼ cup or more of water and shake well.

Maple Syrup Substitute

Most of the time we use pure maple syrup on our pancakes and waffles, but this recipe is good in a pinch and only takes a few minutes to prepare. My family has found they prefer it to most commercial syrups.

Makes approx. 1¼ cups syrup

Place in a small saucepan:

½ cup **sugar**

Turn the heat to medium and cook just until the sugar melts and browns.

Meanwhile in another saucepan, place:

1 cup **boiling water**
1 cup **brown sugar**

Cook on medium heat, stirring often until brown sugar dissolves completely in the water. Then add the browned white sugar. Reduce heat to a simmer and continue to cook on low, stirring often, as syrup thickens, about 5 – 7 minutes.

Once syrup has thickened, remove from heat. Add:

1 teaspoon **extra light olive oil**
1 teaspoon **vanilla** or **maple extract**

Use mixture in any recipe that calls for maple syrup.

> ▪ For those with corn sensitivities: Some maple syrups may use corn oil as an anti-foaming agent when processing. Be sure to check with the manufacturer to see if they defoam their syrup and what they may be using to defoam it.

Mayonnaise

This is a vinegar free mayonnaise recipe, made with extra light olive oil. Mayonnaise is actually very easy to prepare. In five short minutes you can blend together this condiment using an immersion or stick blender. Even works with flaxeggs.

Makes approx. 1½ cups mayonnaise

Place the following in a two cup measuring cup or bowl and blend on high using an **immersion** or **stick blender** for 30 seconds:

2 **eggs** or equivalent substitute
½ cup **extra light olive oil**
2 – 2½ tablespoons **lemon juice** (I prefer 2½ tablespoons.)
1 teaspoon **dry mustard powder**
1 teaspoon **sea salt**

Then slowly pour in:

1 cup **extra light olive oil**

Blend for 30 seconds – 1 minute or until desired consistency is reached.

Store in a tightly covered jar in the refrigerator. Best when used within 7 – 10 days.

- I originally made this in the blender or food processor where you had to slowly dribble the oil in for the mayonnaise to emulsify. Then both the blender and food processor broke at the same time. Decided to give the immersion blender a try and in minutes I had mayonnaise. A total time saver. A great trick is to use a wide mouth storage jar that the mayonnaise can be blended in and stored in when done.

- In the beginning my husband wouldn't eat this mayonnaise. He had a brand he preferred. Finally one day we perfected this recipe to his taste. His version uses only 1½ tablespoons **lemon juice** and we also add 1 teaspoon **sugar**.

Pizza Sauce

This recipe doesn't require any cooking but still has that incredible, perfect pizza sauce flavor. Great when you don't have a lot of time.

Makes approx. 2 cups sauce

Whisk together the following in a medium sized bowl:

1 (15 ounce) can **tomato sauce**
1 (6 ounce) can **tomato paste**
2 **cloves of garlic**, minced
2 teaspoons **dried basil**
2 teaspoons **dried oregano**
1 teaspoon **paprika**
1 teaspoon **sugar**
½ teaspoon **onion powder**
½ teaspoon **sea salt**

Use right away or refrigerate for up to a week. Sauce may also be frozen and used later.

> ▪ My daughter wanted to add a note here: you can also freeze the sauce in ice cube trays. When the sauce is frozen, remove from trays and store in a resealable, plastic bag in freezer to have on hand for personal sized pizzas.

Remoulade Sauce

This sauce goes well with many seafood dishes. Especially good with blackened tuna, swordfish and crab cakes.

Makes approx. 1 cup

Whisk together the following in a small bowl:

½ cup **ketchup** (see page 360)
¼ cup **mayonnaise** (see page 362)
2 – 4 tablespoons freshly grated **horseradish**
1 tablespoon **dried chives**
1 tablespoon **fresh parsley**
1 teaspoon **lemon juice**
¼ teaspoon **paprika**
¼ teaspoon **sea salt**
⅛ teaspoon **black pepper**
⅛ teaspoon **cayenne pepper**

Serve immediately or store in sealed container in refrigerator. Remoulade is a sauce that is best prepared a day in advance of the meal so that all the ingredients can have time to best complement one another.

> ▪ Once by mistake we reversed the amounts of ketchup and mayonnaise, but surprisingly produced an equally good tasting sauce.

Pineapple Salsa

This salsa goes especially well with the Beef Shish Kabobs (see page 106).

Makes 2 cups salsa

Combine the following into a medium sized bowl:

1 (20 ounce) can **crushed pineapple**, drained
1 medium **red onion**, diced
1 large **green** or **red pepper**, cored, seeded and diced
2 tablespoons **grated lime peel**
½ teaspoon **sea salt**

Stir above ingredients well and serve. Refrigerate any leftovers.

Pumpkin Butter

A wonderful spiced spread for toast, rice cakes or pumpkin bread.

Combine the following in a saucepan and mix well with spatula or whisk:

1 (15 ounce) can **100% pure pumpkin**
2¼ cups **sugar**
1½ teaspoons **pumpkin pie spice**
1 (.25 ounce) package **unflavored gelatin**

Place over medium heat. Once mixture reaches a boil, reduce heat to a simmer and continue cooking for 5 – 7 minutes stirring often.

Remove from heat and place in serving container. Refrigerate until serving. Best when used within 5 – 7 days.

- To half this recipe: use 1 cup pumpkin, 1 cup plus 2 tablespoons sugar, ¾ teaspoon pumpkin pie spice and 1½ teaspoons gelatin.

- For those with corn sensitivities and allergies, be sure to use a corn-free gelatin.

Salsa

I've often made salsa and been less than satisfied with the results, but not with this recipe. Whether you use fresh tomatoes or canned you still get an incredibly great tasting salsa.

Makes 4 cups salsa

Combine the following into food processor or a medium sized bowl:

1 **jalapeño**, finely diced and seeds removed (optional)
½ small **sweet onion**, diced (about ½ cup)
2 **large tomatoes**, peeled and diced or 1 (14.5 ounce) **diced tomatoes**
2 tablespoons **chopped cilantro**
1 tablespoon **lemon** or **lime juice**
1 **clove of garlic**, minced
1 teaspoon **olive oil**
¾ teaspoon **sea salt**
½ teaspoon **cumin**
¼ teaspoon **black pepper**

Stir above ingredients well or process in food processor for 30 seconds. Refrigerate and serve chilled.

- For those of you who like to spice things up a notch, add more jalapeno. For those who, like me, are babies when it comes to the fiery kick of a jalapeno, only add half of one.

- This salsa tastes great on tacos made with the taco seasoning (see page 376).

- You can wash and dry fresh cilantro and then chop and store in a plastic bag in the freezer, which makes it handy for recipes like these.

Salsa Verde

Salsa Verde is a Mexican, green salsa. At first when my husband made this I didn't think I'd like it, but the tomatillos produce a highly addictive salsa.

Makes 2 – 3 cups

Place the following into the food processor:

4 **cloves of garlic**
3 **scallions**, cut in thirds
1 – 2 small **jalapeno peppers**, seeds removed
1 medium **onion**, quartered
½ cup **fresh cilantro**
¼ cup **fresh parsley**

Process until all are finely chopped.

Then add:

4 cups **tomatillos**, husked, rinsed and cut in half
1 teaspoon **sea salt**

Process until the tomatillos are pureed, approximately 10 – 15 seconds.

Meanwhile, in a medium saucepan over medium heat, add:

1 tablespoon **olive oil**

Add pureed ingredients and simmer for 12 – 15 minutes, stirring frequently as salsa thickens. Remove from heat and pour into serving bowls. Serve warm or refrigerate and serve cool.

Sour Cream Substitute

This recipe works when you may need a non-dairy sour cream substitute for a recipe.

Makes one cup

Pour into a 2 cup measuring cup:

¾ cup **milk** or **non-dairy milk substitute**
¼ cup **extra light olive oil**
1 tablespoon **lemon juice**
¼ teaspoon **konjac powder** or **xanthan gum**

Mix on high for 30 seconds with an **immersion** or **stick blender** until frothy and thick.
Refrigerate for 30 minutes before using.

> - Although this substitute works in recipes calling for sour cream, it doesn't hold up
>   as well where sour cream is used as a topping – such as on a baked potato, or to top
>   off a bowl of black bean soup.

Tartar Sauce

The perfect accompaniment for most any fish.

Makes 1 cup

Whisk together the following in a small bowl:

1 cup **mayonnaise** (see page 362)
1 tablespoon **dried chives**
1 tablespoon **lemon juice**
1 tablespoon **fresh parsley**
1½ teaspoons **dill**

Serve immediately or store in sealed container in refrigerator.

- • Variation: Add two tablespoons of capers and chopped pickles to the sauce.

Italian Seasoning

A blend of Italian spices to season salads, meats and sauces.

Makes approx. 1 cup

In a small bowl, whisk together the following:

¼ cup **garlic powder**
2 tablespoons **dried basil**
2 tablespoons **dried oregano**
2 tablespoons **dried parsley**
4 teaspoons **onion powder**
1 teaspoon **black pepper**
1 teaspoon **thyme**

Pour ingredients into a sealed container or old spice jar and use when needed.

Jerk Seasoning

This seasoning can be used in a variety of ways. We often use it as a dry rub when grilling chicken breasts, then pair it with the Citrus Vinaigrette Dressing (see page 47). You can also use it as a wet rub or as part of a marinade.

Makes approx. ½ cup

Whisk together the following in a small bowl:

2 tablespoons **onion powder**

1 tablespoon **allspice**
1 tablespoon **brown sugar**
1 tablespoon **dried chives**
1 tablespoon **sea salt**
1 tablespoon **dried thyme**

2 teaspoons **black pepper**
2 teaspoons **cayenne pepper**
2 teaspoons **garlic powder**

½ teaspoon **cinnamon**
½ teaspoon **nutmeg**

The jerk seasoning can be used as a dry rub. Simply sprinkle liberally and rub into food. Cover and let rest for at least 1 hour or overnight in the refrigerator.

For a wet rub, combine ¼ cup olive oil, juice of 1 lemon, and 1 tablespoon of the dry seasoning. Mix together and spoon over beef, chicken or pork and rub into surface or place ingredients in a zip lock bag and massage every so often. Cook or grill the meat immediately or place in refrigerator until ready to cook.

Additionally, two tablespoons of the dry seasoning can be added to 2 cups of orange, lemon, lime or grapefruit juice (or a combination of the juices) to be used as a marinade. Best over chicken or pork. Pour over meat 3 hours before cooking. Keep refrigerated while marinating.

Salt Free Seasoning

A seasoning mix suitable for those on a salt restricted diet.

Makes approx. ⅓ cup

Mix together in a small bowl:

1 tablespoon plus 2 teaspoons **onion powder**
1 tablespoon **dry mustard**
1 tablespoon **garlic powder**
1 tablespoon **paprika**
1 tablespoon **dried thyme**
½ teaspoon **celery seed**
½ teaspoon **black pepper**

Pour mixture into an old spice jar or airtight container.

Seasoning Salt

Seasoning salt is a staple in our house. We use it as a quick way to dress our salads. A sprinkle of seasoning salt, a dash of olive oil and lemon juice and we've made a very easy, simple dressing.

Makes approx. one cup

Mix together in a small bowl or 2 cup measuring cup:

¾ cup **sea salt**
¼ cup **garlic salt**
1½ teaspoons **freshly ground black pepper**
1½ teaspoons **paprika**
½ teaspoon **celery seed**
½ teaspoon **dry mustard**
½ teaspoon **oregano**

Pour mixture into an old spice jar or airtight container.

- Seasoning salt tastes great sprinkled on salads and fresh or cooked vegetables.

- Try seasoning seafood, steaks, burgers and chicken with it both before and after cooking.

Steak Seasoning

Many seasoning blends can often contain wheat. This recipe creates an enticing aroma that seasons steaks perfectly. I enjoy this seasoning so much, I even sprinkle a little extra on as I'm eating my steak.

Makes approx. ¼ cup

In a one-cup measuring cup, mix together:

1 tablespoon **kosher sea salt**
2 teaspoons **black pepper**
2 teaspoons **coriander**
2 teaspoons **dill weed**
2 teaspoons **paprika**
1 teaspoon **garlic powder**

Pour mixed spices into a glass jar or an old glass spice bottle. Sprinkle some of the seasoning blend over both sides of meat before cooking.

Taco Seasoning Mix

When we first starting eating gluten-free, there weren't many taco seasoning mixes on the market that didn't contain wheat. Luckily, things have changed a bit now, but I still have to say I like this mix best. I take an old spice jar and tape a copy of this recipe right to it so it's always handy.

Mix together the ingredients to make a small batch of 2 tablespoons, enough for one meal, or prepare the larger batch to keep on hand.

	Yield: Approx. 2 Tablespoons	Yield: Approx. 1½ cups
minced onion	2 teaspoons	½ cup
sea salt	1 teaspoon	¼ cup
cumin	½ teaspoon	2 tablespoons
garlic powder	½ teaspoon	2 tablespoons
sweet rice flour	½ teaspoon	2 tablespoons
cayenne pepper	¼ teaspoon	1 tablespoon
chili powder	¼ teaspoon	1 tablespoon
oregano	¼ teaspoon	1 tablespoon

To prepare tacos: In a skillet, cook beef over medium heat until no longer pink; drain any fat if necessary. Add 2 tablespoons of taco seasoning mix and ¼ cup water per pound of meat. Reduce heat to low and continue to cook, stirring occasionally, for 10 minutes.

- A funny side note to this is that I used to write this recipe on the side of an old plastic spice container with one of those permanent pens. Sadly though, I found out the ink was not so permanent and much of the recipe had disappeared. Tried many other recipes trying to replicate this one until I was able to decipher the remains of the recipe left on the container. We think this seasoning mix gives tacos just the right amount of kick.

- If you prefer a spicier seasoning, add another ¼ teaspoon of both the cayenne pepper and the chili powder to the smaller yielding mix and an extra 1 tablespoon of each to the larger yielding mix.

- The larger batch stores nicely in a 7-ounce spice bottle.

USEFUL INFORMATION

Cooking Terms

Bake - Cook by dry heat, usually in an oven.

Baking sheet - (also called cookie sheets or trays) A flat pan or sheet of metal that is used to bake products such as cookies.

Barbecue - To roast meat slowly on a spit or grill over coals, or in the oven, basting frequently with a highly seasoned sauce.

Baste - To moisten foods during cooking with drippings, water or seasoned sauce, to prevent drying or to add flavor.

Beat - To smooth a mixture by briskly whipping or stirring it up with a spoon, fork, wire whisk, rotary beater or electric mixer.

Blanch - To plunge foods into boiling water for a few seconds or a few minutes, then quickly remove and place in ice water. This process sets the color of vegetables and allows you to easily peel fruits and vegetables.

Blend - To mix ingredients just until thoroughly combined.

Blind bake – To prebake an unfilled pie shell to prevent puffing and slipping during baking. The pastry is lined with parchment paper and filled with pie weights, dry beans or uncooked rice. These are removed shortly before the end of baking time to allow the crust to brown.

Boil - Cook in boiling liquid in which bubbles rise vigorously to the surface. The boiling point of water is 212 degree Fahrenheit at sea level.

Broil - Cook by exposure to direct heat under the broiler of a gas or electric range, in an electric broiler, or over an open fire.

Brown - To cook food quickly over high heat, usually in a little fat, to help give the food color and flavor.

Brush - To spread food with a liquid such as oil, using a small brush.

Caramelize - To melt sugar slowly over very low heat until sugar is liquid, deep amber in color and caramel flavored.

Chill - To refrigerate food or let it stand in ice or iced water until cold.

Chop – Cutting food into nearly uniform bite-size or smaller pieces.

Coat - To roll foods in flour, sugar, crumbs, etc., until all sides are evenly covered; or to dip first into slightly beaten egg or milk, then to cover with whatever coating is called for in a recipe.

Combine - To mix various ingredients together.

Cook - To prepare food by applying heat in any form.

Core - The process of removing the core, the center section of some fruits such as pineapples and apples, which contains the seeds and tougher fleshy material.

Cream - To whip or beat a mixture until it is soft and fluffy.

Crimp - To create a decorative edge on a pie crust by pinching or pressing dough edges together.

Curdle – When foods such as milk or eggs separate into solids and liquids due to heating or being combined with an acidic ingredient, such as lemon juice.

Cube – Cutting food into squares, generally between ½ to 2-inches or determined by the recipe.

Cut - To divide food into pieces with a knife or scissors.

Cut in - To mix shortening or other solid ingredients with dry ingredients using a pastry blender, knife or fork.

Deep-Fry - To fry foods completely submerged in hot oil.

Dice - To cut food into small cubes of uniform size and shape, usually about ¼-inch in size.

Dissolve - To stir a solid food and a liquid food together to form a mixture in which none of the solid remains.

Dot - Scatter small amounts of specified ingredients, usually oil or chocolate, etc., on top of food.

Dredge – The process of pulling foods through dry ingredients such as flour, herbs and spices or bread crumbs to coat them before cooking.

Drizzle - To slowly pour a liquid, such as melted butter or a glaze in a fine stream, back and forth, over food.

Dust - To sprinkle lightly before or after cooking with dry ingredients, such as flour, granulated or confectioners' sugar or spices.

Emulsify - To bind two or more liquids that do not typically mix together well, such as oil and water.

Fillet - A strip or compact piece of boneless meat or fish.

Fold; **Fold in** - To stir slowly and gently to incorporate a lighter ingredient into a heavier ingredient stirring from the bottom of the bowl and draping or "folding" it over the top.

Fry or Pan-Fry - To cook in a small amount of fat or oil over moderate or high heat on top of the stove.

Garnish - To decorate any foods. Parsley, dill and citrus zest are often used as garnishes to add the finishing touch to a dish.

Glaze - To coat with a thin sugar syrup.

Grate - To reduce a large piece of food to coarse or fine threads by rubbing it against a rough, serrated surface, usually on a grater.

Julienne - To cut vegetables such as carrots into very thin strips, the size of matchsticks.

Knead - To work and press dough with the heels of your hands so the dough becomes more pliable.

Leavening - Any agent that causes a dough or batter to rise. Leaveners in this book include cream of tartar and baking soda.

Marinate - To soak foods in a seasoned liquid mixture, usually an acid-oil mixture of oil and vinegar or lemon juice, often flavored with spices and herbs to flavor and tenderize meats.

Melt - To heat solid food, like sugar or fat, until it becomes liquid.

Mince - To cut with knife or scissors into very fine pieces.

Mix - To beat or stir until ingredients are thoroughly combined.

Pan-Fry - To cook or fry on top of the range in a hot, uncovered skillet with little or no fat. Steaks, chops and potatoes are frequently cooked this way.

Peel - To strip away the outer coverings of some fruits or vegetables.

Pipe - To force a food (typically frosting) through a pastry tip to use as a decoration.

Pit - To remove the seed or pit.

Pound - To flatten meats and poultry to a uniform thickness using a kitchen mallet to ensure even cooking and also help tenderize.

Preheat - To heat oven to stated temperature before using.

Prick - To pierce a food usually with a fork in many or a few places often to prevent buckling such as in crackers and pie crusts.

Puree - To blend, process, sieve, or mash a food until it is very smooth and has the consistency of a fine-textured substance.

Reduce - To evaporate some of the liquid in stock or sauce by boiling.

Roast – Cooking or baking by dry heat in an oven, over charcoal, or in an electric rotisserie.

Roux - A blend of flour and oil used to thicken sauces and gravies.

Rub - A mixture of spices or herbs that is applied to food, wet or dry, for the purpose of adding flavor.

Sauté - To fry and brown food first on one side and then on the other in a small quantity of fat or oil.

Scald - To heat liquid such as milk to a temperature just below the boiling point.

Score - To cut narrow cuts or slashes with the point of a knife.

Sear – To quickly cook the surface of food by exposing it to extremely high heat to produce a crusted surface and seal in the juices.

Shred - To cut food into slivers or slender pieces, using a knife or shredder.

Sift - To pass dry ingredients such as flour through a fine sieve to insure it is lump free.

Simmer - To cook in a liquid that is kept just below the boiling point which produces bubbles which form slowly and break below the surface.

Skewer - A long shaft or thin rod inserted through pieces of meat and other foods to hold several pieces together while cooking over a grill or roasting.

Skim - To remove fat or froth from the surface of a liquid, such as stock.

Steam - To cook on a rack or holder over a small amount of boiling water in a tightly covered container.

Stew - To cook foods, in enough liquid to cover, very slowly maintaining a temperature below the boiling point.

Stir - To mix, usually with a spoon or fork, until ingredients are blended together.

Stir-fry - The food is tossed about in a hot wok or fry pan with very little oil, in a process similar to sautéing.

Stock - The flavorful juices that are produced when meat and vegetables are cooked in water for long periods of time.

Temper - To heat food gently before adding it to a hot mixture so it does not separate or curdle. Eggs are often tempered with a little hot liquid to raise their temperature before they are stirred into a hot sauce or soup.

Toast - To brown by baking or placing food such as bread under direct heat.

Toss - To quickly and gently mix ingredients together, such as a salad or pasta in a dish, using a large spoon and fork.

Whip - To rapidly beat eggs, liquids or batter in order to incorporate air and expand volume.

Whisk - To beat ingredients with a looped wire utensil to mix or blend, or incorporate air.

Zest - To remove the colored peel of a citrus fruit using a grater or zester.

Conversion Charts

Flours and Dry Ingredients Conversion Chart

1 cup *Celeste's Best Gluten-Free Flour Mix*	5.4 ounces	155 grams
1 cup *Celeste's Best Baking Mix*	4.2 ounces	120 grams
1 cup amaranth flour	4.2 ounces	120 grams
1 cup arrowroot starch/flour	4.0 ounces	115 grams
1 cup ivory teff flour	5.0 ounces	140 grams
1 cup quinoa flakes	3.8 ounces	105 grams
1 cup quinoa flour	3.9 ounces	110 grams
1 cup sweet potato flour	4.5 ounces	125 grams
1 cup sweet rice flour	4.9 ounces	140 grams
1 cup tapioca flour	4.2 ounces	120 grams
1 cup white bean flour	5.0 ounces	140 grams
1 cup white rice flour	5.3 ounces	150 grams
1 cup unsweetened cocoa	3.25 ounces	92 grams

Sugars and Syrups Conversion Chart

1 cup confectioners sugar	4 ounces	115 grams
1 cup granulated sugar	7 ounces	200 grams
1 cup dark brown sugar	8.4 ounces	240 grams
1 cup molasses	11.25 ounces	322 grams
1 cup honey	11.75 ounces	335 grams

Oils and Fats Conversion Chart

1 cup vegetable shortening	6.75 ounces	190 grams
1 cup extra light olive oil	7.5 ounces	215 grams

Oven Temperature Conversion Chart

275 F	140 C	Gas Mark 1
300 F	150 C	Gas Mark 2
325 F	160 C	Gas Mark 3
350 F	180 C	Gas Mark 4
375 F	190 C	Gas Mark 5
400 F	200 C	Gas Mark 6
425 F	220 C	Gas Mark 7
450 F	230 C	Gas Mark 8
475 F	250 C	Gas Mark 9

U.S. Volume Equivalents Chart

1½ teaspoons	½ tablespoon	
3 teaspoons	1 tablespoon	
2 tablespoons	⅛ cup	1 ounce
4 tablespoons	¼ cup	2 ounces
8 tablespoons	½ cup	4 ounces
1 cup	½ pint	8 ounces
2 cups	1 pint	16 ounces
2 pints	1 quart	32 ounces
4 quarts	1 gallon	128 ounces

Metric Volume Conversion Chart

⅛ teaspoon	.5 ml
¼ teaspoon	1.23 ml
½ teaspoon	2.5 ml
1 teaspoon	5 ml
1 tablespoon	15 ml
2 tablespoons (1 ounce)	30 ml
¼ cup (2 ounces)	60 ml
⅓ cup (2.67 ounces)	75 ml
½ cup (4 ounces)	120 ml
¾ cup (6 ounces)	180 ml
1 cup (8 ounces)	240 ml

Metric Weight Conversion Chart

½ ounce	14 grams
1 ounce	29 grams
1½ ounces	43 grams
2 ounces	57 grams
4 ounces	113 grams
8 ounces	227 grams
16 ounces (1 pound)	454 grams

Baking Pan Size Volumes and Conversions

If the recipe calls for	Volume	You can use this instead
8-inch round cake pan	4 cups	8x4-inch loaf pan; 9-inch round cake pan; 9-inch pie plate
9-inch round cake pan	6 cups	8½x4½-inch loaf; 11x7x2-inch baking pan
8-inch square baking pan	6 cups	11x7x2-inch baking pan; 9-inch round; 8½ x4½ -inch loaf
9-inch square baking pan	8 cups	9x5-inch loaf pan; 11x7x2-inch baking pan; 9-inch deep dish pie plate
11x7x2-inch baking pan	6 cups	9-inch round cake pan; 8-inch square baking pan; 9-inch square baking pan
13x9x2-inch baking pan	14 cups	(2) 8-inch square baking pans; (1) 10½x15x1-inch jellyroll pan
10½x15x1-inch jellyroll pan	10 cups	(2) 9-inch square baking pans; (1) 13x9x2-inch baking pan
8x4-inch loaf pan	6 cups	8-inch round cake pan; 11x7x2-inch baking pan
9x5-inch loaf pan	8 cups	9-inch square baking pan; 9x2-inch deep dish pie plate

Baking Pan Conversion Chart

If the recipe calls for	You can use this instead
8x1½-inch round	20x4-cm cake tin
9x1½-inch round	23x3.5-cm cake tin
11x7x1½-inch	28x18x4-cm baking tin
13x9x2-inch	30x20x5-cm baking tin
15x10x2-inch	30x25x2-cm baking tin
9-inch pie plate	22x4 or 23x4-cm pie plate
9x5x3-inch loaf	23x13x7-cm or 2 pound narrow loaf tin

INDEX

W

Waffles
  Baking Mix Waffles 232
  Chocolate Waffles with Chocolate Sauce 209-210
  replacing waffle iron 207, 209, 232
  Waffles 207
White Cake 299, 313
White rice flour 10-11, 13-15, 383
White Sauce 93

X

Xanthan Gum 11, 13-14, 16, 169

Y

Yeast, sensitivity 168
Yeast-Free Pizza Crust 194-195
Yeast-Free Pizza Crust #2 198-199
Yellow Cake 3, 22, 312-313

Z

Zucchini
  Beef Shish Kabobs 106, 365
  Roasted Italian Vegetables 80
  Zucchini Boats 84-85
  Zucchini Bread 244-245
  Zucchini Fritters 86

Made in the USA
Middletown, DE
12 November 2018